COGNITIVE THERAPY

COGNITIVE THERAPY
Applications in Psychiatric and Medical Settings

Edited by

Arthur Freeman
Center for Cognitive Therapy
University of Pennsylvania
Philadelphia, PA

Vincent B. Greenwood
Director
Washington Center for Cognitive Therapy
Washington, DC

HUMAN SCIENCES PRESS, INC.
72 FIFTH AVENUE
NEW YORK, N.Y. 10011

Copyright © 1987 by Human Sciences Press, Inc.
72 Fifth Avenue, New York, New York 10011

All rights reserved. No part of this work may be reproduced or utilized in
any form or by any means, electronic or mechanical, including
photocopying, microfilm and recording, or by any information storage
and retrieval system without permission in writing from the publisher.

Printed in the United States of America
987654321

Library of Congress Cataloging-in-Publication Data

Cognitive therapy.

  Includes index.
  1. Cognitive therapy. I. Freeman, Arthur M.
II. Greenwood, Vincent B. [DNLM: 1. Behavior Therapy.
2. Cognition. 3. Mental Disorders—therapy.
WM 400 C676]
RC489.C63C648 1986   616.89'142   86-10399
ISBN 0-89885-285-4
ISBN 0-89885-311-7 (pbk.)

CONTENTS

Contributors   7

Foreword by James L. Stinnett, M.D.   9

Introduction   13

PART I.   APPLICATIONS IN PSYCHIATRIC SETTINGS

1. **Cognitive Therapy: An Overview**   19
   Arthur Freeman
2. **Cognitive Therapy and Medication as Combined Treatment**   36
   Jesse H. Wright
3. **Day Hospital Treatment of Alcoholics**   51
   Meyer D. Glantz
4. **Inpatient Treatment of Adolescents**   69
   G. Randolph Schrodt, Jr. and Jesse H. Wright
5. **Problem-Solving Training: A Cognitive Group Therapy Modality**   83
   Erich Coché
6. **Cognitive Therapy with the Young Adult Chronic Patient**   103
   Vincent B. Greenwood

7. **Fully Integrated In- and Outpatient Services in a Psychiatric Sector: Implementation of a New Model for the Care of Psychiatric Patients Favoring Continuity of Care**   117
   Carlo Perris, Karin Rodhe, Astrid Palm, M. Abelson, Siv Hellgren, Carola Lilja, and H. Soderman

8. **A Cognitive Approach to Group Therapy with Hospitalized Adolescents**   132
   Robert W. Grossman and Beverly Freet

PART II: APPLICATIONS IN MEDICAL SETTINGS

9. **Cognitive Therapy with Cancer Patients**   155
   J. William Worden

10. **Cognitive Approaches to Management of the Type A Behavior Pattern**   162
    Julaine Kinchla

11. **Issues in the Diagnosis and Cognitive Therapy of Depression in Brain-Damaged Individuals**   183
    Mary Ruckdeschel Hibbard, Wayne A. Gordon, Susan Egelko, and Karen Langer

12. **Problem-Solving Training and Institutionalized Elderly Patients**   199
    Richard A. Hussian

13. **Group Cognitive Behavior Therapy for Sexual Rehabilitation of Spinal Cord–Injured Clients**   213
    Janie S. Weinberg

Index

CONTRIBUTORS

M. Ableson, Umea University, Department of Psychiatry, and WHO Collaborating Centre for Research and Training in Psychiatry, Umea, Sweden

Erich Coché, Partner, Coché & Coché, Clinical Psychologists, Philadelphia, Pennsylvania

Susan Egelko, Department of Rehabilitation Medicine, Rusk Institute of Rehabilitation Medicine, New York University Medical Center, New York, New York

Arthur Freeman, Center for Cognitive Therapy, University of Pennsylvania, Philadelphia

Beverly Freet, Western Michigan University, Department of Psychology, Kalamazoo, Michigan

Meyer D. Glantz, National Institute on Drug Abuse, Division of Clinical Research, Rockville, Maryland

Wayne A. Gordon, Department of Rehabilitation Medicine, Rusk Institute of Rehabilitation Medicine, New York University Medical Center, New York, New York

Vincent B. Greenwood, Director, Washington Center for Cognitive Therapy, Washington, D.C.

Robert W. Grossman, Western Michigan University, Department of Psychology, Kalamazoo, Michigan

Siv Hellgren, Umea University, Department of Psychiatry, and WHO Collaborating Centre for Research and Training in Psychiatry, Umea, Sweden

Mary Ruckdeschel Hibbard, Department of Rehabilitation Medicine, Rusk Institute of Rehabilitation Medicine, New York University Medical Center, New York, New York

Richard A. Hussian, Terrell State Hospital, Terrell, Texas

Julaine Kinchla, Institute for Cognitive and Behavioral Therapies, Presbyterian-University of Pennsylvania Medical Center, Philadelphia

Karen Langer, Department of Rehabilitation Medicine, Rusk Institute of Rehabilitation Medicine, New York University Medical Center, New York, New York

Carola Lilja, Umea University, Department of Psychiatry, and WHO Collaborating Centre for Research and Training in Psychiatry, Umea, Sweden

Astrid Palm, Umea University, Department of Psychiatry, and WHO Collaborating Centre for Research and Training in Psychiatry, Umea, Sweden

Carlo Perris, Umea University, Department of Psychiatry, and WHO Collaborating Centre for Research and Training in Psychiatry, Umea, Sweden

Karin Rodhe, Umea University, Department of Psychiatry, and WHO Collaborating Centre for Research and Training in Psychiatry, Umea, Sweden

G. Randolph Schrodt, Jr., Assistant Professor, University of Louisville School of Medicine; Associate Clinical Director, Norton Psychiatric Clinic, Louisville, Kentucky

H. Soderman, Umea University, Department of Psychiatry, and WHO Collaborating Centre for Research and Training in Psychiatry, Umea, Sweden

Janie S. Weinberg, Health Maintenance Organization of Delaware, Wilmington, Delaware

J. William Worden, Department of Psychiatry, Harvard Medical School, Massachusetts General Hospital, Boston

Jesse H. Wright, Associate Professor, University of Louisville School of Medicine; Medical Director, Norton Psychiatric Clinic, Louisville, Kentucky

FOREWORD

Cognitive therapy has clearly demonstrated its robustness as a psychotherapeutic technique. Recent studies have shown that cognitive therapy is as effective as antidepressant drugs in the treatment of unipolar depression. If further studies support this initial view, then cognitive therapy will have even wider appeal than it now enjoys since both therapists and patients would presumably prefer to use a psychotherapeutic treatment modality over a pharmacologic one. In addition, psychotherapeutic techniques would have fewer side effects and a longer "duration of action" than pharmacological ones. An additional benefit is that learning how to cope with Life and to use that skill in solving psychological and other problems, is more compatable with our notion of "humaness" and free will, in that it implies that we are doing something with our minds and are exerting some degree of control over the solution of our problems.

The therapeutic effectiveness of cognitive therapy has been demonstrated initially in the treatment of mood and anxiety disorders occurring in the context of traditional, one to one psychotherapy. The scope of application of cognitive therapy has, however, spread from the treatment of mood and anxiety disorders to include numerous other disorders (pain, substance abuse, and various social problems, to name a few). Its application has spread to other psychiatric treatment settings such as group, family, marital counselling, inpatient psychiatric treatment units, and residential treatment settings. One of the most exciting extensions of the use of cognitive therapy has been to medical settings. There are numerous behavioral disorders resulting from both medical and psychological causes that are extremely difficult to treat. These are, *inter alia*, substance abuse, chronic psychosis, the terminal illness, and behaviors that are associated with high health risk factors such as "type

A behavior." The mental health needs of *these* patients with these disorders have not been adequately served by traditional mental health approaches. This is particularly important since these disorders are so prevalent in our society. The morbidity of these disorders and their impact on society in social and economic terms is in excess of its actual prevalence. Treatment interventions that can be shown to be effective in these disorders are particularly deserving of attention. That is the focus of this book.

This book focuses on disorders that either do not lend themselves to traditional forms of treatment or which, for a variety of other reasons, have not attracted the focused and sustained efforts of the mental health profession. Usually this is because these disorders are intrinsically difficult to treat. Looking through the table of contents will indicate the truth of that statement. The disorders addressed in this volume range from the patient with cancer to patients with brain damage to patients with sexual disorders and spinal cord injuries. Cognitive behavioral treatment, as described in this book, uniquely lends itself to the treatment of these disorders because it focuses on target symptoms and describes in specific sequential steps how to carry out the therapy.

The use of cognitive therapy in non-conventional settings to treat a wider range of disorders must be viewed within the context of the major changes in the sociology and economics of health care delivery that has occurred in this country. One major change is in reimbursement for psychiatric services and the other is the marked influx of psychiatric health care providers who have different theoretical orientation than traditional medically trained psychotherapists. Economic forces have a powerful influence on who provides treatment and how that treatment is provided. In medical treatment settings we have seen how reimbursement has shifted from reimbursement for costs of health care to a formula where reimbursement is dependent on a particular disorder, the Diagnostic Related Groups (DRG). This simple fact alone has had, and will continue to have, in the future, far reaching influences on the way medicine is practiced in the United States. It places a particular premium on developing treatment interventions that are rapid and effective, and, most important, can be tied to measureable changes in behavior. Although the aforementioned changes in reimbursement have been limited to medical disorders in traditional medical treatment settings, it is clear that it is only a matter of time before patients with psychological and behavioral problems will have the cost of their treatment determined on the same basis.

Traditional forms of psychiatric treatment have emphasized psychodynamic types of approaches. No matter what the data show about the effectiveness of this approach or its theoretical and metapsychological validity, this type of treatment usually takes a long time to produce effects. Although there have been no comparison studies that I am aware of comparing the effectiveness and efficiency of cognitive therapy vs. traditional psychodynamic therapy, it is the considered clinical experience of those clinicians who are trained in both cognitive therapy and psychodynamically oriented therapy that cognitive therapy, which focuses on specific cognitive and behavioral goals, works more rapidly. If this clinical impression is born out by later studies, then Cognitive Therapy, will clearly have an advantage over more traditional approaches in the economic climate of the 80's and 90's, regardless of the setting in which it is practiced.

The editors and contributors to this volume are uniquely qualified as both experienced clinicians in their respective settings and Cognitive Therapists. They have broken new ground and offered new programs for the reader to study, utilize, adapt and develop further.

James L. Stinnett, M.D.
Department of Psychiatry
University of Pennsylvania

INTRODUCTION

Cognitive-Behavior Therapy (CBT) as an approach to treating a wide range of psychological and behavioral disorders is currently riding the crest of a wave of enthusiasm. This enthusiasm is well founded, as many practitioners from the disciplines of psychology, psychiatry, nursing, counseling, and social work have found that the documented successes of CBT, combined with its appealing common sense, have made it a powerful addition to the therapeutic armamentarium. Smith (1982), in his survey of members of Division 12 (Clinical) and 17 (Counseling) concluded that Cognitive Behavioral strategies were among the most powerful therapeutic tools available.

The inherent common sense of the model has helped to encourage a rather rapid proliferation of creative and exciting applications of the CBT model to new patient populations and clinical problems, with the CB model becoming an important development in the health care delivery system. The present volume grew out of the expressed need of therapists working in inpatient settings for a resource volume that would help to initiate CBT applications with psychiatric and medical patients. Given the increasing popularity of CBT, scant attention has been paid, to date, to the applications of this collaborative, empirically based and clear-cut theory of human functioning and behavior change to this large and diverse population.

Part I of the book focuses on applications in psychiatric settings.

In the initial chapter, Freeman offers an overview of the theory, technique, and practice of Cognitive Therapy. In presenting the basic CT model, Freeman's chapter is a good review for the clinician experienced and knowledgeable in CT and an excellent introduction for those first studying the model.

In a number of studies, Cognitive Therapy has been combined with medication as a joint treatment and found to be more effective than either CT or medication alone. In this chapter Wright discusses the combined use of CT and medication. He offers to the reader a rationale and guidelines for the use of medication, and makes a strong case for the noncompetitive nature of the two treatments.

In chapter 3, Glantz describes a group therapy program for the treatment of alcoholism in a day hospital setting. This patient group has complex needs for biomedical, social service, and psychotherapeutic treatment. Glantz describes the assessment, treatment, and evaluation phases of this comprehensive treatment program.

Schrodt and Wright, in chapter 4, discuss a cognitive behavioral strategy for helping adolescents through the turmoil and crises of this difficult developmental stage. Adolescents who are referred for inpatient treatment are often the most difficult to reach. The authors set out a developmental perspective for the use of CBT, and then discuss the specific applications to treatment.

In chapter 5, Coché offers a group approach to developing better coping skills. This Problem Solving Training (PST) approach, designed for in-patient use, has been found to be effective as an adjunct to the treatment regimen that can increase patient self-efficacy, increase patient confidence, and can contribute to better institutional functioning.

Greenwood's chapter on the chronic young adult is most timely. He describes the modifications necessary to make the model applicable to the so-called revolving door population of young adults. This population has come to the attention of the public as the "street people," that for many reasons have the experience of multiple hospitalizations, often with little lasting effect.

Offering a continuum of treatment is often difficult, making multiple hospitalizations more likely. In chapter 7, Perris and his associates describe an integrated system of treatment that follows the patient through the inpatient and outpatient experience. Without this integration, the patients can become the revolving door patients discussed in the previous chapter.

In the final chapter in this section, Grossman and Freet offer another CBT approach to working with adolescents. In their model, rational self-awareness was coupled with skill building to give the adolescent the tools to function more effectively in the world.

Part II deals with the applications of the CBT model in medical settings. While the problems described in the chapters that comprise this part of the book have psychiatric elements, the chapters deal with the medical patient.

Cancer is the second greatest killer of adults. Worden, in chapter 9, describes a therapeutic program designed to improve coping ability and to reduce the emotional stress that is an essential part of the overall treatment of cancer. Problems of low morale, feelings of helplessness, overwhelming hopelessness, and discouragement are common in these patients. This program has been found to be effective in helping patients change their view that no change is possible.

Kinchla's contribution in chapter 10 is an important contribution to the treatment of Type A behavior, a recognized contributor to numerous cardiac problems. If patients can be helped to reduce their Type A behavior, their lifespan can be prolonged. This cognitive behavioral appraoch can be an important and essential part of the treatment program for this often chronic and potentially fatal problem.

In chapter 11, Hibbard and her associates describe the issues and treatment possibilities in treating the depression that is part of the neurological syndrome of right brain stroke. Given the serious sequelae of the cerebrovascular difficulty, the concomitant depression makes treatment even more difficult. They have described their evaluation strategies in great detail, and have illustrated them with case material that helps to make their work readily adaptable with a variety of patient groups.

Hussian's chapter on treatment of the institutionalized elderly is an important contribution to the CBT literature. This growing patient has often been underserved not only in practice, but also in the treatment literature. By utilizing the PST approach, Hussian has developed another CBT approach that demonstrates that CBT approaches do not have to be obviated by the concomitants of aging.

In the book's final chapter, Weinberg describes the uses of the CBT model with spinal cord injured patients. Utilizing a group approach, she deals with the sexual rehabilitation process with great success. Her goal is to assist the injured patient to live more effectively as a physically disabled person in an able-bodied world.

A volume of this kind could not exist without a number of people working together. First and foremost, we wish to thank our contributors for sharing their clinical experience, insights, and time. We know that the time to write these chapters came out of their personal time as we know them all to be very active in their professional work. The editors wish to thank Norma Fox of Human Sciences Press for her encouragement and per patience. Donna Matthew of Human Sciences Press was the liaison who shepherded the volume to completion. Candi Parente was an invaluable help in coordinating time and effort. Shelly Nowlin and Eileen Swartz turned very rough draft into finished fine typescript. Dr. Karen M. Simon is a partner and collaborator who has helped to develop this and other projects (AF). (VG) would like to thank his father Joseph Greenwood for his support and encouragement over the years. Finally, the editors wish to thank Flora Zaken-Greenberg, Ph.D., for her help in the final editing of the volume.

Part I

APPLICATIONS IN PSYCHIATRIC SETTINGS

Chapter 1

COGNITIVE THERAPY

An Overview

Arthur Freeman

The goal of this introductory chapter is to offer the reader an overview of the basic cognitive therapy model, with specific focus on understanding the broad cognitive-therapy perspective. For the therapist sophisticated in the theory, conceptualizations, and applications of cognitive-behavioral techniques, this chapter can serve as a brief review. For the therapist trained in another model (whether dynamic or behavioral) and for whom this model is new, this can serve as an introduction.

The basic premise of the cognitive-behavioral therapy (CBT) model is that there is an essential interaction between the way individuals feel and behave and the way in which they construe their world, themselves, and the prospects for their future. The cognitive therapist does not avoid or dismiss the affective and behavioral issues that arise in therapy. It is the contention of cognitive therapy that the focus in therapy be primarily a cognitive focus. By maintaining this focus the therapist can help patients change behaviors, adapt more functionally to the world, and generally feel better.

DEFINITION OF COGNITIVE THERAPY

Cognitive therapy is a relatively short-term form of psychotherapy that is active, directive, and collaborative between patient and therapist. The goal of therapy is to help patients uncover their dysfunctional and irrational thinking, reality-test their thinking and behavior, and build more adaptive and functional techniques for responding both inter- and intrapersonally. Specifically, cognitive therapists work directly with their patients, proposing hypotheses and strategies for testing them, developing specific skills, and teaching a model for coping/adaptation. The focus is collaborative—that is, the therapist and patient working together as a team, rather than the patient being "in therapy." Collaboration is not always 50-50. With the severely depressed individual, the therapist's activity level must be high enough to supply the initial energy to complete the therapy work so that the collaboration might be 80-20, or even 90-10. The CBT therapist would rely not only on restatement but also restructuring, active intervention and interaction rather than simply interpretation, problem focus and direction rather than a vague and aimless therapeutic wandering, and collaboration rather than confrontation.

Cognitive therapy is a coping model of psychotherapy as opposed to a mastery model. The goal of cognitive therapy is not to "cure" but rather to help the patient to develop better coping strategies to deal with his life and work. By helping the patient uncover his dysfunctional thoughts and irrational belief systems, the cognitive therapist begins to teach a model for patients to utilize on their own.

The historical roots of CBT are mixed. On one hand, Kelley and Dowd (1980) see cognitive therapy as growing out of the behavior modification model, with the work of Bandura (1977a, 1977b, 1985) being an important milestone. The psychodynamic foundations, however, are an essential ingredient in CBT. In point of fact, both Beck and Ellis credit their early training in Adlerian and Horneyan models as central to their formation of a cognitive model of psychotherapy. Cognitive therapists have borrowed from the behavioral school the scientific method, a focus on behavioral change, and a variety of behavioral techniques and strategies (i.e., graded task assignments, scheduling, behavior rehearsal, and role playing). From the psychodynamic schools cognitive therapy has taken the notion of the importance of understanding the internal dialogue and process. Although avoiding the pitfalls of the construct of the unconscious, the cognitive therapist nevertheless works to give voice to the unspoken and to help patients redirect their thinking, attitudes, and behavior with a goal of increased function, amelioration of symptomology, and better adaptive strategies for life.

Cognitive therapy generally has come to mean the work of Aaron T. Beck (1976, 1979), but there are several cognitive therapies (or more correctly, cognitive behavior therapies), including Albert Ellis's (1962, 1973, 1977) rational-emotive therapy, Arnold Lazarus's (1976, 1981) multimodal therapy, Donald Meichenbaum's (1977) cognitive-behavior modification, and Maxie Maultsby's (1975) rational behavior therapy. The issue of cognition as an essential issue or central focus of psychotherapy also has been proposed by psychoanalysts of several analytic schools; Sullivanian, (Arieti 1980; and Crowley, 1985); Adlerian, (Shulman, 1985); Logotherapy (Frankl, 1985); Horneyan (Rendon, 1985); and Freudian (Bieber, 1981).

Common Misunderstandings of the CBT Model

Before discussing further what cognitive therapy is, it is important to discuss what it is not. There are several common misunderstandings about the theory and practice of CBT

1. The myth of simplicity. Implicit in this misunderstanding is the simplistic notion that CBT is as easy as ABC. The idea may be "Oh, it's easy. All I have to do is tell them what they are doing wrong," or "I just have to get them to say more positive things."

2. The power of positive thinking. CBT is not the "power of positive thinking" or looking for the silver lining in the dark clouds. That view is far more reflective of the works of Norman Vincent Peale (1978), Dale Carnegie (1982), or Bishop Fulton J. Sheen (1978).

3. Symptom relief versus "deep cure." One of the common (though misplaced) criticisms of the CBT approach is that it is a "Band-Aid" or surface model of psychotherapy as opposed to working on the "deep" problems or getting to the "core" issues. Inasmuch as the cognitive therapist is interested in dealing with the internal dialogue of the individual, there is clearly a dynamic focus.

4. Thought and affect. The goal of CBT is not to produce clear thinking in dysfunctionally behaving people with severe affective instability. The focus of the work will involve dealing with depressive affect, pain problems, anger control, or anxiety symptoms via cognitive behavioral strategies.

5. Focus on the past. There can be no argument that individuals are a product of their past experiences. Individuals learn ways of responding, both emotionally and behaviorally, from early socializing agents such as parents, home, school, religion, and peers. The CBT focus is not so much on what was but rather on what is and what maintains or reinforces dysfunctional behavior.

6. Fifteen sessions or less. The cognitive therapist would not generally set a limit on the number of sessions that a patient may come to for treatment. Research studies (Blackburn et al., 1981; Murphy et al., 1984; and Rush et al., 1977) have clearly demonstrated that there is a major amelioration of symptoms in 12 to 20 sessions over 16 weeks. Unless the patient is in an outcome study, the amount of time that the patient spends in therapy is dependent on the nature of his problems, the level of motivation, availability for sessions, and the number of presenting life issues.

7. Avoidance of medication. CBT has been found to be as effective as pharmacotherapy in the treatment of unipolar depression (Murphy et al., 1984). Medication would be recommended as an adjunct to CBT with certain patients, i.e., bipolar depressives, psychotics, or those patients whose depression has made them vegetative and unable to respond to the therapy.

8. Transference. Good therapy requires that the therapist be mindful of a number of nonspecific factors in therapy, including the ability to establish and maintain a working relationship, demonstrating empathy and caring, active listening, and the like. The reality of the patient's having specific reactions to the therapist cannot be denied, and it is essential for the cognitive therapist to deal with these reactions directly by having the patient look at the cognitions that are generating the behavior.

9. *Cognitive-behavioral eclecticism.* The acquisition of a number of CBT techniques, thrown into a grab-bag to be used as part of a so-called eclectic approach, places the therapist in the situation of possibly coming to the bottom of the bag, and having no further gimmicks to use. An essential part of the model is the ability to conceptualize patient problems within the cognitive-behavioral framework and then to *generate* additional strategies as needed.

Cognitive Model of Emotion

Beck (1976, 1979) posits the existence of three factors in emotion: (1) the cognitive triad, (2) cognitive distortions, and (3) schema.

The concept of the triad, initially developed to understand the verbalizations and thinking of depressed patients involves the depressed patient's idiosyncratic negative veiw of self, world, and future.

The negative view of self is evidenced in the statements "I'm no good," "I'm fat/ugly/stupid/a failure," or "I'm a loser." Statements typical of the negative view of the world (that is, the patient's idiosyncratic world) might include "It's unfair," "They're unfair," "It's too hard." Finally, the negative view of the future involves a pessimism or hopelessness that is the prime ingredient in suicidality. Verbalizations include "It will never change" or "I'll always be this/that way." The model is, however, more generally useful. In anxiety problems there is the tendency also to see problems as related to self, world, or future in terms of focus, locus, and direction of dysfunctional thinking.

All humans appear to have a capacity to distort reality in a number of significant ways. If the distortion is severe enough, the individual may lose touch with reality and be labeled psychotic. However, the neurotic (to use that old *DSM II* term) distorts reality in particular significant and dyfunctional ways. Beck (1976), Beck et al. (1979) and Burns (1980a,b) have classified particular types of distortions that are most commonly seen. These distortions are fueled by the basic life schemata or underlying assumptions (similar to Ellis's rational and irrational beliefs). These irrational belief systems or rules for living become a substrate or wellspring from which the basic cognitive distortions emerge. These schema are often established early in childhood. When an external event stimulates a particular schema, certain specific distortions or more general styles of distortion are seen. Schema may be family schema, religious schema, cultural or personal schema. They can be simple or complex, compelling or noncompelling. The schema may be isolated or appear in various constellations. They may be accessible or guarded, or any combination of the above.

Cognitive Distortions

Distortions may be in either a positive or negative direction. If one were to distort in a positive direction, one might unrealistically engage in activities that may be harmful, i.e., continuing to exercise after feeling severe chest pains while saying "It's nothing, I can do it, I'm invincible." Or, one might be the "fool" who rushes in "where angels fear to tread" and enter a business that everyone predicts will fail—and end up rich and successful. It is the negative distortions that are the major focus of the CBT, though dysfunctional positive distortions are also grist for the therapeutic mill. These distortions do not appear in isolation but in a number of combinations and permutations. For the purpose of illustration, the major types of distortions will be discussed. Examples of these distortions include the following:

Figure 1-1. Depression triad/"catch"

SELF
(Focus of Threat)

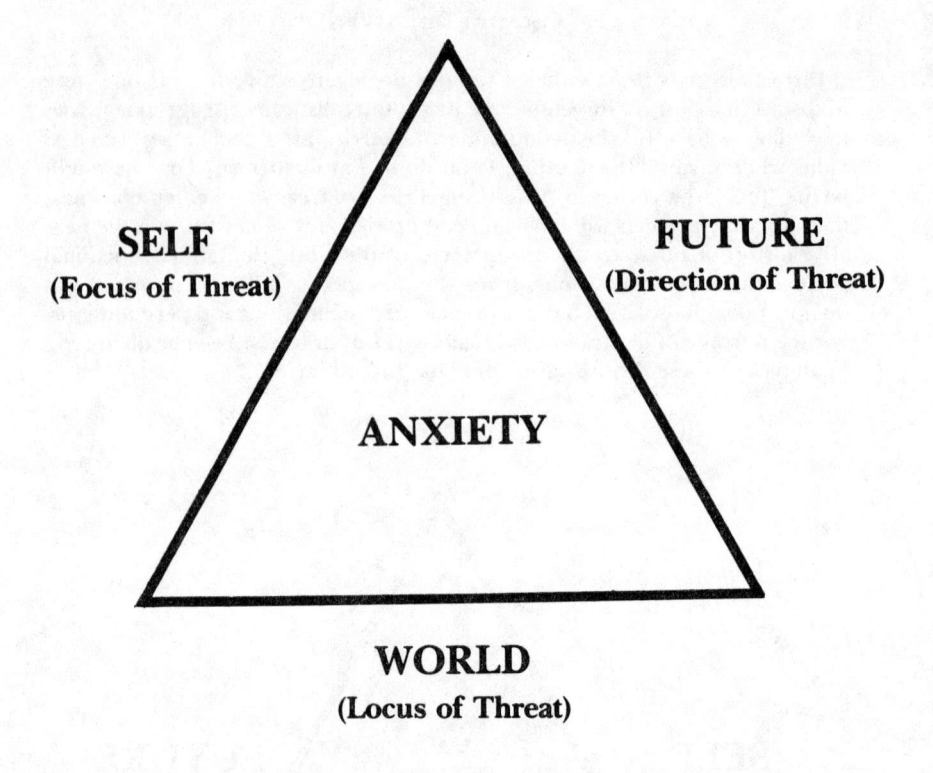

FUTURE
(Direction of Threat)

ANXIETY

WORLD
(Locus of Threat)

Figure 1-2. Anxiety triad/"catch"

All-or-nothing thinking. This refers to the tendency to evaluate performance or personal qualities in extremist, black-and-white categories. For example, a doctoral student was referred subsequent to a serious suicide attempt. He had written his dissertation and submitted it to his committee chair. A meeting with the chairperson was held to discuss the scheduling of an oral defense. At this meeting the student inquired as to whether the committee saw his dissertation as being "with merit" (an honors designation). On being informed that the committee saw the dissertation as being an excellent piece of work but not with the designation of "with merit," the student asked for the dissertation back and held it for a year to try to make it better. After a year he tried to kill himself because he thought that he had done his best work and it was only excellent. "Why be just one more PhD?" he asked.

Catastrophizing. This is the "Chicken Little" approach to life. The individual who continually catastrophizes sees the cloud (or creates it) around every silver lining. This exaggeration of difficulty to disaster causes the individual to live in rather constant fear of the imminent end of the world. For example, socially anxious individuals live in fear of social contact because they might say or do something that they are sure will cause them to be shunned by civilized (and possibly uncivilized) persons.

Overgeneralization. You arbitrarily conclude that a single negative event will happen over and over again. For example, a twenty-six-year-old man entered therapy to help him start dating. He reported that he had asked a girl out once while in college. She turned him down, which gave him the evidence that he would *never* have a date: "Girls will always turn me down." When I questioned him about his evidence, he stated that he had never tried again; he was generalizing that single event to all events of a similar category for the future.

Selective abstraction. In this distortion individuals selectively choose the single or few pieces of evidence that validate or support their depressive ideas while ignoring all of the other available data. In effect they pick out the negative details in any situation and dwell on them exclusively, thus concluding that the whole situation is negative. A thirty-year-old woman entered therapy as a way of "getting back into the swing of things" after her divorce. Her complaint was one heard too often, "All of the nice men are either taken or gay." She was employed as a nurse at a large teaching hospital. When questioned about the availability of eligible men or about her interest in someone, she reported that their was a senior resident attached to her service that she found attractive, but she "knew" that he wasn't interested in her. Her evidence was that he had never asked her out. He had, however, on a number of occasions had coffee waiting for her in the morning, had come in to "check" on his patients even on days and at times that he wasn't scheduled to be on duty, and had cut out cartoons and left them at the nursing station for her. Despite all of the other evidence, his not asking her out was the operative fact. When she finally asked him to go for coffee, she discovered that he thought that she was still married and that was why he hadn't sought to become more involved than by what he saw as flirting. (They did get together and lived happily, albeit briefly.)

Disqualifying the positive. This is truly an amazing skill, constantly snatching defeat from the jaws of victory. A forty-five-year old woman had recently been graduated from a large university with a major in accounting. Her grade point average at graduation was 4.0. Her explanations for her success were (1) she was lucky, (2) she had easy teachers, (3) her teachers felt sorry for her because of her advanced age, and (4) it took her 5 years rather than the expected 4 years (she discounted the fact of her caring for her home, cooking, shopping, cleaning, caring for three children, all in addition to going to school).

Arbitrary inference. This involves jumping to an arbitrary, negative conclusion that is not justified by the facts of the situation or is in direct contradiction to the facts. Two types of arbitrary inference are mind reading and negative prediction.

1. *Mind reading.* Mind reading involves the idea that others should be able to read one's mind and know what one would like. It might also involve the idea that a person has the skill to "know" what others think of him/her and therefore do not bother to check it out. This is often seen in working with couples. For example:
PARTNER A: "You're angry. I can tell that you're angry because of the way your eyebrow goes up."
PARTNER B: "No, I'm not angry. I had something in my eye."
PARTNER A: "You can't tell me that. I know you too well. You are angry."
PARTNER B *(shouting):* "I said I'm not angry."
PARTNER A: "See, I told you that you were angry."
2. *Negative prediction.* The person imagines, and in fact predicts, that something bad is about to happen, then takes this prediction as fact even though it may not be realistic. Predictions of failure even though well prepared for an examination, doing poorly on an interview, or doing a poor job are all examples of negative predictions. The danger in these predictions is that they may become self-fulfilling prophecies.

Magnification or minimization. This may be called the binocular distortion because the individual is either exaggerating things out of proportion or shrinking them. For example, when looking at mistakes or flaws or at what one sees to be the skills or talents of others, there is a tendency to make things seem bigger than they really are. In contrast, looking at either the strengths one sees for oneself or at the problems or flaws of others, the minimizer will probably look through the opposite end of the binoculars, which makes things seem small and distant. Because one magnifies imperfections and minimizes good points, the net result is that the person ends up thinking that he/she is inadequate and inferior to other people and feeling depressed.

Emotional reasoning. This distortion involves taking one's emotions as evidence for the way things really are. The logic is "I feel, therefore I am." Examples of emotional reasoning include "I feel guilty. Therefore, I must be a bad person." "I feel overwhelmed and hopeless. Therefore, my problems must be impossible to solve." "I feel inadequate. Therefore, I must be a worthless person." "I feel very nervous around elevators. Therefore, elevators must be very dangerous."

"Should/must/ought" statements. These self statements always seem to have a finger wagging under the nose. Their focus depends on trying to motivate an individual with guilt. By saying, "I/you should do this" or "I/you must do that," the imperative seems clear. These statements have the potential to gen-

erate guilt, pressure, and resentment. Interestingly, the result of this type of distortion may not be to motivate but rather to de-motivate and leave you feeling helpless and apathetic.

When one directs "should" statements toward others, a likely reaction is to have been frustrated, angry, or indignant. For example: It is not unusual for the desk in my office to be stacked with papers, some stacks neatly piled, others askew. A patient came in and demanded to know why my desk was a mess. Her statement was that a therapist *should* be able to organize his desk.

Labeling and mislabeling. Personal labeling involves creating a negative identity that is based on one's errors and imperfections, as if these revealed one' true self. Labeling is an extreme form of overgeneralization. The philosophy behind this tendency is "The measure of a man is the mistakes he makes." There is a good chance that someone is involved in self-labeling whenever they describe themselves with sentences beginning with "I am . . ." For example, when an individual goofs up in some way, he might say, "I'm a loser," instead of "I lost out on this," or one might think "I'm a failure," instead of "I made a mistake."

Mislabeling involves describing an event with words that are inaccurate and heavily emotionally loaded. For example, a physician on a diet ate a dish of ice cream and thought: "How disgusting and repulsive of me. I'm a pig." These thoughts made him so upset that he ate the whole quart of ice cream.

Personalization. This involves taking events that have nothing to do with one and making them personally meaningful. (We see this at its extreme in the paranoid.) If they were on their way somewhere, in a rush, and found traffic tied up, they might say to themselves, "This always happens when I'm in a rush." If they were questioned as to whether this *always* happened, they would probably say, "Of course not, it doesn't *always* happen."

Although all of the preceding distortions are negative and can lead to dysfunctional behavior, it should be noted that at some point each of them most likely would have had a functional use. The ability to monitor and assess our behavior and experience is an important part of this function. When this is taken to an extreme, however, it becomes dysfunctional. It is important for individuals to learn to monitor nonverbal cues, but when they monitor them and make inferences about behavior (arbitrary inference) it may be dysfunctional. Striving for success is an important part of the American ideal, but taken to the extreme of all or nothing, it becomes a perfectionism that leads to dysfunction.

UNDERLYING ASSUMPTIONS AND IRRATIONAL BELIEFS

The source of the distortions is irrational belief systems. Beliefs are of various strengths and include social learning—i.e., being polite and always saying "please" and "thank you"; religious learning—i.e., the strong belief in religious values and commandments, the "shalt and shalt nots"; and internalization of legal codes—i.e., living in accordance with the rule of law. This would include everything from not killing or stealing to "walk/don't walk." The individual's degree of belief in these underlying assumptions or rules of living will determine the strength that the beliefs have as a wellspring of distortions.

An example of the distortion-belief can be seen in the following reconstruction. A child of elementary school age comes home from school with a 98 on a math test. The parents either overtly or covertly inquire about the other two points with statements such as "I thought you knew that work?" or "What happened to the other two points?" When the child comes home with a perfect exam paper, he is greeted with smiles, hugs, and kisses (a 98 warranted only a pat on the back and "better luck next time"). A basic rule of life that might develop from this treatment would be "To be accepted/loved/thought well of/prized, I must/should/ought to be perfect." With this as a basic underlying belief, the individual dichotomizes experiences as success (100%) or failure (99.9% or below). The underlying belief, or schema, is not necessarily good or bad but neutral.

It is how we interpret the schema that can cause problems. If one has the belief that "people should always love me," one might become dependent and helpless, always worried that others might get angry or annoyed with one. On the other hand, an individual may become a superior teacher, an actor, or other professional who constantly gets approval or "love." Certain schema may be dormant and come into play only in certain situations and under specific circumstances. Two apparently contradictory schema can coexist. One might believe that killing is bad but might kill to protect oneself, one's family, or one's property. Overall, the major thrust of the therapy work can be on the schema, so that changes are more lasting. Further, the therapeutic interventions aimed at the schema can be far more powerful.

TREATMENT

In the course of cognitive therapy treatment, the first issue addressed would be the distortions. The style, type, and content of the distortion would be considered as signposts to the underlying assumptions. A patient often will terminate therapy having learned to cope successfully with his distortions but leaving the underlying assumptions untouched. The more elegant solution, however, would be to have the individual cope not only with the distortions but with the assumptions.

Structure is an essential issue in therapy. A case might be made that patients enter therapy because they have lost the ability to structure their lives, their thinking, or their overall life experience. The goal of therapy is to structure both the course of therapy and the individual therapy session. This will allow us to make the best use of time, effort, and energy. The cognitive therapist works with the patient to develop a list of specific problems to be worked on. Patients coming into treatment to work on depression or communication or—the most ambiguous of all—"to get their heads together" do not present symptoms that can be worked on or problems that can be ameliorated. The cognitive therapist first needs to assess the problems and then prioritize them. Lazarus (1981) spells out the need for specificity in his BASIC ID model, where the clinician evaluates problems in terms of *B*ehavior, *A*ffect, *S*ensation, *I*magery, *C*ognition, *I*nterpersonal relationships, and *D*rugs/*D*iet (physiological issues).

Having taken a problem or task focus in the therapy, the cognitive therapist takes a focused approach to the session. Just as we might formulate an agenda for a meeting to allow the most efficient use of time, it is helpful for the therapist and the patient to generate an agenda for the session. Typical agenda items might include a review of the week (brief and focused on items of relevance), a review of the session in the last 3 to 5 minutes, review of homework, and particular items to be worked on within the session. Once the agenda is set and prioritized, it is not engraved in granite but should be flexible. If the patient digresses and begins to free-associate, the therapist can either take a task focus and ask whether the patient wants to continue with this line of work or whether he/she wants to return to the agenda. (For a more elaborate discussion of the agenda-setting strategy, see Beck et al., 1979; Freeman et al., in press.) The "meat" of the session depends on what the problems are. The particular strategies and interventions will depend on the type of problem and the skills of the patient and the therapist. The final few minutes of the session can be used to evaluate the session, go over homework for the next session, get feedback of therapist behavior, and have the patient capsulate what it is the patient has learned during that session and will be taking home with him. It also allows a more gradual ending of the session than the traditional "We have to stop here."

COGNITIVE AND BEHAVIORAL STRATEGIES

A number of cognitive strategies are utilized to help patients test the reality of their cognitions. We can divide them roughly into cognitive and behavioral techniques, though some cross the boundary between the two. We do not choose a particular technique and doggedly follow that technique to the bitter end. The goal is to have the therapist develop an array of techniques that can be utilized as needed.

Cognitive Strategies

Idiosyncratic meaning. Therapists cannot assume that they always know what a patient means by a term or statement. They need to ask directly for their meaning. If one were to ask a group of professionals to indicate what they considered the prime descriptor of depression, out of 100 responses there would be a large number of prime descriptors including sad, hopeless, sleep difficulty, and eating problems. Given the differing ideas, one cannot be sure what patients mean when they say "depressed" or "anxious" or "upset."

Questioning the evidence. People use certain evidence to maintain their ideas and beliefs. It is essential to teach patients to question the evidence that they are using to maintain and strengthen an idea or belief.

Reattribution. A common statement made by patients is "It's all my fault." This is commonly heard in situations of relationship difficulty, separation, or divorce. Although one cannot dismiss this totally, it is doubtful that a single person is totally responsible for everything. The therapist can help the patient distribute responsibility among all relevant parties.

Examining options and alternatives. Suicidal patients are prime examples of individuals who see themselves as having lost all options. Alternatively, they see their options and alternatives as so limited that among their few choices death might be the easiest or simplest. The goal is to work with the patient to generate additional options.

De-catastrophizing. Given the patient's catastrophic thinking, this may be termed the "what if" technique. This involves helping patients to see that they are overestimating the catastrophic nature of a situation. Questions that might be asked of the patient: "So what?", "What is the worst thing that can happen?", or "And if it does occur, what would be so terrible?"

Fantasized consequences. In this technique patients fantasize a situation and describe their concerns. Often patients describe their worst concerns and see the irrationality of their ideas. This technique allows patients to bring into the consulting room imaged events, situations or interactions that have happened previously or are going to happen in the future.

Advantages and disadvantages. Having patients list the advantages and disadvantages of a particular belief or behavior can help them to gain balance and perspective. This may be seen as a scaling technique, having patients move away from an all-or-nothing position to one that focuses on the advantages and disadvantages to a particular behavior or way of thinking.

Turning adversity to advantage. There are times that a seeming disaster can be used to advantage. Losing one's job can be a disaster but may in some cases be the entry point to a new job or even a new career. Having a deadline imposed may be seen as oppressive and unfair but may be used as a motivator.

Labeling of distortions. Many patients like to label the particular distortions that they are utilizing as a way of monitoring and altering their dysfunctional thinking.[Dave Burns's *Feeling Good* (1980) is excellent for this purpose.] The patient can see the "personalizing" or "mind reading" they are doing.

Downward arrow. This also can be called the "then what" technique. This involves a guided association approach. By having patients follow their reasoning through to each succeeding level of reasoning/belief, they can be helped to understand the underlying schematic issues.

Paradox or exaggeration. By taking an idea to an extreme, the therapist often can help to move the patient to a more central position vis-a-vis a particular belief. Care must be taken not to insult, ridicule, or embarrass the patient. Given a hypersensitivity to criticism and ridicule, some patients may experience the therapist as making light of their problems.

Scaling. For the patient who sees things as all or nothing, the technique of scaling or seeing things as existing on a continuum can be very helpful.

Replacement imagery. The patient's imagery and dreams can be used as grist for the therapeutic mill. [For a fuller description see Freeman (1980)]. We can help patients to generate more effective and functional coping images to replace the depressogenic or anxiety-producing ones.

Externalization of voices. By having the therapist take the part of the dysfunctional voice, the patient can get practice in adaptive responding. The therapist can first model being adaptive to the patient's verbalization of dysfunctional thoughts. After modeling the functional, the therapist can, in a graded manner, become an increasingly more difficult dysfunctional voice for the patient to respond to.

Cognitive rehearsal. By visualizing an event in the mind's eye, the patient can practice particular behaviors. A number of athletes are using this technique to enhance performance, i.e., lifting more weight, jumping higher jumps, scoring more baskets, or taking a horse over a higher jump.

BEHAVIORAL TECHNIQUES

The goal in using behavioral techniques is twofold: first, to work at changing behavior through the use of a broad range of behavioral techniques; second, and more important, to utilize the behavioral techniques as short-term interventions in the service of a longer-term cognitive change. The behavioral work can be the "laboratory" work of the therapy and a way of collecting data for the therapy.

Activity scheduling. A common self statement for many professionals is "There aren't enough hours in the day to do all that I need to do." How often do individuals who are feeling overloaded consider scheduling time 1 or 2 weeks in advance so as to maximize the potential for productivity of the available time? By utilizing the activity schedule in the very first session as a homework assignment, the therapist can (1) assess the patient's present use of time, (2) help to plan better and more productive use of time, and (3) begin to socialize the patient to the idea of doing homework.

Mastery and pleasure ratings. Utilizing the activity schedule, the patient can begin to examine mastery, M (how well they see themselves doing something) and their pleasure, P (how much they enjoy something). Utilizing the activity schedule, the patient not only can assess the M and P but begin to plan more mastery and pleasure.

Behavioral rehearsal. The session can be used to practice potential interactions, i.e., discussing a problem with a significant other, a boss, or a friend. The therapist can give feedback on the patient's performance and coach the patient on more effective responses or response styles. This strategy may be used for skill building or practice of existing skills.

Social skills training. When patients describe having social difficulty or the therapist assumes the patient having social difficulties based on the therapeutic intervention, we cannot assume that it is because they do not want to behave differently. There may be a skills deficit and not just a motivational deficit. Part of the work of therapy is to help patients gain the social skills that they have missed as part of their normal developmental.

Bibliotherapy. For the patient for whom it is appropriate, reading can be very helpful. Readings like *Feeling Good* (Burns, 1980b), *Cognitive Therapy and the Emotional Disorders* (Beck, 1976), *Coping with Depression* (Beck & Greenberg, 1974), *Talk Sense to Yourself* (McMullin & Caesy, 1975), or *Own Your Own Life* (Emery, 1982) can help patients do much of the therapy work on their own with, of course, the therapist's guidance. It should be stressed that bibliotherapy is part of the overall psychotherapy and not the sum total of the therapy work.

Graded task assignments. By establishing a hierarchy of difficulty, tasks can be arranged so that the patient can learn to approximate the final goal in a step-by-step manner, starting with the simplest and moving to the complex. This may involve starting by collecting data and moving to more direct interactions.

Assertiveness training. Like social skills training, assertiveness training involves the therapist in taking the very directive role of teaching the patient certain skills, in this case assertiveness skills.

In vivo work. For many problems, the most effective manner of intervention may be direct modeling in an in-vivo setting. Agoraphobia, social phobia, or social anxiety difficulties respond well to the therapist's working with the patient in the very situations that generate the "heat." This is far more effective than getting reports of the problems a week later.

Relaxation, meditation, and breathing. For anxious patients the use of progressive relaxation, focused breathing, and meditation can be helpful to distract themselves and begin to gain a sense of control over their anxiety. The use of hyperventilation as a technique for demonstrating ways of mastering overbreathing through the use of focused breathing activities is very useful.

Shame-attacking exercises. This technique, much favored by Ellis and his colleagues, has patients actively performing activities that test their catastrophic thinking in regard to what others will think of them; for example, having a patient call out the stops on an elevator, bus, or subway and seeing that most people do not care or respond. Further, the patient can be helped to see that it matters little what they/the observers think.

Homework

An important part of cognitive therapy is the idea that therapy does not happen 1 or 2 hours a week in the therapist's office but needs to be a process that is constantly lived. The cognitive therapy patient is not being "therapized" so much as collaborating with the therapist. An important part of the collaboration is doing self-help work at home. Clinical experience has indicated that the patients who do more self-help work make progress more quickly in therapy and are able to meet their stated therapy goals more quickly. Self-help work includes any and all of the cognitive and behavioral techniques indicated above. The particular homework needs to be appropriate to the problem, within the skills of the patient, and collaboratively arrived at.

Summary

In this introduction the goal was to lay down a basic groundwork for all of what follows in this volume. No single chapter can fill the gap that needs to be filled by training or workshop experiences. The goal was to cover the basic areas as briefly, though completely, as possible. The contributors to this volume have taken this basic model and expanded it to new populations and new problems. Their creativity is not an end point for therapy but rather a beginning.

References

Arieti, S. (1980). Cognition in psychoanalysis. *Journal of the American Academy of Psychoanalysis, 8,* 3–23.

Bandura, A. (1977a). Self-efficacy: Towards a unifying theory of behavior change. *Psychological Review, 84,* 191–215.

Bandura, A. (1977b). *Social learning theory.* Englewood Cliffs, NJ: Prentice-Hall.

Bandura, A. (1985). Model of causality in social learning theory. In *Cognition and psychotherapy,* M. Mahoney & A. Freeman (Eds.). New York: Plenum Press.

Beck, A. T. (1976). *Cognitive therapy and the emotional disorders.* New York: International Universities Press.

Beck, A. T., Rush, A. J., Shaw, B. F., & Emery, G. (1979). *Cognitive therapy of depression.* New York: Guilford.

Bieber, I. (1981). *Cognitive psychoanalysis.* New York: Jason Aronson.

Blackburn, I., Bishop, S., Glen, A. I. M., Whalley, L. J., and Christie, J. E. (1981). The efficacy of cognitive therapy in depression: A treatment using cognitive therapy and pharmacotherapy, each alone and in combination. *British Journal of Psychiatry, 139,* 181–189.

Burns, D. D. (1980a). *Definitions of cognitive distortions.* Unpublished manuscript.

Burns, D. D. (1980b). *Feeling good.* New York: Morrow.

Carnegie, D. (1982). *How to win friends and influence people.* New York: Pocket Books.

Crowley, R. (1985). Cognitive elements in the work of Harry Stack Sullivan. *Cognition and psychotherapy,* In M. Mahoney & A. Freeman (Eds.). New York: Plenum Press.

Ellis, A. (1962). *Reason and emotion in psychotherapy.* New York: Lyle Stuart.

Ellis, A. (1973). *Humanistic psychotherapy: The rational-emotive approach.* New York: Julian.

Ellis, A. (1977). The basic clinical theory of rational-emotive therapy. In *Handbook of rational-emotive therapy,* A. Ellis & R. Grieger (Eds.). New York: Springer.

Emery, G. (1982). *Own your own life: How the new cognitive therapy can make you feel wonderful.* New York: New American Library.

Frankl, V. (1985). Cognition and logotherapy. In *Cognition and psychotherapy,* M. Mahoney & A. Freeman (Eds.). New York: Plenum Press.

Freeman, A., Simon, K. M., Pretzer, J., & Fleming, B. (in press). *Clinical applications of cognitive therapy.* New York: Plenum Press.

Freeman, A. (1980). Dreams and imagery. In *New directions in cognitive therapy,* G. Emery, S. D. Hollon, & R. C. Bedrosian, (Eds.). New York: Guilford Press.

Kelley, F. D., & Dowd, E. G. (1980). Adlerian psychology and cognitive behavior therapy: Convergences. *Journal of Individual Psychology, 36,* 119–135.

Lazarus, A. (Ed.) (1976). *Multimodal behavior therapy.* New York: Springer.

Lazarus, A. A. (1981). *The practice of multimodal therapy.* New York: McGraw-Hill.

Mahoney, M. J. (1974). *Cognition and behavior modification.* Cambridge, MA: Ballinger.

Maultsby, M. (1975). *Help yourself to happiness.* New York: Institute for Rational Emotive Therapy.

McMullin, R. E., & Caesy, B. (1975). *Talk sense to yourself: A Guide to cognitive restructuring therapy.* Counseling Research

Meichenbaum, D. (1977). *Cognitive-behavior modification.* New York: Plenum Press.
Murphy, G. E., Simons, A. D., Wetzel, R. D., Lustman, P. J. (1984). Cognitive therapy versus tricyclic antidepressants in major depression. *Archives of General Psychiatry, 41,* 33–41.
Peale, N. V. (1978). *Power of positive thinking.* New York: Fawcett.
Rendon, M. (1985). Cognition and psychoanalysis: A Horneyan perspective. In *Cognition and psychotherapy,* M. Mahoney & A. Freeman (Eds.). New York: Plenum Press.
Rush, A. J., Beck, A. T., Kovacs, M. & Hallon, S. (1977). Comparative efficacy of cognitive therapy and imipramine in the treatment off depressed outpatients. *Cognitive Therapy and Research, 1,* 17-37.
Sheen, F. J. (1978). *Life is worth living.* New York: Doubleday.
Shulman, B. H. (1985). Cognitive therapy and the individual psychology of Alfred Adler. In *Cognition and psychotherapy,* M. Mahoney & A. Freeman (Eds.). New York: Plenum.
Smith, D. (1982). Trends in counseling and psychotherapy. *American Psychologist, 37,* 802–809.
Wachtel, P. (1977). *Psychoanalysis and behavior therapy: Toward an integration.* New York: Basic Books.

Chapter 2

COGNITIVE THERAPY AND MEDICATION AS COMBINED TREATMENT

Jesse H. Wright

Most hospitalized patients receive some form of combined pharmacotherapy and psychotherapy. Medication usually is offered as "standard" treatment for inpatients. However, there is considerable variation in the application of psychotherapy on inpatient units. Some hospitals are oriented toward providing intensive long-term psychodynamic psychotherapy. Others ascribe to a strongly biological model and actively discourage psychotherapy. Only a few inpatient units have attempted to use a cognitive behavioral treatment approach.

Regardless of the particular treatment model, it could be argued that pharmacotherapy is never used alone with hospitalized patients. There are multiple opportunities for psychotherapeutic experiences in the hospital milieu. Physicians, nurses, psychologists, social workers, occupational therapists, activities workers, aides, and even other patients provide a complex network of helping individuals who interact in specific and nonspecific therapeutic ways with the hospitalized patient (Chase, Wright, & Ragade, 1980).

Cognitive therapy is a recent addition to the list of specific psychotherapies used with inpatients. Although originally developed for outpatients, this approach also appears to be of considerable benefit to hospitalized patients (see other chapters, *this volume*). Controlled research on outcome of cognitive therapy in hospitalized patients has not yet been reported, but several centers, including our unit at the Norton Hospital and the University of Louisville, have now had several years of experience in treating inpatients with cognitive therapy. A recently completed study from our unit on combined treatment with cognitive therapy and nortriptyline will be reported elsewhere.

The focus of this chapter will be on clinical issues in using combined pharmacotherapy and cognitive therapy. Major emphasis will be placed on the treatment of depression, since this is the most common diagnosis in psychiatric inpatients in short-term hospitals. However, an effort will be made to describe general treatment techniques that can be applied to treatment of other disorders.

A Rationale for Combined Treatment

Although some depressed inpatients have been successfully treated with cognitive therapy alone, Rush has reported that a small series of depressed patients with abnormal dexamethasone suppression tests failed to respond to cognitive therapy without medication (Rush, 1983; Shaw, 1981). He has recommended that depressed patients with melancholic features or abnormal dexamethasone suppression tests be given biological treatments as the primary therapy. (Rush, 1983). There is little doubt that psychopharmacologic treatments are effective for severe psychiatric disorders. The usual response rate for patients treated with tricyclic antidepressants is about 70% whereas the response rate for those treated with placebo is approximately 40% (Baldessarini, 1977). The relapse rate for patients treated with tricyclic antidepressants is one-half the rate of patients given placebo (Baldessarini, 1977). Antipsychotic drugs also have been shown to be consistently superior to placebo in suppressing psychotic symptoms (Clark & Del Giudice, 1978; Baldessarini, 1977).

Despite the recognized effectiveness of psychotropic drugs, there are a number of questions that remain unanswered. Could combined pharmacotherapy and psychotherapy improve the rate of treatment response? Are there certain types of hospitalized patients who can be successfully treated with cognitive therapy alone? Can cognitive therapy facilitate the effects of medication? Can medication help with the process of cognitive therapy? What are the possible sites of interaction between treatments? Since there are no definite answers available for these questions at the present time, the use of combined treatment must be based on theoretical and practical considerations.

It would appear unlikely that depression or any other common psychiatric disorder has a single cause or only one possible treatment. Akiskal and McKinney (1975) have suggested that there is a "psychobiological final common pathway" in which multiple forces (e.g., genetic, biological, psychodynamic, behavioral, cognitive, social) coalesce in disease expression. Treatment can be directed at any single one of these sites. However, it is possible that the use of multiple treatments, matched to the individual patient's unique blend of psychological pathology, could maximize the chances for a good treatment response.

A rather straightforward working formulation for the interaction between pharmacotherapy and cognitive therapy is that drugs suppress symptoms (e.g., insomnia, agitation, low energy, impaired concentration, distorted thoughts, and psychotic symptoms) and thereby help the patient to participate in psychotherapy—a process in which attention, concentration, rationality, and ability to remember are required for learning. Conversely, enhanced rapport and understanding from psychotherapy help with drug compliance and enhance hopefulness of a response to treatment.

Two well-controlled outpatient research studies that compared cognitive therapy alone, tricyclic antidepressants plus medication checks, and combined cognitive therapy and tricyclic antidepressants in the treatment of major depression found no evidence of superior short-term outcome (e.g., symptom relief) in patients treated with combined therapy (Hollon, DeRubeis, & Evans, 1983; Murphy, Simons, Wetzel, & Lustman, 1984). However, there was also no evidence of negative interactions between treatments. In another study, Blackburn and co-workers (1981) found that patients from a hospital outpatient clinic responded better to combined treatment than cognitive therapy or pharmacotherapy alone, but patients from a general practice setting had equal responses to cognitive therapy and combined therapy. The latter groups of patients had a poor response to drug treatment alone. Hollon and co-workers (1983) have reported long-term follow-up results that suggest a superior outcome for combined therapy. It has been argued that the addition of cognitive therapy could lead to better long-term results because the patient learns new patterns of thinking and behaving.

Cochran (1982) recently has reported that cognitive therapy added to lithium in the treatment of bipolar outpatients improves drug compliance. Cognitive therapy helped the patients to understand their disorder and to make rational decisions about following the treatment protocol. This study may be more relevant to clinical issues in combined treatment than the previously mentioned outcome studies. Cochran (1982) attempted to integrate the treatments conceptually and to communicate this to patients treated with combined therapy. The larger controlled studies with unipolar patients delivered the two treatments as separate entities without having therapists or patients work at integrating treatment concepts or methods.

Even if all of the evidence from outpatient trials suggested that pharmacotherapy and psychotherapy do not facilitate one another, a case could still be made for combining treatments with inpatients. It is not yet known whether the results of outpatient experiments can be extrapolated to hospitalized patients. Furthermore, a majority of inpatients would not fit the strict categorization requirements for treatment assignment in outpatient randomized trials. patients who are admitted to hospitals frequently have multiple and complex problems—both psychiatric and medical. Symptoms are more severe, social support systems are usually broken down, and social and occupational function frequently has been lost (Maxmen, Tucker, & LeBow, 1974). These patients usually require intensive treatment, including pharmacotherapy, individual psychotherapy, family therapy, and vocational/occupational therapy.

It also should be noted that most patients ask for combined treatment and seek it out if it is not offered. Weissman and co-workers (1979) found that the dropout rate in their study of pharmacotherapy and interpersonal therapy was lower in the combined treatment group than with either treatment alone, and patients who dropped out and sought other therapy usually selected combined treatment. Our clinical experience has been similar. Requests for treatment with drug alone are extremely rare. Although a few patients ask not to be treated with medications, this is often the result of dysfunctional attitudes, a topic that will be explored later.

INDICATIONS FOR COMBINED TREATMENT

Depressed inpatients treated at the Norton Psychiatric Clinic, University of Louisville, have responded well to combined cognitive therapy and pharmacotherapy. In a study of 38 patients with primary, major depression, the mean Hamilton Depression Rating Scale (HRS) score fell from 29.53 to 15.87 after 2 weeks of combined inpatient treatment and to 10.39 after 4 weeks of treatment (Wright, Barrett, Linder et al.) Only a few of the patients in this study failed to show substantial improvement. One of these cases illustrates the possibility of improving outcome by adjustments in treatment. After completion of a 4-week double-blind trial with cognitive therapy three times per week and nortriptyline, a twenty-six-year-old woman had shown some improvement but remained significantly depressed and had persistent suicidal ideation. Her HRS was 16. Lithium was added to her treatment regimen because lithium may facilitate recovery in patients who have been resistant to tricyclic antidepressants (deMontigny, Cournoyer, Morissette et al., 1983). She was soon able to concentrate much better, and she began to have more energy to participate in activities. Cognitive therapy became more meaningful to her as she was able to follow through with cognitive and behavioral assignments. She improved dramatically within 2 weeks. A recently completed 6-month follow-up found this patient to be in complete remission, with a HRS score of 0.

We usually treat hospitalized major depressives with individual, family, and group cognitive therapy combined with a tricyclic antidepressant. The medication is given in sufficient doses to obtain therapeutic plasma levels. At times, other pharmacological approaches such as lithium, monoamine oxidase inhibitors, new antidepressants, or thyroid hormone are needed. The indications for such treatments and description of pharmacological techniques are beyond the scope of this chapter. However, it should be noted that there are many possibilities for combined treatment and that a broad availability of treatment choices can widen the range of indications for combined treatment of inpatient depressives. For example, a patient with recurrent major depression and subclinical hypothyroidism could be treated with an antidepressant, thyroid supplementation, and cognitive therapy. Another patient with major depression with psychotic features (e.g., delusions and paranoia) might receive combined pharmacotherapy (a tricyclic antidepressant plus an antipsychotic drug) and limited cognitive therapy (primarily behavioral techniques) at the beginning of treatment. The patient would then receive more intensive cognitive therapy as the psychotic elements of the disorder resolve.

There are occasional cases of major depression in which pharmacotherapy is relatively contraindicated and cognitive therapy must be used alone. Examples include patients with severe cardiac disease with heart block or very recent myocardial infarction, women who are pregnant, or patients with a history of severe drug reactions. There is only one major contraindication to starting cognitive therapy in hospitalized depressives. Patients with major depression with extreme psychotic features and intense suicidal preoccupation are at high risk for suicide. They usually respond quickly to electroconvulsive therapy, the treatment of choice for severe psychotic depression. Cognitive therapy can be started later when the acute psychotic phase of the illness has abated.

We have observed that unilateral electroconvulsive therapy to the nondominant hemisphere of the brain can be used together with cognitive therapy. The conventional treatment is to stop psychotherapy altogether when electroconvulsive therapy is being used. However, unilateral electroconvulsive therapy does not impair memory function (Fromm-Auch, 1982; Strömgren, 1973). Electroconvulsive therapy together with cognitive therapy is a form of combined treatment that may have considerable utility in the management of especially severe cases of psychotic depression.

Bipolar depressives also can benefit from combined therapy. As noted earlier, cognitive therapy and lithium have been found to be effective partners in the maintenance phase of treatment (Blackburn, Bishop, Glen, et al.). Combined therapy also can be used in the acute depressive phase of bipolar illness, but cognitive therapy is probably of little value in hypomania. A hypomanic patient can benefit from structuring techniques such as agenda setting and directive procedures. However, formal cognitive therapy requires more collaboration and concentration than are possible during most hypomanic episodes.

There are many other possible applications of a combined treatment approach with inpatients. A partial listing of situations in which we have used combined treatment is contained in Table 2-1. Cognitive theories and techniques have been described previously for most of these disorders, and the pharmacological approaches to these disorders have been studied extensively (Baldessarini, 1977; Beck, Rush, Shaw, et al., 1979; Clark & Del Giudice, 1978; Emery, Hollon, & Bedrosian, 1981). Cognitive therapy techniques can have a primary role in the treatment of some of these disorders (e.g., depression, panic disorder, anorexia nervosa) but may play a more supportive or adjunctive role in the treatment of illnesses in which biological features predominate (e.g., bipolar illness, chronic schizophrenia). A full discussion of the cognitive and pharmacological approaches for each of these disorders will not be attempted here. However, the general principles of combined treatment described in this chapter can be applied to any of these clinical problems.

Table 2-1
Applications of Combined Cognitive Therapy and Pharmacotherapy

Disorder	Drugs Used with Cognitive Therapy
Depression, unipolar and bipolar	Tricyclic antidepressants, monoamine oxidase inhibitors, hormones (thyroid, estrogen) Lithium New nontricyclic antidepressants (e.g., trazodone, amoxapine)
Anorexia nervosa and bulimia	Tricyclic antidepressants Antipsychotics
Alcohol dependency	Benzodiazepines for withdrawal Antabuse Antidepressants or lithium if depression present
Severe phobias or panic disorder	Monoamine oxidase inhibitors Tricyclic antidepressants Benzodiazepines
Psychophysiologic disorders and chronic pain syndromes	Beta blockers Tricyclic antidepressants Benzodiazepines
Chronic mental illness (e.g., schizophrenia, schizoaffective disorder)	Antipsychotics Lithium
Borderline personality disorder	Antidepressants Antipsychotics Benzodiapines

COMBINED THERAPY TECHNIQUES

The Therapeutic Relationship

One therapist can perform both treatments in combined therapy if this individual has a medical degree and has been trained in cognitive therapy. Although there are few psychiatrists as yet who have had extensive experience in cognitive therapy, several psychiatric residency training programs have begun courses in cognitive therapy. It is likely that there will be a growing number of psychiatrists who can competently treat patients with both pharmacotherapy and cognitive therapy. However, at present the more common arrangement is to have two therapists—a physician who prescribes drugs and another cognitive therapist (e.g., psychologist, social worker, or nurse) who performs congitive therapy.

The therapeutic relationship is considerably more complicated with dual therapists than with a single therapist (see Figure 2-1). The patient has thoughts and feelings, not only about each of the two therapists as individuals but also about the relationship between the two therapists. Similarly, each of the ther-

```
Pharmacotherapist  ←————————→  Cognitive Therapist
              ↘         ↕        ↙
                     Patient
```

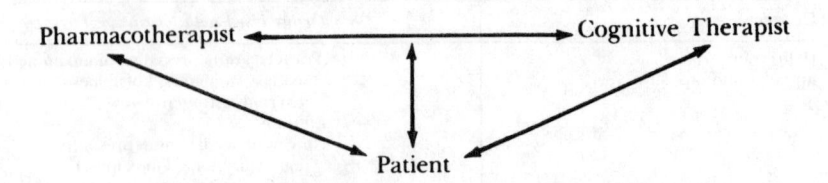

Figure 2-1. The therapeutic relationship with dual therapists

apists has significant relationships with the patient and with each other. Nonspecific treatment variables such as rapport, kindness, empathy, understanding, and remoralization are operative in all of the relationships in this triangle. (Barrett & Wright, 1984; Frank, 1978; Marmor, 1976).

It is likely that the quality of the relationship between the therapists will affect the patient. Do the therapists have mutual respect for one another—or are they angry, jealous, and protective of their own professional territory? Do they understand and accept the conceptual model and treatment techniques of the other's therapeutic approach? Ideally, the pharmacotherapist and psychotherapist should know each other quite well, work together on virtually a daily basis, have a good fundamental understanding of both treatments, communicate freely with one another, and agree on a clear model for combined treatment that can be communicated to the patient. They also should be able to adjust their treatment techniques as the therapy proceeds based on shared information and mutual agreement. Problems in any of these areas can impair the quality of combined treatment. For example, a pharmacotherapist who appears on the surface to understand and respect cognitive therapy actually may hold a rather firm view that cognitive therapy is just adjunctive treatment that really doesn't make much difference. This therapist might believe that the patient will start to get better only when the tricyclic antidepressant "kicks in" at about 10 to 14 days. On the other hand, a nonphysician cognitive therapist may harbor professional jealousy at not being able to prescribe drugs and may wish to prove that his/her efforts with cognitive therapy are superior to the "symptom relief only" action of drugs. These attitudes can be perceived by the patient, leading to a conflicted understanding of the methods and goals of treatment. Expectations, motivation, and adherence to the combined approach could be significantly impaired.

These two examples underscore the need for dual therapists to understand their own attitudes about the different treatments and to do the best job they can of learning about the strengths and weaknesses of each treatment. Most importantly, they need to work together to develop a conceptual model that can be accepted not only by both therapists but also by the patient. Table 2-2 contains some suggested steps for forming an effective pharmacotherapist/

Table 2-2
Steps in Forming a Dual Therapist Team

Work together regularly
Learn about the "other" therapy and about the other therapist's techniques
Get to know your associate personally
Only work together if you find you like and respect your associate
Develop together a conceptual model for combined therapy
Decide what you will communicate to the patient about the theory and techniques of using two therapies together
Communicate frequently during the course of therapy
Present yourselves as a team to the patient
Be sure that the patient understands and is willing and able to collaborate with combined treatment delivered by two therapists

---

psychotherapist team. It may be somewhat easier to follow these procedures in a hosptial setting than in outpatient practice. Inpatient therapists on wards that emphasize teamwork and integrated treatment planning have frequent opportunities to talk with one another in treatment conferences and in less formal contacts, whereas outpatient therapists who are in separate offices may have infrequent opportunities to meet with one another (Chase, Wright, & Ragade, 1980; 1981).

We have found that a weekly therapy supervision meeting for inpatient therapists has provided an excellent forum for in-depth discussions and for the formation of effective teams of therapists. Since we now do individual, family, group, and milieu cognitive therapy, usually combined with drugs, there can often be four or more therapist involved in treating a single patient. The need for clear communication becomes even greater when this is the case.

The optimal therapeutic relationship in treatment of a hospitalized patient is one in which collaborative empiricism is maximized in all of the multiple therapeutic relationships, role confusion is minimized, and the nonspecific treatment variables such as rapport and kindness are actually heightened by the collaborative work of the therapists. Placing medication issues on the cognitive therapy agenda, psychoeducational techniques and eliciting and testing cognitive distortions about combined treatment can enhance the formation of good patient/therapist relationships. These topics will be discussed in more detail and illustrated with case examples.

Agenda Setting in Combined Treatment

Agenda setting, a standard cognitive therapy technique, can be adapted easily to treatment with combined therapy. Physician/cognitive therapists in our unit always suggest that medication issues be placed on the agenda. It is important to know what positive or negative effects have been associated with a medication and then to use this information to make decisions about continuing or changing the pharmacotherapy regimen. In addition, the therapist is interested in the patient's perception of the effects of medications. Cognitions about medication can provide valuable therapy material, as will be illustrated later. Placing medication issues on the agenda also signifies to the patient that this is an important part of therapy deserving the attention of both patient and therapist.

When there are two or more therapists, medication issues can be placed on the agenda for cognitive therapy (with a focus on cognitions about the medication), and agenda setting in pharmacotherapy can provide a structural link between the two treatments. In both situations the patient is asked to work together with the therapist to identify significant problems or issues, to prioritize agenda items, and to work on these problems efficiently during the session. A typical agenda for a pharmacotherapy session (in the dual-therapist situation) might include (1) general symptom review, (2) side effect review, (3) how long to take medication, and (4) how the cognitive therapy is coming along.

Psychoeducational Techniques

Experienced pharmacotherapists usually do a good job of educating patients about what to expect from drug treatment. Patients are prepared for possible side effects and what to do if they occur. The time of onset of action of drugs is explained. At times pamphlets, books, and other informational packets are given to patients about drugs and psychobiology. Rapport and compliance is heightened by giving clear information about what to expect from treatment.

Cognitive therapists also consider psychoeducational techniques an important part of treatment. Theories and techniques are explained in detail and considerable checking for understanding occurs throughout treatment. Reading assignments such as "Coping with Depression" (Beck & Greenberg, 1974) or self-help books are often used to reinforce the learning process.

Although psychoeducational approaches are compatible with both treatments, there can be conflicts in the information provided. Psychoeducational materials should be reviewed carefully by members of the treatment team to be sure that information does not conflict with the model of combined treatment. An example of information that might be ruled out is a pharmaceutical company pamphlet on depression that presents a unitary view of the cause and treatment of depression.

Eliciting and Testing Cognitions About Drugs

The taking of medication has powerful meaning to most individuals. This is particularly apparent in the placebo response, in which curative or even magical powers are attributed to a pill or potion, even though it has no active ingredients. It is well known that placebos have pronounced psychological effects and can promote relief of both psychic and physical symptoms (Barrett

& Wright, 1984; Clark & Del Giudice, 1978). The majority of medicines used in modern psychiatric practice have been found to relieve symptoms more effectively than placebo (Baldessarini, 1977; Clark & Del Giudice, 1978). Yet, the placebo response is probably still a part of the activity of psychotropic drugs. When an active drug is given, the total response is a summation of both the psychophysiologic and placebo effects of the drug.

If symptom relief is a goal of treatment, then a positive placebo response should be encouraged. This is, in a sense, a promotion of a cognitive distortion—a positive one that should be adaptive for the patient. Yet there can be maladaptive positive cognitive distortions about medications that can disrupt treatment and undermine the chances for recovery. An example of a potentially damaging distortion is "I have a biochemical defect; the drug will take care of the problem; talking couldn't possibly help." Some proponents of biological psychiatry may encourage such attributions. Yet even in conditions such as bipolar disorder where there is a good deal of support for genetic and biochemical etiologies, it is unlikely that psychotherapy would be of no use. The patient still has to understand the illness and adjust to it psychosocially. In other instances positive drug attributions counteract underlying negative views of self, such as in the statement, "If the drug works it means I have a medical problem, and I am not so weak after all."

Negative expectations and beliefs about drugs and their effects are the most common cognitive distortions encountered in combined therapy. Some of these negative cognitions are listed in Table 2-3. As with positive distortions, there are some therapists who may believe that such statements are valid. However, a combined therapy approach attempts to avoid either/or categorizations. Instead, a balanced, but generally positive view of both therapies is encouraged. Research from outcome studies is supportive of this stance, as there is good evidence for the effectiveness of both cognitive therapy and pharmacotherapy (Baldessarini, 1977; Clark & Del Giudice, 1978; Wright, 1985; Wright & Beck, 1983).

The techniques for eliciting and testing cognitive distortions about drugs are the same as those used in standard cognitive therapy (Wright & Beck, 1983; 1985). Questioning is the most common technique. Patients are usually

---

Table 2-3
Common Negative Distortions About Drugs

"Drugs are just a crutch."
"Drugs are really dangerous."
"I am the one who will get the severe side effects."
"People that take drugs are weak."
"You should be able to do it by yourself."
"I'll get addicted."
"I won't be able to work if I'm taking medication."
"A drug couldn't really work; I'm having an existential crisis."
"How could a drug help when the problem is really my wife?"
"Drugs are overused; my doctor is just a pill pusher."

able to talk about their attitudes toward drugs when questioned directly. However, at times imagery, role-playing, and other similar exercises can be helpful. The Daily Thought Record is another potential source of cognitions about drugs.

Cognitive errors such as absolutistic thinking, personalization, selective abstraction, and arbitrary inference are very common in cognitions about drugs. The examples in Table 2-3 contain many of these errors in logic. For example, personalization is involved in the statement "I am the one that will get the severe side effects." Identification and modification of cognitive errors, automatic thoughts, and other cognitive distortions promote reasonable expectations about drug therapy and help to facilitate good collaborative treatment relationships in combined therapy. The patient also can learn about the relationship between cognition, emotion, and behavior by uncovering maladaptive cognitive responses to medication use.

Case Illustrations

Three brief vignettes will be used to illustrate possibilities for combined pharmacotherapy and cognitive therapy.

Case 1: Cognitive Therapy in a Patient with Drug Noncompliance. A forty-two-year-old woman had a history of four significant depressive episodes and one period of hypomania. She had been placed on lithium 2 years previously but had stopped taking the medication after about 2 weeks, reportedly because of side effects. There had been two episodes of recurrent depression since stopping lithium.

This patient described her response to lithium as "terrible." She recalled that it "didn't help at all" and "it made me a total basket case." Furthermore, she reported that she couldn't concentrate and that she "didn't have any feelings" while on lithium. Her previous doctor had concluded that she could not take this drug because of severe side effects.

The physician/cognitive therapist who saw this patient in consultation recognized that her reports of side effects may have been heavily influenced by cognitive distortion. Questioning and imagery techniques were used to elicit a number of cognitions about taking drugs and to understand the relationship between these cognitions and several important underlying schemas. Eventually, it was found that the patient believed that she was basically an inferior, weak person and that taking any drug confirmed this fact. Schemas relating to self-concept were activated when her previous doctor had suggested that she had a biochemical defect that would require lifelong treatment. Although she did actually experience some physiological side effects from lithium (e.g., mild tremor and transient nausea), her rejection of this potentially useful treatment had much more to do with her cognitive state than with her physical reaction to the medication.

Eliciting and testing automatic thoughts and underlying schemas, coupled with educational material on lithium, gave this patient a more rational view of the risks and benefits of this treatment. She responded well to her second trial of lithium. Mild nausea and muscle weakness occurred in the first 2 weeks of therapy, but these problems disappeared and no further side effects were encountered.

Case 2: Treatment-Resistant Depression. A fifty-six-year-old professional man was admitted to the hospital after having made a very serious suicide attempt with barbiturates. He had been treated with supportive individual psychotherapy and a tricyclic antidepressant as an outpatient but had not responded. On admission he told his doctor, "Just leave me alone; my life is over and I just want to die." He was abjectly hopeless about any treatment working because he believed that it was impossible to solve his problem. His wife had left him and had taken his only child, a fourteen-year-old daughter, with her. He reported, "Without my wife, I'm nothing."

All the classic neurovegetative symptoms of depression were present, including sleep disorder, loss of appetite and weight, decreased concentration, loss of libido, and poor energy. The psychiatrist, who was also a trained cognitive therapist, diagnosed major depression without psychotic features and started the patient on nortriptyline. However, he knew that despite the use of plasma-level monitoring the likelihood of a rapid treatment response to drugs was not high. He reasoned that it might take 10 to 14 days for the medication to have substantial effects, although sleep might improve earlier if the drug was given as a once-daily dose at bedtime.

Therefore, the psychiatrist focused heavily on treating hopelessness with cognitive therapy in the first 24 hours of hospitalization. Several gross cognitive distortions were identified, and the patient was asked to complete a particularly important homework assignment—to call his daughter to check out his thought that "she never wants to see me again." His daughter's response was quite positive. She told him she had been terribly worried about him and that she loved him. She wanted to visit him just as soon as possible. His hopelessness diminished rapidly as he saw that he had misread the situation and that he might be misinterpreting information from many other sources. Suicidal ideation decreased, and a clear improvement in his attitude about self and future was noted. However, his energy and appetitie did not start to improve until about a week later. He was discharged from the hospital after 3 weeks. Full recovery was evident within 5 weeks, and follow-up visits for 3 years revealed no evidence of return of depression.

Although it is possible that either cognitive therapy or pharmacotherapy would have been effective alone, the combined approach seemed justified in this case of severe depression. Each treatment appeared to have a particular role to fill. This case illustrates one important advantage of using cognitive therapy with medication instead of drug treatment alone. Hopelessness and suicidal ideation can be reduced immediately with cognitive therapy while the later onset of action of drug effects is awaited.

Case 3: Anorexia Nervosa. A nineteen-year-old woman was admitted to the hospital for the second time when her weight dropped to 79 pounds and she became profoundly depressed. A diagnostic interview revealed typical features of anorexia nervosa, including self-induced emesis, binge eating, refusal to eat, distorted body image, and hyperactivity. In addition, she had symptoms of major depression with delusions of guilt and mild paranoia. Her previous treatment had been individual and family psychodynamically oriented psychotherapy together with a tricyclic antidepressant.

This patient was judged to be so severely ill that intravenous feedings and aggressive pharmacotherapy were needed. She was treated with a continuation of the tricyclic antidepressant plus the addition of low doses of an antipsychotic drug. She was extremely weak, had very poor concentrating ability, and was moderately delusional. These symptoms interfered with the use of psychotherapy.

Unfortunately, the chemotherapy regimen was not effective, and her depression intensified. She started to beg to be allowed to die. A short course of electroconvulsive treatment was then initiated. Her depression improved significantly, and she began to take some foods again. Suicidal thoughts disappeared. At this point the patient started with cognitive therapy and was placed on a new antidepressant. She started to work on distortions about self-image and agreed to a behavioral component of the treatment plan. She then continued with combined cognitive therapy and pharmacotherapy on an outpatient basis. Although recovery was slow, she attained a normal weight for her height and a complete remission of symptoms of depression and anorexia nervosa within 5 months.

This case illustrates the importance of being able to shift treatment modes depending on the type and severity of symptoms. Biological treatments including electroconvulsive therapy were probably life-saving for this young woman. Yet, the cognitive therapy played a significant part in her eventual recovery.

Summary

The "psychobiological final common pathway" model suggests that there are multiple etiologies for common psychiatric problems and that treatments can work together effectively if they are integrated in theory and practice. The rationale for combining cognitive therapy with pharmacotherapy is based on this model and on the clinical experience of inpatient therapists who have found combined therapy to be a useful treatment strategy.

There are several "generic" techniques for combined therapy that can be applied to the treatment of a wide variety of disorders. These include procedures to enhance collaborative working relationships, agenda setting, psychoeducational efforts, and eliciting and testing cognitions about drugs.

Several specific applications for combined cognitive and pharmacotherapy also are suggested and illustrated.

It is concluded that cognitive therapy and pharmacotherapy should be noncompetitive. These two treatments share a common interest in learning, memory, and information processing (Wright, 1985). Perhaps future neurobiological and cognitive research will clarify the central nervous system processes that link these two treatments and provide clues for development of new combined treatment techniques.

REFERENCES

Akiskal, H. S., & McKinney, W. T. (1975). Overview of recent research in depression: Integration of ten conceptual models into a comprehensive clinical frame. *Archives of General Psychiatry, 32,* 285–305.

Baldessarini, R. J. (1977). *Chemotherapy in psychiatry.* Cambridge, MA: Harvard University Press.

Barrett, C. L., & Wright, J. H. (1984). Therapist variables. In *Issues in psychotherapy research,* M. Hersen & A. S. Bellack (Eds.). New York: Plenum Publishing.

Beck, A. T., & Greenberg, R. L. (1974). *Coping with depression.* New York: Institute for Rational Living.

Beck, A. T., Rush, A. J., Shaw, B., & Emery, G. (1979). *Cognitive therapy of depression.* New York: Guilford Press.

Blackburn, I. M., Bishop, S., Glen, A. I. M., Whalley, L. J., & Christie, J. E. (1981). The efficacy of cognitive therapy in depression: A treatment using cognitive therapy and pharmacotherapy, each alone and in combination. *British Journal of Psychiatry, 139,* 181–189.

Chase, S., Wright, J. H., & Ragade, R. (1980). The inpatient psychiatric unit as a system. *Behavioral Sciences, 26,* 197–205.

Chase, S., Wright, J. H., & Ragade, R. (1981). Decision making in an interdisciplinary team. *Behavioral Sciences, 26,* 206–215.

Clark, W. G., & Del Giudice, J. (1978). *Principles of psychopharmacology.* 2nd ed. New York: Academic Press.

Cochran S. D. (1982). Effectiveness of cognitive therapy in preventing non-compliance with lithium regimens. Presented at the Annual Meeting of the American Psychological Association, Washington, D.C.

deMontigny, C., Cournoyer, G., Morissette, R., (1983). Lithium carbonate addition in tricyclic antidepressant-resistant unipolar depression. *Archives of General Psychiatry, 40,* 1327–1334.

Emery, G., Hollon, S. D., & Bedrosian, R. C. (Eds.). (1981). *New directions in cognitive therapy.* New York: Guilford Press.

Frank, J. D. (1978). *Psychotherapy and the human predicament: A psychosocial approach.* New York: Schocken Books.

Fromm-Auch, F. (1982). Comparison of unilateral and bilateral ECT: Evidence for selective memory impairment. *British Journal of Psychiatry, 141*, 608–613.

Hollon, S. D., DeRubeis, R. J., Evans, M. D. (1983). Final report of the cognitive-pharmacotherapy trial: Outcome, prophylaxis, prognosis, process, and mechanism. Presented at the 17th Annual Convention of the Association for the Advancement of Behavioral Therapy, Washington, DC.

Marmor, J. (1976). Common operational factors in diverse approaches to behavior change. In *What makes behavior change possible?* A. Burton (Ed.). New York: Brunner-Mazel.

Maxmen, J. S., Tucker, G. J., & LeBow, M. (1974). *Rational hospital psychiatry.* New York: Brunner/Mazel.

Murphy, G. E., Simons, A. D., Wetzel, R. D., Lustman, P. J. (1984). Cognitive therapy versus tricyclic antidepressants in major depression. *Archives of General Psychiatry, 41*, 33–41.

Rush, A. J. (1983). Cognitive therapy of depression. *Psychiatric Clinics of North America, 6*, 105–127.

Shaw, B. F. (1981). Cognitive therapy with an inpatient population. In *New directions in cognitive therapy*, G. Emery, S. D. Hollon & R. C. Bedrosian (Eds.). New York: Guilford Press.

Strömgren, L. S. (1973). Unilateral versus bilateral electroconvulsive therapy. *Acta Psychiatrica Scandinavica Supplementum, 240*, 8–26.

Weissman, M. M., Prusoff, B. A., DiMascio, A., et al. (1979). The efficacy of drugs and psychotherapy in the treatment of acute depressive episodes. *American Journal of Psychiatry, 136*, 555–558.

Wright, J. H. (1985). The cognitive paradigm for treatment of depression. In *Psychiatry: The state of an art*, (Vol. 4), P. Berner (Ed.). London: Plenum Publishing

Wright, J. H., Barrett, C. L., Linder, L. H., Chase, S., Weinstein, G., & Hurst, H. *Nortryptitive effects on cognition in depression.* Unpublished research.

Wright, J. H., & Beck, A. T. (1983). Cognitive therapy of depression: Theory and practice. *Hospital and Community Psychiatry, 34*, 1119–1127.

Wright, J. H., & Beck, A. T. (1985). Cognitive therapy. In *Depression*, K. Sultz (Ed.), Munich: Ernest Reinhardt, GMBH.

Chapter 3

DAY HOSPITAL TREATMENT OF ALCOHOLICS[1]

Meyer D. Glantz

DAY HOSPITAL APPROACH

More than any other class of psychotherapy patients, alcoholics often require a broad range of intervention services. They frequently are in need of biomedical and social services as well as psychotherapeutic treatment. Biomedical needs might include detoxification, emergency medical care for injuries and disease conditions, and basic medical care to improve their frequently deteriorated physical states; neuropsychiatric and other special medical services also are often called for. In terms of social services, many alcoholics are indigents in need of basic subsistence support; others require assistance related to employment, educational, basic financial, institutional, and legal problems. Perhaps their greatest needs, if not always their most immediate, are their psychiatric ones.

There are four general psychologically related areas of concern and foci for intervention. Foremost, of course, is the drinking behavior itself, an intervention target which is all too often not specifically dealt with in psychotherapy. Second is the inevitably concurrent psychopathology, which, though it may be seen as being antecedent, concomitant, facilitative and/or consequent

---

[1] The development and practice of the therapy described here was done at the Center for Problem Drinking, Veterans Administration Outpatient Clinic, Boston, Massachusetts, and was supported by the VA Medical Research Service. The views expressed here are not necessarily those of the Veterans Administration or the National Institute on Drug Abuse.

to the drinking, must be dealt with in order for there to be a real possibility for therapeutic success. Third is the area of coping abilities and adaptive cognitive conceptualization skills; alcoholic patients typically have inadequate skills for conceptualizing and solving problems and require focused intervention in order to improve their functioning in this critical area. Fourth, alcoholics usually live in social environments that at least permit and often support their drinking. An important area of intervention involves assisting the alcoholic patient to change his environment or to move to a new environment.

It is assumed here that the most appropriate therapy is the least intrusive intervention that is feasible for each particular patient. To the extent possible the patient should remain in the environment in which he will have to function in order to learn to cope with the particular stresses and problems of that environment and to permit the patient to utilize the interpersonal and other resources available to him in that environment. Given this, it is important to identify which patients are capable of making sufficient gains from outpatient therapy and which require the broader and more intensive intervention of the day hospital.

The patients who were the "average" patients in the program on which this report is based all met the *DSM III* criteria of alcohol abuse and/or alcohol dependence. They typically had a history of alcohol misuse spanning 10 to 20 years and had problems similar to, but often more serious than, the "heavy intake" and "binge drinking" alcoholics described by Cahalan and Room (1974). Most obviously suffered from some detrimental consequences of chronic alcohol abuse and almost without exception they met the "instant identification" criterion of drinking a weekly average of more than four "standard drinks" per day. Whereas there is often a question with more moderate drinkers as to whether their drinking has become alcoholic, with these patients there was rarely a question as to whether they were alcoholics or a question about whether they would benefit from and be appropriate for the day hospital.

Although many of the patients often "maintained sobriety" while being treated at the day hospital, their control over their drinking was usually quite tenuous at best. This is perhaps the single most important discriminator for distinguishing between those drinkers who can be treated on a conventional outpatient basis and those who require a more intensive intervention. Those drinkers appropriate for outpatient treatment are able to exercise a fair degree of control over their drinking; although they are at risk for getting intoxicated, they are not at high risk for an extensive drinking episode that will place them at physical risk, that will have disastrous consequneces for their social or support environments, or that will have a strongly detrimental effect on their psychological state or their progress in therapy. Because of their low level of internalized control, the day hospital candidates require the external support that a structured non-drink-supporting environment provides and a relatively high number of hours of therapeutic contact.

The appropriate candidates for day hospital often require very basic biomedical and social support services; they frequently need assistance in a number of areas, including detoxification, emergency medical care, subsistence assistance, and aid in obtaining employment. A comprehensive day hospital program can provide at least some of these needed services and can refer to and coordinate the other needed services through community and other health and care providers; few outpatient programs have the resources to do this. Most of the appropriate candidates have fewer and more impoverished interpersonal resources than the average mental health outpatient, and they often cannot access the potential of the resources that are available to them. Many have never been married or are divorced, and few have many friends. The appropriate candidates typically have difficulty making positive changes or gains in their environments and, in fact, their environments typically permit and often support their alcohol abuse. The day hospital alcoholics are often unable to find or enter healthier environments, and the day hospital provides a transitional environment not unlike that provided by halfway houses. Finally, in addition to needing psychotherapy, many of the appropriate candidates need to learn practical skills (such as those involved in finding a job) and more psychologically oriented skills (such as assertiveness or deep muscle relaxation); the day hospital readily allows for involvement in a variety of different interventions, which are coordinated into a coherent supervised program designed for the individual patient. This is not to imply that a patient in need of a more moderate level and scope of services will not benefit from the day hospital program; in fact, the more resources the patient has, the more likely and the more easily they are to make significant therapeutic gains. It is also not meant to imply that a patient requiring a greater level or scope of intervention may not require, at least initially, the services of an inpatient program.

The program that is to be described here is based on a program that was conducted at the Center for Problem Drinking (CPD) of the Veterans Administration Outpatient Clinic in Boston. The CPD has created an excellent alcoholism day hospital treatment program that serves the Boston area and provides treatment for hundreds of alcohol abusers every year.[2] As part of a multitreatment research program, the author developed and conducted a cognitive behavior therapy program at the CPD.[3] Based on experience with the CPD program, the author has developed a model for a more integrated cognitive behavior day hospital program for alcoholics, and that model is to be presented here. The model to be presented follows but is an "idealized" version of both the CPD day hospital program and the cognitive behavior

---

[2] The original Boston VA Center for Problem Drinking day hospital program was developed by the staff of the Center, in particular, William McCourt, M.D., Allan Adinolfi, Ph.D., Lacey Corbett, Ph.D., and Paul Duffly, Ph.D.

[3] William McCourt, M.D., was one of the co-therapists who worked with the author while the cognitive therapy treatment program was being developed, and he made several contributions to it.

therapy treatment that was integrated into it. This will allow the author to recommend an optimal program that is not limited by the particular constraints of any individual setting and that has the ability to expand the cognitive behavior therapy emphasis. Although most effective alcoholism day hospital programs will include many of the same services and facilities, a cognitive behavior therapy program will be based on cognitive therapy and appropriate ancillary supports. To best describe the cognitive therapy, it is necessary to present first a cognitively oriented model of alcholism.

A Cognitively Based Model of Alcoholism

The model asserts that the fundamental nature of and defining characteristic of substance abuse of any kind is the reliance of the abuser on use of the drug as a primary coping mechanism. Thus, alcohol is not only a problem for the alcoholic, but it is also a mechanism, albeit a poor one, for solving problems. The particular problems may be emotional (e.g., anxiety or feelings of helplessness), environmental (e.g., job or family stress) and/or interpersonal (e.g., loneliness or conflict with another person); they may even be psychiatric as in the case of an individual (e.g., a schizophrenic) attempting to medicate himself. Although alcohol is a central nervous system depressant, its effects on a particular individual at a given time depend on a variety of factors, including dosage, the user's physical state, the circumstances of use, the user's expectations, and so on. Because of this, alcohol may serve as a problem-solving mechanism in a variety of different ways, seemingly performing opposite and contrasting purposes for different individuals. It might be used to reduce anxiety or any strong affect; to disinhibit internal restrictions on thoughts or behaviors; to distort perceptions of the self, of others, or of situations; to stimulate or terminate fantasies; to facilitate escape through unconsciousness; or to facilitate the forgetting of or distortion of a memory of past events or one' involvement in them. It may be used by the drinker as an excuse for failure or for other unacceptable behaviors, as a means of avoiding responsibility or escaping situations, or as a facilitator of or a substitute for some aspect of normal functioning.

The use of alcohol as a coping mechanism can be established in the same way that any other behavior can become established and identified by the individual as a coping mechanism. It is hypothesized that for most alcoholics the etiology of their alcohol abuse begins very early in their lives. A number of researchers have reported that alcoholics typically have some difficulty in functioning normally even before the onset of their alcoholic drinking (see, for example, the study by McCord and McCord, 1960, 1962; McCord, 1972). Jessor and Jessor (1977) and Robins (1980) have proposed the notions of, respectively, a "problem behavior proneness" and a "deviance syndrome," which hypothesize that many types of adult deviant "antisocial" behaviors are preceded during late childhood and early adolescence by a concurrence of psychological, environmental, and behavioral factors that not only involve moderate-level deviance and support for deviance but that also facilitate and predispose the individual toward still more deviant behaviors, which, coupled with increasing life stresses, in turn lead to still greater deviance, including the possibility of some form of substance abuse. It is hypothesized here that primary factors in the problem behavior proneness are maladaptive conceptualizations in both the cognitive contents and processes of the individual. The maladaptive conceptualizations are hypothesized to develop early in the individual's life. For many of these individuals the maladaptive conceptualization processes and contents develop in concert with and at least partially in consequence of early dysfunctions in sensory processing, experiential organization and representation, and other basic personality-related systems. In general, these early compromised functions do not usually manifest themselves as severe, blatant, highly dysfunctional childhood psychopathologies but rather as moderate to severe deviations and deficits in functioning that are exacerbated rather than compensated for by the environment. The dysfunctions often go unrecognized as may their significance and their relation to the developing maladaptive conceptualizations and the associated psychopathology and alcohol abuse; for a related discussion on the early etiology of other forms of psychopathology, see Greenspan and Porges (1984).

Accompanying and partly caused by the development of these maladaptive conceptualizations is the development of maladaptive and ultimately inadequate coping mechanisms and strategies. Although these mechanisms and strategies may be adequate and perhaps even successful during early and middle adolescence, by late adolescence or early young adulthood they are likely to begin to fail when the stresses of adult life are encountered. Failing to cope adequately using these maladaptive problem-solving approaches, some individuals will begin to rely on alcohol. The more often an individual employs alcohol as a coping mechansim, the more likely that he/she will rely on that mechanism in the future and come to believe that he/she cannot cope without alcohol. As these individuals increasingly use alcohol as a problem-solving mechanism, they are likely to become increasingly ineffective at solving problems through more normal and adaptive means. At this point the overt behaviors associated with alcoholism will begin to become evident, and abusers will begin to believe that alcohol use is necessary. Even if they recognize that their drinking is causing problems, their ability to use other more adaptive coping strategies and their belief in the possibility and the efficacy of other methods for them may be inadequate to induce them to stop drinking. They are likely to continue until they come to believe that not using alcohol is possible and that the consequences of drinking are worse than the consequences of not drinking.

The maladaptive conceptualizations of the alcoholic have a crucial role, not only in the etiology of alcohol abuse but also in its maintenance and exacerbation; most relevant here, the maladaptive conceptualizations of the alcoholic are the primary target of the cognitive behavioral psychotherapy. For this reason it is important to describe some of the conceptualization patterns that are common among alcoholics. Beck (1972) has proposed a conceptualization-based model of depression in which he describes errors in the processes of thinking that are common among depressed individuals; for example, drawing conclusions in the absence of or contrary to available evidence. He describes how these dysfunctional processes can lead to depressive thought contents; for example, a depression-prone woman might think, "John didn't call me tonight; it must mean that he doesn't love me anymore." Although alcoholics may be a more heterogeneous population than depressives, the basic model of maladaptive thoughts and processes as the foundation of the psychopathology still applies, and some of the more common patterns can be described. The maladaptive thought processes of alcoholics generally seem to involve a failure to utilize the typical parameters, range, content, number, and relationships of categories or attribution classes.

Alcoholics demonstrate the maladaptive processes that Beck (1972, 1976) has described for depressives. These include drawing arbitrary inferences, making dichotomous evaluations, and making gross overgeneralizations. They also demonstrate a number of other maladaptive processes. Alcoholic patients frequently exhibit thinking that is either global, abstract, and undifferentiated or thinking that is highly narrow, concretized, and specific. Their evaluations are often compromised or based on a single criterion, standard, or dimension; or the criteria and categories used in their evaluations are not sufficiently discriminated from each other and/or are applied incorrectly (e.g., sobriety may be seen as the measure for entitlement). Although alcoholic's appraisals are frequently emotionally dominated to an abnormal extent, they are often unable to identify and differentiate affects or the origin or object of the affect (e.g., "I don't know why, but I'm angry all the time at nothing"). Their beliefs and assumptions often are not tested against reality or readily subject to disconfirmation by contradictory evidence, and at least some of their attributions are likely to be unrealistic. Many fail to see interrelationships between factors in a situation, and they often demonstrate an aribitrary and narrow focus of attention on a single aspect of a situation or person. Partly as a consequence of this, alcoholics are often unable to generate or consider alternatives or change their perspective or point of view. This is not an exhaustive list of maladaptive processes, and these processes are neither confined to nor definitive of alcoholics; no one individual exhibits all of these processes, but rather they seem consistently to utilize a limited number.

These maladaptive conceptualization processes not only support ineffective problem-solving strategies, but they also lead to a number of frequently occurring maladaptive themes, or thought contents, in alcoholic populations. There is not an invariant one-to-one relationship between each process and each theme; any process may lead to any one or more of the themes, and conversely, any theme may be determined by any one or more of the processes. The most common of the maladaptive themes among alcoholic populations will be described briefly.

Some alcoholics believe that they are totally powerless and/or victimized.

Many have either very low *or* (less commonly) very high self-images, and many either overaccept *or* underaccept responsibility for either good *or* bad outcomes. Alcoholics' evaluations and anticipations are frequently unrealistically negative and pessimistic. Some have an unreasonably high *or* an unreasonably low sense of entitlement. Finally, most believe that for them alcohol is the only alternative to bad feelings and difficult problems. As was the case with the list of maladaptive processes, this list is not meant to be exhaustive, and these content themes are neither confined to nor definitive of alcoholics. No one patient exhibits them all; instead, each seems to demonstrate consistently a limited number.

There has not been much research on the conceptualization systems of alcoholics; the maladaptive conceptualization processes and contents described above are based primarily on the author's observations. The findings of one particularly relevant study (Glantz, Burr, & Bosse, 1984) that support these observations will be mentioned briefly. In this recent study, the Situations Rep Test (a modified Kelly Rep Test that uses situations as objects for construal) was used to explore the conceptualization systems of 44 alcoholic adult men in comparison with a sample of 36 nonalcoholic, nonpsychotic (neurotic) adult male outpatients and 62 normal adult men. The structural (process-related) and the content (theme-related) analyses of the elicited-conceptualizations samples indicated significant differences between the groups' conceptualizations. Both the alcoholic and the neurotic patients had more monolithic construct systems than the normal subjects, which indicates a lower degree of object discrimination and a lower degree of independence of their construct dimensions (constructs are attribution characteristics used in conceptualizations or appraisals). When categorizing events, the alcoholics tended to overapply constructs, whereas the neurotics tended to underapply them. The alcoholics' process-related abnormalities would lead to some of the evaluation problems described above. Both patient groups most commonly construed situations primarily in terms of general positive or negative affective states, whereas the normals most commonly defined situations primarily in terms of affiliative interpersonal concerns. Further content analyses showed that the alcoholics were less likely than the normals to conceptualize situations in terms that would facilitate predicting and manipulating events. They were less likely to construe situations in terms of evaluative standards and more likely to construe situations in terms of ability, self- or other image, and responsibility-oriented constructs that reflect image and coping-related concerns. These content-related findings are closely related to the maladaptive contents described above for alcoholics.

COGNITIVE BEHAVIOR TREATMENT APPROACH

The cognitive behavior day hospital treatment program has two main parts. The first is a cognitive behavior therapy group supplemented with individual cognitive behavior therapy, and the second is the larger day hospital program into which these are organized. The specific cognitive behavior therapies will be described first; they can best be described by the general stages that are involved.

In the earlier stages of the therapy, the therapist diagnoses each patient to identify his particular psychopathology and maladaptive conceptualization processes and contents. The therapist also introduces the patients to the general model of cognitive behavior therapy. Patients are introduced to the ideas that (1) the ways in which they think about things has a strong influence on all aspects of their lives, including their problems and their ability to cope with and enjoy life; (2) there are alternative ways to view things, which lead to more desirable feelings and behaviors; and (3) it is within the power of each patient to control thinking processes and through these to control his feelings and behaviors. Although the topics of the therapy discussions and exercises usually focus on personal, interpersonal, or environmental problems that the patients identify or on content (theme)-oriented issues that the therapist raises, the therapist uses these activities as a medium to attempt to modify the patients' maladaptive conceptualization processes. The ultimate target of the therapy and the modality through which it operates are cognitive in nature. As part of this the therapist tries to make evident to each patient his own particular maladaptive conceptualization contents and themes, helps each patient to understand the negative consequences of these maladaptive conceptualizations, and shows each the alternatives and the improvements that would result from their employment. The therapist then helps the patients to explore and adopt the more adaptive conceptualizations and the other relevant cognitive and behavioral skills. Therapy and support services also are provided for any other problems that may face the patient. A primary goal of the therapy is the teaching of generalized coping and reconceptualizing skills that go beyond the specific content of the problems that are openly dealt with in the therapy. Patients are helped to develop the self-insight, the self-monitoring abilities, and the analytic models and skills necessary to "become their own therapist" and to continue the work of the therapy on their own after the formal therapy is concluded. Even during the therapy patients are very strongly encouraged to be active collaborators in rather than passive recipients of the treatmtent.

Additionally, patients are helped to develop alternative and more successful coping and self-regulatory skills and encouraged to substitute more adaptive behaviors for those that support maladaptive conceptualizations and behavioral symptom patterns. Although the therapy is specifically designed for the treatment of alcoholism, its focus is on maladaptive conceptualizations and behaviors, only some of which involve or are related to alcohol use. Although drinking is often a therapy focus, the use of alcohol is considered in the same way as any other maladaptive behavior or unsuccessful coping strategy. Patients are helped to learn to substitute a more adaptive behavior for a maladaptive one rather than being encouraged simply to stop the maladaptive one, such as drinking. Although the larger therapy program does involve some behavioral skills training, for the most part it is assumed that the patients have, at least to some degree, most of the necessary adaptive practical and interpersonal skills and that the problem is to help the patients to identify and use those skills when appropriate. For some patients, instruction in relaxation training, assertiveness training, and social skills training, and sometimes instruction in practical skills (such as job hunting) can provide an important supplement to the patients' repertoire of adaptive alternative behaviors, and perhaps more important, can increase their confidence in their ability to exert self-control and use an alternative adaptive strategy.

Patients who have benefited from the therapy seem to have four characteristics in common: (a) they were motivated to change; (b) they accepted the general cognitive behavior model and its implications; (c) they felt that they had been able to exercise some degree of increased insight into and control of their conceptualizations; and (d) they had some experience in which they benefited from a reconceptualization and the application of some of the cognitive skills they learned. Not surprisingly, those patients with greater personal, interpersonal, and practical resources and supports were more often able to benefit from the therapy program; however, this is not saying much more than noting that those who have less far to go and have more help getting there are more likely to reach the goal. Many of the concepts of the cognitive therapy model and the directions for individual change must be presented didactically, but a number of patients seem to have great difficulty assimilating ideas from a verbal presentation. For this reason discussion must be supplemented by in vivo experiences, role playing, homework assignments, reality testing, behavioral change experiments, and guided exercises in self- and other monitoring skills. For many patients another factor in their ability to benefit from the therapy is the extent to which they are able and willing to engage in these experiences.

Cognitive Behavior Treatment Program

The therapy relies on many of the established general principles and techniques that define cognitive behavior therapy. Of particular relevance are the strategies and methods developed by Beck and associates (1976, 1979), and Meichenbaum (1975, 1977), and Meichenbaum and Turk (1976) and the skills training procedures developed by D'Zurilla and Goldfried (1971) and Novaco (1977). Therapists who are considering using the program described here are encouraged to familiarize themselves with these works. The treatment program involves both a group intervention and an individual therapy component. A specific protocol for the group will be described; since the individual therapy is an extension of the group, only a brief description of it will be necessary.

The group therapy relies on the development of a facilitative group process of open interaction among the group members. Therefore, in addition to skills as cognitive therapists, the therapists who lead the groups in the day hospital also must have some expertise in group intervention approaches.

There are usually sufficient similarities between the alcoholic patients' pathologies and a sufficient likelihood that most of the patients will have at least some of the maladaptive cognitive characteristics common to alcoholics and common to at least some of the other members of the group to make the use of a group modality not only possible but particularly advantageous; nevertheless, it is important to develop an individual diagnosis and treatment plan for each patient. Although the general intervention strategy described above is applied to all patients, specific goals and intervention attempts are developed for each individual patient based on his particular maladaptive conceptualizations and coping strategies, personality and psychopathology, social and environmental resources and circumstances, drinking history and pattern, and so on. For this reason several assessments are administered for diagnostic and planning purposes.

Patients are asked to complete a Beck Depression Inventory, a Spielberger Trait Anxiety Scale, a California Psychological Inventory, a detailed problem-drinking history report, an assertiveness measure, and a Situations Rep Test (Glantz, 1980, 1982) that provides information about the organization and content of the subject's conceptualizations. The Rep Test is an extremely powerful assessment for cognitive therapy and makes a major contribution to diagnosis and treatment planning. During the course of the therapy patients also describe their beliefs about themselves, make a short presentation introducing themselves to the group, and fill out a Goal Attainment Scale (GAS) that describes the current status of four important areas of their lives. Other personality and neuropsychological assessments are administered at the discretion of the therapists. The information from all of the assessments is organized into a diagnostic picture; the problems and strengths of the patients and therapeutic goals and potential interventions are determined; and the diagnostic picture and the goals and plans for each patient are constantly checked and revised as new information becomes available. The treatment goals for the individual patient are coordinated with the therapy protocol, and the therapists attempt to accomplish the scheduled tasks for each therapy session while at the same time taking advantage of presented opportunities to advance the therapeutic plans developed for the individual patients.

The cognitive therapy groups are led by two therapists and consist of from 8 to 10 patients; in those cases where the patients and both therapists are men, a female therapist may sometimes be asked to assist in role-playing exercises (for convenience it will be assumed that the patients are men as was the case in the program on which this discussion is based[4]). For the program

---

[4]The therapy program and the description of alcoholics' maladaptive conceptualization characteristics were developed at the VA and based primarily on its mostly male population. Although it has been the author's experience that the cognitive model and the list of maladaptive conceptualization characteristics is also descriptive of female alcoholics and although the author has used an individual therapy version of the cognitive behavior therapy program with female alcoholics, the reader should note that the applicability of these materials to female alcoholics is more speculative than its applicability to male alcoholics.

recommended here, each group should meet twice weekly with each meeting lasting for 1½ to 2 hours. Group meetings should be videotaped if possible. Certain rules are established with the patients. No patient may attend a meeting if he is intoxicated. Patients are asked to commit themselves to come for 2 months and are then asked to renew their contract every 2 months; if a patient misses more than two consecutive meetings or more than five meetings in a 2-month period, he may continue to attend only if the other group members agree to allow him to continue. If the therapists feel that the group has become too small to continue productively, it is combined with another group that has also completed the initial 35-session protocol. All patients in the group are assigned to one of the cotherapists for individual therapy, which meets weekly or more frequently at the discretion of the therapist. These individual therapy sessions are also cognitive therapy–based and are intended to provide for each patient the individual therapeutic intervention that the therapist believes will benefit the patient the most. Patients are encouraged to participate in the skills training groups at the day hospital (e.g., relaxation training, assertiveness training, etc.) and also are encouraged to participate in the recreational and other activities. If the therapist feels that it is appropriate, the patient also may be offered the opportunity to engage in other therapy activities,—for example, cognitively oriented family therapy, a special support group, or training in cognitive compensation skills. Following is a general therapy protocol for the initial sessions of the cognitive therapy group for alcoholics.[5]

Group Therapy Protocol

Sessions 1 and 2

Patients are introduced to the group, and a general description of the therapy and its processes is provided; the rules and expectations for the group also are discussed. Patients complete several exercises that will be used for diagnosis and as a basis for future group activities. The first exercise is the (GAS), for which each patient, usually with considerable help from a therapist, describes his current status, his 5-week, 10-week, and 3- to 6-month goals in four areas of his life: (1) home or residence, (2) recreation, (3) employment/education/skills, (4) social/interpersonal/affiliative relationships and activities. All of the goals must be at least somewhat realistic and must be stated in specific concrete behavioral terms, which is difficult for most alcoholics. The second exercise is the self-presentation, in which each patient is asked to pre-

---

[5]The reader may find it helpful to refer to "Cognitive therapy in groups with alcoholics" (Glantz & McCourt, 1983), which contains a description of an outpatient treatment program that shares many of the basic principles employed in this program. This earlier chapter includes some discussion of relevant research and a more extensive description of some treatment aspects common to both programs.

pare a 3-minute talk about himself that is videotaped in the following session before an audience of three unfamiliar staff members. After the completion of the exercises the group reconvenes, and each patient is asked to introduce himself to the group and to tell the group a little about himself, including when he was happiest and when saddest and what he thinks the future holds for him. This introduces the patients to each other and establishes the expectation that personal information will be shared in the sessions. Patients are asked to complete the Beck Depression Inventory, the Spielberger State Anxiety Scale, and the California Psychological Inventory between the sessions.

Sessions 3 and 4

The therapists role-play several vignettes to demonstrate that the different possible behavioral and emotional responses to a given situation are the product of different thoughts and different conceptualizations; other aspects of the general cognitive model also are illustrated. Reality testing is discussed and illustrated by having the patients check their opinions against the videotape; in many sessions patients are asked to compare a belief with a tape or with the group's opinion. The patients' videotaped self-presentations also are used to demonstrate that one's self-concept is an opinion that others may not necessarily share. The assignment for session 5 is for each patient to list the five most important beliefs he has about himself. Patients are assigned to one of the therapists for individual therapy, which begins on a weekly basis.

Sessions 5 and 6

A patient is selected, and the group attempts to guess what the patient listed as his beliefs about himself. Although the group members have usually had very little contact with each other prior to the formation of the group, they are usually fairly accurate in guessing at least the general tone of the list. The group also is asked to list their impressions of the patient, which is usually more favorable than the patient's assessment. The implications of each list are discussed, as are related issues such as whether group members feel that they would respond differently to the patient if his self-image were different. At least one patient usually has not done the assignment and makes an excuse to avoid responsibility. This is discussed and is a good example of the ways in which the therapists attempt to use events in the group to deal with maladaptive behaviors and conceptualizations. After the self-presentation exercise is done with each patient, the therapists again present the cognitive model emphasizing the framework that thoughts determine feelings, which together determine behaviors; the potential benefits for controlling one's thoughts and feelings is discussed. For the seventh meeting, the patients are assigned the "monitoring" task, in which they are asked to describe in writing two strong feelings that they had during the past week, the thoughts that preceded the feelings, and the behaviors that followed.

Sessions 5 through 7

The therapists use the patients' monitoring assignments as a means to discuss the thought–feeling–behavior (TFB) model and its implications; events in the group also are often analyzed in a similar manner, and this type of analysis is sometimes enhanced with behavioral or imaginal role playing. The assignments are analyzed with the assistance of the group and discussed in great detail. In between the sessions the patients meet with one of the therapists, who administers the Situations Rep Test, which is scored and later discussed with the patient.

Sessions 8 and 9

The progress the patients have made on the goals they listed on the GSA is discussed and related to their adaptive and maladaptive conceptualizations; patients are given the chance to revise their goals if they feel that they can identify more realistic or more desirable goals. A monitoring assignment is given for the tenth session.

Sessions 10 through 14

The monitoring assignments are discussed, with increasing emphasis on the importance of monitoring one's thoughts and with a greater focus on patients' particular maladaptive conceptualization contents and processes. A greater emphasis also is placed on the implications of alternative conceptualizations and on methods such as adaptive self statements that can be used to increase adaptive thinking. Alternate thought experiments are encouraged. A monitoring assignment is given for the fifteenth session.

Sessions 15 through 18

A simplified version of Schacter and Singer's model of affective reaction is presented and is the basis for a discussion on resisting and controlling strong undesirable emotions. The monitoring assignments are used as illustrations. Meichenbaum's stress inoculation procedure (1975) and a version of Novaco's anger control technique (1977) are taught and practiced. Simple relaxation techniques also are taught. Patients who have a particular problem with affect or impulse control may attend a special therapy group at the day hospital and/or continue to work on their problem in individual therapy.

Sessions 19 through 22

A version of D'Zurilla and Goldfried's (1971) problem-solving strategy is presented and related to the TFB model. Patients identify problems that they would like to work on (often related to their GAS goals), and the group analyzes and tries to suggest adaptive problem-solving strategy steps. The therapists assign each patient to a two-person problem-solving team. Each team is made up of a pair of patients who have very different, preferably incompatible, conceptualization system characteristics. Each of the pair identifies a problem that he would like to work on, and it is the homework assignment for the team to try to solve, or at least work out a method for solving, the two problems. This seems to help the patients to learn how alternate, though often maladaptive, conceptualizations can influence problem solving; they also learn about the effects of their own conceptualization. The team often becomes an important interpersonal relationship for many of the patients, and for some it is the first time they have ever really worked collaboratively with someone. Intra-team interpersonal problems often are raised during the group as difficulties to be focused on and resolved. A monitoring assignment is given for the twenty-third session.

Sessions 23 through 26

The monitoring assignments are discussed, with the patients assuming an increasing responsibility for the analyses. Patients also are encouraged to bring up issues that they would like to discuss or problems that they would like to work on. When appropriate, the therapists may recommend between-session exercises in which patients play extended roles designed to encourage understanding and adopting alternative conceptualizations [cf. Kelly's Fixed Role Therapy (Kelly, 1955)]. Patients also are offered the opportunity to read some of the self-help guides available (e.g., Beck & Greenberg, 1974; Ellis & Harper, 1975). Patients are asked to prepare a new 3-minute self-presentation, which they deliver between sessions to the same audience as before.

Session 27

The videotapes of the self-presentations are played for the group, sometimes (at the discretion of the therapists) in conjunction with their original presentation. Patients often are surprised at their own improvements, and these are related to changes in their conceptualizations. A monitoring assignment is given. Patients are asked to complete a Rotter Incomplete Sentences Blank.

Sessions 28 and 29

The progress the patients have made on the goals they listed on the GAS is discussed as before, and the monitoring assignments are also discussed. The patients are encouraged to take a major role in the analyses and in identifying possible adaptive alternatives. The suggestion is made that patients keep a private diary, which they are then encouraged to review periodically to gain some additional insight about themselves. Patients are given the chance to select one or more "special therapy topics," such as weight loss, being an absentee father, overcoming a phobia, and the like.

Sessions 30 through 32

The special therapy topics are the focus of these sessions, and they are handled as the therapists feel is appropriate. Dailey Programmed Case Assessments (1971) are administered between sessions.

Session 33

The Dailey Programmed Case Assessments are used as a focus for group discussions on understanding and predicting others' behavior. Patients are assigned to new problem-solving teams and work on problems as before. Platt and Spivack Problem Solving Assessments are administered between sessions to identify areas of problem solving inadequacy.

Sessions 34 and 35

These sessions are used to focus on the areas of problem-solving inadequacy identified by the tests. Patients complete new GASs.

Further Sessions

Although the group is expected to continue, there is no specific protocol for the sessions, and the therapists develop therapy plans based on the needs of the patients. Many types of activities of the previous sessions are repeated but often at a more sophisticated level.

THE DAY HOSPITAL

The day hospital itself provides the services and facilities associated with this type of intervention, including the ancillary supports and interventions referred to above. The distinguishing characteristic of the cognitive behavior therapy day hospital is that the cognitive interventions make use of the occurrences and activities of the day hospital to further the goals of the therapy. Not only are the identified therapies an intervention, but the other aspects of the day hospital are also an intervention rather than just an alternative custodial environment.

SPECIAL ISSUES

There are several special issues that are important to consider. The first of these is the issue of whether the specific alcohol-related goal of the therapy should be complete abstinence from alcohol or whether controlled drinking is a feasible goal for most alcoholics. There is some controversy over this question. Although controlled drinking is possible for some alcoholics, experience has shown that the percentage who are able to stay in control for a prolonged period of time is far too small to suggest that this is a chance worth taking, particularly since the consequences of relapse are so great and there is no reliable way to identify even the few who can drink in a controlled fashion. Certainly it is easier to learn not to do a behavior at all than to learn to engage in it only to a certain point but no further. This difficulty is exacerbated in the case of alcohol use because any degree of alcohol use disrupts and limits exactly those cognitive control functions that are necessary to exercise the self-control required to prevent further drinking and intoxication. For this reason patients are encouraged to adopt abstinence as a goal.

Contemporary psychotherapy often involves the use of psychotherapeutic medications, and the treatment of alcoholism is not an exception. However, because of the special nature of the substance abuse patient, the use of some of these medications (outside of special medical circumstances such as detoxification) involves some unique considerations with this population. Of particular concern are those psychoactive drugs that have a high abuse liability, notably the minor tranquilizers and the sedative hypnotics, many of which have effects that are similar to those of alcohol. There are not many occasions when it makes sense to give an abusable drug to a substance abuser with the expectation that it will have a therapeutic result. Although some therapists feel that the patient's use of these drugs can be controlled and is not likely to become part of an abuser pattern, it is suggested that the use of these drugs with this population usually works against the goals of the therapy. Therefore, the use of these drugs with alcoholics entails considerable risk and is not generally advised.

Related to this is the question of the use of disulfiram (Antabuse®) as a treatment adjunct. Use of disulfiram does help some alcoholics remain sober, and for some it reduces their feeling that their drinking cannot be controlled; it also can help some to create the opportunity to learn that they can cope without alcohol and can even change their environment. Alternatively, its use reinforces the idea in patients that they cannot control and are not responsible for controlling their drinking and that if their drinking is to be controlled it will be only through some external agent. Although the therapist must judge each case individually, the gains usually outweigh the losses; however, since most patients are unwilling to use disulfiram and since even those who do use it can still abuse other drugs or can stop taking the drug and soon go back to drinking, the issue seems to make a difference less often than might be expected.

Finally, many alcoholics, particularly the older ones, suffer some degree of neuropsychological impairment. Although abstinence will in some cases allow at least partial recovery of some functions, it is most often the case that recovery is not complete. It is the author's experience that teaching these patients cognitive-behaviorally oriented compensating skills can be of benefit to some individuals. Organized planning and problem solving, use of environmental aids, development of self-monitoring and self-talk, ability to bring performance anxiety under control, and belief in the power of cognitions assist some patients to reach a level of performance that they report brings them much closer to their former level of function. This type of therapy has been used with several patients, and the results are encouraging if only anecdotal. Though this type of intervention is not being proposed as a substitute for biomedically oriented treatments, it may prove to be a powerful supplement. The potential of a cognitively oriented therapy for those demonstrating neuropsychological decrement is an exciting possibility that deserves more attention from other researchers.

Conclusion

Although it is not possible to discuss all of the aspects of cognitive behavior therapy treatment of alcoholics in this chapter, it is hoped that a sufficiently useful introduction was provided. Cognitive therapy is a powerful intervention modality for alcoholics, and therapists who treat this patient population are encouraged to explore its potential.

References

Beck, A. (1972). *Depression: Clinical, experimental, and theoretical aspects.* Philadelphia: University of Pennsylvania Press.
Beck, A. (1976). *Cognitive therapy and the emotional disorders.* New York: International Universities Press.
Beck, A., & Greenberg, R. (1974). *Coping with depression.* New York: Institute for Rational Living.
Beck, A., Rush, A., Shaw, B., & Emery, G. (1979). *Cognitive therapy of depression.* New York: Guilford.
Cahalan, D., & Room, R. (1974). *Problem drinking among American men.* New Brunswick, NJ: Rutgers Center of Alcohol Studies.
Dailey, C. (1971). *Assessment of lives.* San Francisco: Jossey-Bass.
D'Zurilla, T., & Goldfried, M. (1971). Problem solving and behavior modification. *Journal of Abnormal Psychology, 78,* 107–126.
Ellis, A., & Harper, R. (1975). *A new guide to rational living.* North Hollywood, CA: Wilshire.
Glantz, M. (September 1980). Developments in the elicitation and analysis of constructs. Paper presented at the meeting of the American Psychological Association, Montreal.
Glantz, M. (April 1982). Diagnosis and assessment for cognitive behavior therapies: A Rep Test approach. Paper presented at the meeting of the Eastern Psychological Association, Baltimore.

Glantz, M., Burr, W., & Bosse, R. (1985). *Constructs used by alcoholics, nonpsychotic outpatients and normals.* Submitted.

Glantz, M., & McCourt, W. (1983). Cognitive therapy in groups with alcoholics. In *Cognitive therapy with couples and groups,* A. Freeman (Ed.) (pp. 157–181). New York: Plenum Press.

Greenspan, S., & Porges, S. (1984). Psychopathology in infancy and early childhood: Clinical perspectives on the organization of sensory and affective-thematic experience. *Child Development, 55,* 49–70.

Jessor, R., & Jessor, S. (1977). *Problem behavior and psychosocial development: A longitudinal study of youth.* New York: Academic Press.

Kelly, G. (1955). *The psychology of personal constructs.* New York: Norton.

McCord, J. (1972). Etiological factors in alcoholism: Family and personal characteristics. *Quarterly Journal of Studies on Alcohol, 33,* 1020—1027.

McCord, W., & McCord, J. (1960). *Origins of alcoholism.* Stanford, CA: Stanford University Press.

McCord, W., & McCord, J. (1962). A longitudinal study of the personality of alcoholics. In *Society, culture and drinking patterns,* D. Pittman & C. Snyder (Eds.). New York: Wiley Press.

Meichenbaum, D. (1975). A self-instructional approach to stress management: A proposal for stress inoculation training. In *Stress and anxiety,* (Vol. 2.), C. Spielberger & I. Sarason (Eds.). New York: Wiley.

Meichenbaum, D. (1977). *Cognitive-behavior modification.* New York: Plenum Press.

Meichenbaum, D., & Turk, D. (1976). The cognitive-behavioral management of anxiety, anger, and pain. In *The behavioral management of anxiety, depression, and pain,* P. Davidson (Ed.). New York: Brunner/Mazel.

Novaco, R. (1977). A cognitive therapy for anger and its application to a case of depression. *Journal of Consulting and Clinical Psychology, 45,* 600–608.

Robins, L. (1980). The natural history of drug abuse. In *Evaluation of treatment of drug abusers. Acta Psychiatrica Scandinavica, 62* (Supplement 284).

Chapter 4

INPATIENT TREATMENT OF ADOLESCENTS

*G. Randolph Schrodt, Jr.
Jesse H. Wright*

Most adolescent inpatient psychiatric units have adopted a treatment philosophy based on psychodynamic or behavioral principles (Kahn & Boyer, 1980). Probably the most common approach is a combination of these two models. An emphasis is placed on psychodynamic theories for psychotherapy and on behavioral techniques for control of the ward milieu. In some treatment settings the roles of the psychodynamically oriented therapist and the ward behavioral manager are purposely kept quite separate. However, in other units some attempt is made to integrate these two approaches.

We have recently introduced the cognitive-behavioral model to a 16-bed adolescent inpatient unit. This unit had previously utilized an eclectic blend of psychodynamic, behavioral, biological, and family systems theories to direct its activities. The treatment program is still in the early phases of development, but we have observed that the goal-oriented, here-and-now focus of cognitive behavior therapy is well suited for work with adolescents. This therapy also appears to provide a stimulus for cognitive maturation in many teenagers. In this chapter we will describe a developmental perspective for use of cognitive-behavioral techniques with adolescents and then discuss specific applications of cognitive-behavioral therapy on an adolescent inpatient unit.

TREATMENT OF ADOLESCENTS: GENERAL ISSUES

The Developmental Perspective

Adolescence is a time of dramatic biological, affective, cognitive, and behavioral change. The adolescent is challenged to accommodate these physical and psychosocial changes to societal norms. Although most adolescents manage this transition without major difficulty (Offer et al., 1981), some adolescents exhibit serious behavioral problems. Violence, depression, suicide, pregnancy, substance abuse, and school failure are some of the more common manifestations of a significant disruption in adolescent growth and development.

Sociocultural factors are among the most powerful forces in this developmental process. The adolescent's attitudes and values often are influenced more by peers and cultural models than by adults. There is a progressive separation and individuation from the family of origin. At the same time, the family system serves as a source of modeling and structure. Psychologically healthy adolescents usually have a stable social ecology that can provide a point of reference for testing old and new ideas, beliefs, and behaviors (Petersen & Offer, 1979). Conversely, adolescent psychiatric patients often come from disorganized families that have experienced sociocultural or emotional poverty, divorce, or death.

Cognitive Maturation in Adolescents

Adolescence is also a time of maturation of cognitive style. Piaget has noted that formal operational thinking is achieved during this developmental phase (Anthony, 1982). Most adolescents acquire the capacity to think in formal, abstract, and hypothetical dimensions—abilities that have strong adaptive value in problem solving throughout adult life. In contrast to children and preadolescents, whose interpretations of environmental events are usually based on direct observation, adolescents can form alternative explanations and consider different perspectives of themselves and the world. Preverbal representational models of the world and self are formalized and solidified by these new cognitive abilities. The ability to think abstractly and consider alternatives is nurtured in cognitive behavioral therapy with teenagers. An important goal of this treatment is to supplant immature and flawed reasoning with more mature cognitive processes.

A second distinctive feature of adolescent cognition is egocentrism. David Elkind (1967) has described the characteristic tendency of teenagers to believe that their interpretation of the world is the accurate perspective. He emphasized the importance of idiosyncratic distortions such as "personal fables," which influence decision making and behavior. For instance, the belief that one cannot get pregnant even if one does not use birth control can lead to behavior with profound negative effects. Elkind also describes the "imaginary audience" phenomenon in teenagers who believe that others share their highly personalized obsession with appearance and behavior. This self-consciousness is noted in clinical work with adolescents. Their egocentric and rigid beliefs, acute sensitivity to criticism, and intense emotional responses require considerable patience and understanding from the therapist.

Cognitive processes are involved in complex psychological activities such as the refinement of self-concept (Guidano & Liotti, 1983), the regulation of self-esteem, the elaboration of a social niche, and the actualization of personal goals. Personal identity is defined by the dynamic set of beliefs and attitudes that individuals have about themselves in relation to the world. Experiences that validate these beliefs provide a sense of integrity, coherence, and cohesiveness. An adolescent's representational model of self and world is also a product of early life experiences and biological influences.

An important component of the adolescent's self-concept is "self-efficacy"—the personal belief in one's ability to deal adequately with situations. Albert Bandura (1977) describes self-efficacy as an integral component of behavior and behavior change. The strength of an adolescent's belief in self-efficacy is related to abilities such as adequate intelligence, problem-solving skills, and physical prowess, and it is affected by past experience, social feedback, and social learning. Belief in self-efficacy also has been related to the persistence and strength of behavioral efforts made in solving tasks when faced with problems and obstacles (Bandura, 1977). As a teenager searches for an acceptable adult role, self-efficacy may be impaired by actual deficiencies in skills or by distortions in self-appraisal. These may have profound effects on other areas of adolescent identity formation.

Distorted or dysfunctional information processing may result from a variety of factors, including depression, cognitive immaturity, and substance abuse. Beck and associates (1979) have described "primitive" modes of thinking that are seen in high frequency in adult depressives. These include arbitrary inference, selective abstraction, overgeneralization, magnification and minimization of events, personalization, and absolutistic thinking. These cognitive distortions are extremely common in hospitalized adolescents but are also rather common in normal teenagers. The maturation of more rational and flexible modes of thinking is usually associated with an improvement in self-concept and self-esteem regulation, both in normal teenagers and in those with significant psychopathology.

The Therapeutic Attitude

Cognitive-behavioral therapy requires a collaborative and empirical working relationship with the teenager. Therapist characteristics that are operative in all effective psychotherapies (e.g., warmth, empathy, genuineness, and respect) are also of great importance in cognitive psychotherapy with teenagers. Patience, tolerance, and a noncritical, nonjudgmental attitude are essential.

Many authors have emphasized the need to modify adult techniques for work with teenagers (Gittelson, 1948; Meeks, 1980). For instance, Gittelson (1948) has suggested that an active "synthetic" approach is preferable to a passive "analytic" approach with adolescents. In this regard, cognitive therapy would appear to be quite appropriate for teenagers. The cognitive therapist is active, engaging, and goal-oriented. The collaborative problem-solving approach of cognitive therapy helps to counter difficulties that adolescents have in engaging in a working relationship with an adult therapist.

Psychotherapy with adolescents is complicated by the inherent power imbalance in the therapeutic relationship. Teenagers often distort and magnify the actual power that the therapist possesses. Some adolescents have doubts about the intentions and motives of therapist and staff. The therapist must clearly acknowledge that there are parental, legal, and ethical issues in dealing with a minor. At the same time, the therapeutic contract must be primarily for the teenager's benefit. The teenage patient usually demonstrates a strong skepticism of parents and other adults. This attitude can impair effective, honest communication in psychotherapy. However, the egalitarian, empirical approach of cognitive-behavioral therapy encourages healthy skepticism. If the therapist can maintain that his perceptin of a situation is but one possible alternative, and if the teenager can be encouraged to reciprocate by looking at his own thoughts with the same critical analysis, then collaborative empiricism can be attained. Thus, cognitive-behavioral therapy can proceed.

COGNITIVE-BEHAVIORAL THERAPY ON AN ADOLESCENT UNIT

Organizing Philosophy

A multidisciplinary approach is used in most inpatient adolescent psychiatric units. The mixture of treatments often includes individual psychotherapy, intensive group therapy, family therapy, recreational therapy, and educational remediation. It is important that adolescent inpatient programs have a clear organizing philosophy. Work with severely disturbed adolescents who are in need of safety, structure, and consistency often places an extreme demand on staff and patients alike. Combining different therapies without an overall model for care can lead to a chaotic therapeutic milieu with resultant confusion, splitting, and destructive behavior. Many units have handled this problem by developing a behavioral program in which staff and patients are clearly aware of and bound to a set of the ward rules. We have found that adding a cognitive perspective to the behavioral model gives a greater depth of perspective of the adolescent and provides many opportunities for meaningful therapeutic work.

The Admission

The cognitive-behavioral treatment of adolescent inpatients begins with the referral. Teenagers are admitted to psychiatric units for a variety of reasons. At times, the failure of outpatient treatment prompts hospitalization. In other cases, suicidal or other dangerous behavior leads to inpatient treatment. Severe psychosomatic disorders may also require treatment in a medical setting. Cognitive-behavioral therapy emphasizes the need for specificity in target symptoms and goal setting. For example, significant individual variations exist in motivation for treatment, available resources, and the "fit" with the treatment milieu. The adolescent usually has diverse and complex problems that must be identified and prioritized.

Intake information usually is biased in some manner by the referring party. It is important to recognize the inherent limitations of these data. Initial assumptions are frequently incorrect, and they can bias the treatment staff and have a negative influence on treatment. For instance, when a teenager is referred for "out of control" behavior or physical violence, the staff may focus unduly on this aggressive behavior and inadvertently exclude other data. Distorted perceptions also can be critical in the problem of recidivism. A patient who is readmitted to the adolescent unit often can provoke a sense of helplessness and therapeutic impotence. These attitudes must be addressed before effective treatment can be delivered.

Referral information is an important factor in the decision to admit to the hospital and is helpful in staff preparation for working with a teenager on initial entry into the system. However, a thorough diagnostic evaluation is needed before setting treatment goals and initiating therapy. In addition to the routine psychosocial history and medical examination, inquiry about adolescents' perceptions of self and environment adds a cognitive dimension to the initial diagnostic evaluation. A collaborative approach to treatment is facilitated when teenagers believe from the outset that their thoughts and feelings are appreciated.

The Family

Cognitive-behavioral therapy with the family of the adolescent emphasizes the eliciting and testing of underlying assumptions and beliefs. For instance, a family who brings their teenager for treatment may have a primary goal of stopping antisocial behavior (e.g., drug or alcohol abuse) but may have little understanding or appreciation of the existence or need to treat associated psychiatric illness (e.g., depression). It is not uncommon for some families to have the implicit expectation that the hospital should "fix" the patient and that there should be little input or involvement from themselves in the treatment process. Conversely, some families have expectations of intense involvement, including control of the inpatient therapeutic process. They can become disappointed or angry when they are excluded in any way from the treatment. Generally, there is a considerable amount of family system instability and ambivalence at the time of admission, and it is useful to explore the expectations of treatment and assumptions concerning the hospital's role as "helper" versus "punisher." Successful contract negotiation also can be helped by addressing certain basic but often neglected issues such as the goal of returning to the family system or placement outside the home following hospitalization. This decision usually cannot be made at the time of initial referral or admission, but any preexisting thoughts or assumptions need to be explored early in the course of hospitalization.

After initial assumptions have been identified about the goals of hospitalization, they can be tested against the realities of the situation. For instance, in a brief period of time a thorough evaluation may be possible but with minimal behavior change. Broad and ambitious goals such as extensive personality changes or "improving family communication" may be possible only after long-term treatment and may not be realistic goals for inpatient treatment. The agenda for treatment is established most effectively if the family, the adolescent, and the treatment team collaborate in this process.

Providing information to families about the role of family therapy in the hospital setting can correct many distorted ideas. At times, the family can be engaged as a "surrogate therapist" and can provide support for the teenager in completing homework assignments or other tasks. At other times, the family is involved more as "the patient." Dysfunctional attitudes, cognitive distortions, and maladaptive behavior patterns within the system are treated by family therapy. When a family member other than the teenager exhibits clinical psychopathology, appropriate referral is indicated.

Many patients require education in the basics of appropriate parenting. Parenting workshops can provide families an active role in treatment and offer a coherent framework for discipline, responsibility, and negotiation within the family. At times parents need help in understanding adolescent development and in distinguishing between "normal" and dysfunctional adolescent behavior.

Initial Phase of Hospitalization

The adolescent's problems often are manifested in dysfunctional behavior that can undermine psychotherapy. Teenagers also may have difficulty in identifying the goals of treatment or in understanding their role in the process. Generally, the teenager does not initiate treatment. At the time of admission, most adolescents are unwilling participants. Although attempts are made at the outset to establish a good working relationship, it is usually necessary to be rather straightforward with the teenager in the early stages of hospitalization.

It was noted earlier that an adolescent must have a stable and consistent milieu within which to develop a cohesive sense of identity. Furthermore, many teenagers who require inpatient hospitalization present with self-destructive behaviors and poor impulse control that must be managed before any effective treatment can take place.

Expectations for behavior on the ward must be presented with consistency and clarity. A patient manual that explains the role of various personnel, the treatment process, and specific behavioral rules and consequences can be very helpful in this regard. It is not the intention to present an autocratic or repressive attitude, but it is necessary to apply behavioral standards without hesitation and to attempt to clarify the social necessity of such rules for life in an inpatient unit. It is not uncommon, however, for adolescents to distort and thereby react to the treatment staff as "wardens" of the ward. Exploration and examination of such distorted views usually enhances effective behavioral control.

Staff members in an established, well-functioning therapeutic milieu will anticipate problem situations before they arise and will respond empathically yet consistently, in keeping with the overall therapeutic philosophy. The adolescent will find rules and clear contingencies immediately on admission. Any initial rebellion against the system usually subsides when collaborative working relationships are established.

Behavioral Techniques

Countertherapeutic boredom and anxiety can be avoided if the adolescent program has a clear structure and purpose. The use of a daily activity schedule with specific planned activities, including school, groups, and recreational time, serves several purposes. These include giving structure to the day, providing behavioral reinforcers, and serving as a method of engaging teenagers in modification of their own behavior. Later in hospitalization, after effective collaboration has been attained, the adolescent is given more freedom to alter the schedule on an individual basis. Some teenagers show the maturity to design their own schedule for the day. Activities enhancing self-esteem can be scheduled and used as contingencies for reaching mutually established goals.

A level system of privileges can be useful. Therapeutic levels and other privileges, such as phone calls and inclusion in recreational and social events, can serve as potent reinforcers for maintaining behavior within appropriate social limits. Requests for change in levels, schedules, and other privileges are initiated by the patient through a written request that is considered in the daily staff meeting. Specific feedback as well as reasons for the decision are offered in writing or in person by the therapist or a member of the treatment team. Inclusion of the patient in therapeutic planning meetings is another way of promoting adaptive behavior while enhancing collaborative therapeutic relationships.

Inappropriate ward behavior often can be modified by room restriction. In many cases this behavior is motivated by a need for attention from the staff or peers. When inappropriate behavior is observed, staff members instruct the teenager to go to his room. The teenager then completes a written restriction form that is designed to elicit perceptions of the incident and associated thoughts and feelings. These forms are reviewed with the staff member who placed the patient on restriction. Enhanced mutual understanding and cognitive resolution are frequent outcomes of this exercise.

The cognitive-behavioral milieu seeks to do more than just shape behavior. The adolescent is encouraged to take active responsibility for behavior and to learn about individual, family, and group methods for change. For example, the weekly patient-staff meeting, which is chaired by "officers" elected by the patient group, provides an opportunity for this type of experience. In general, adolescents handle these positions with maturity and a sense of pride. Important ward issues are often discussed and resolved in this forum.

Initially, many adolescents are unable or unwilling to manage issues "outside" the hospital, but are easily engaged in issues surrounding the daily ward routine. A positive experience on the ward often encourages collaboration on problems prompting hospitalization. Unfortunately, there are occasions when, despite intense effort on the part of the staff, it is impossible to establish a working alliance with a teenager. However, when collaboration is possible and when particular goals for treatment can be established, the formal work of cognitive therapy can begin.

Eliciting and Testing Cognitions

The process of cognitive therapy involves bringing automatic thoughts, schemas, and other cognitions into full awareness. Adolescents vary in their capacity for formal operations or, more specifically, in the capacity to think about thinking. However, there are many opportunities to elicit automatic thoughts and images and to identify the critical association between thought, feeling, and behavior. In psychotherapy sessions, cognitive material is gathered by guided questioning and other standard cognitive therapy procedures such as imagery and role-playing (Watkins & Rush, 1983).

Direct questioning was used in the following example to elicit and test significant, negative automatic thoughts. A 15-year-old male, who was admitted for fights with his father, depression, and suicidal thoughts, related that a family visit over the weekend had gone very poorly, and he had been left feeling very depressed. His father had appeared preoccupied and quiet. The patient was asked to try to remember what he thought when he was with his father. He answered: "My father was mad at me because I'm here in the hospital. He thinks I should never get sick or have any problems." These thoughts were accepted uncritically and had led the teenager to withdraw and not talk with his family during the visit. The therapist and patient agreed to test out the validity of these automatic thoughts at the next family conference. The father admitted that he had been preoccupied, but his pensiveness had been about a serious problem at work. He hadn't mentioned this to his son "because I didn't want to worry him."

We also have used the Daily Record of Dysfunctional Thoughts (DRDT) with many of our hospitalized adolescents (Meeks, 1980; Watkins & Rush, 1983). Teenagers generally require more direction and guidance in the use of this instrument than do adults. However, adolescents can learn to analyze their own perceptions of events (such as family conferences or patient/staff or patient/patient interactions) effectively and record and test these thoughts on the DRDT.

For example, an eighteen-year-old with anorexia nervosa and depression used the DRDT to describe a situation involving her eating behavior. The situation was "sitting with everyone while they were eating; they bug me and pester me that I'm not eating." She described her emotional response as "I'm mad," and then listed a very interesting series of automatic thoughts, including "I wish they would leave me alone, they never cared before, why should they now; it's not my fault they stuff themselves with fattening food; at least I'm in control; they're not and they'll pay for it later."

Several core ideas expressed in this DRDT were examined in therapy, including the effect of her "audience" and the absolutistic nature of her attitudes about "control." The use of techniques such as the DRDT, which help the adolescent to "de-center" and gain an objective view of thinking, can lead to a sense of mastery as well as insight into particular dysfunctional and distorted patterns of thought.

Another technique for eliciting and testing cognitions is the hour included in each teenager's daily schedule for "room reflect." During this time period, the teenager writes a page on a topic of his choosing or one that has been agreed on with the therapist. Room reflects often reveal important thoughts, perceptions, and feelings that can be examined in therapy. For example, a fourteen-year-old girl admitted for running away and oppositional behavior wrote the following:

> You know I'm tired of looking at things in a positive way. I always say well I'll go home and I'll try and I'll ignore the things that upset me and I'll take my punishments and I'll get through it all. But I'm sick of always wanting to try and willing to do better and not getting any effort back.
>
> No one cares about trying; no one cares, period. They just sit back and watch me struggle and try but they don't want to help me carry my load.
>
> So I come to the conclusion that I'm not worth it and I say forget it, I've done lost the fight.

This written statement conveys the teenager's hopelessness and helplessness and reveals possible cognitive errors, particularly absolutistic thinking, that may be amenable to change in cognitive therapy. This excerpt also suggests a therapeutic focus on the teenager's use of language. Words such as *all, no one, forever, can't* and other emotively colored or judgmental words such as *good* and *bad* are targeted. An exploration and refinement of these concepts in therapy can lead to new perceptions of self and others.

Another more extensive room reflect report from a sixteen-year-old boy admitted for depression and violent threats shows a change in perspective during the process of writing down thoughts and feelings:

> Today I would like to write about how stupid room reflect is because I really hate having to come in my room and write about boring topics with a boring pen and piece of paper. I would think that everyone else would

agree that this is the most boring part of the day for all the patients. (Except for school). Some people would like to relax and smoke cigarettes instead of sit in quiet and try to think of something silly to write about. I mean some people just aren't that creative when it comes to writing and probably have no interest in it. So why should we be forced to write this stuff? I have to do this sort of thing in English class at school all the time, but now it is the summer and it is time for me to relax and try as hard as I can to forget how much I hate school. It's not like I need the practice in creative writing because I've been doing it all my life, and personally I think it is quite boring.

O.K. I can't write this whole paper about the negative aspects of room reflect because it does have it's good points. Well, I can think of one. That is, the room reflect can help psychiatrists and staff figure out what the patient is thinking, what he/her feels, and what is exactly wrong with them, quicker. That itself is a good enough reason to do it, because the quicker we can figure out what is wrong with us and try to correct it, the sooner we can leave the hospital. Even I have been able to express feelings and thoughts which I have not been able to talk about. And oftentimes try to avoid even thinking about. So I am beginning to learn more about myself and what makes me angry. Now that I have gotten into this paper I realize that room reflects are not such a bad idea because they do make you think about yourself inside and that is what I need to do to learn how to control myself better.

Use of structured instruments such as the Dysfunctional Attitude Scale (Weissman, 1979), the Cognitive Response Test (CRT) (Watkins & Rush, 1983), or sentence-completion tests also can assist in eliciting basic thoughts and assumptions and can promote work toward elucidation of underlying schemas, particularly with patients who are relatively nonverbal. An example of the use of structured tests for cognitive distortion can be found in the CRT responses of a sixteen-year-old girl who was admitted for running away, drug use, fights with her family, and depression. The CRT uses short vignettes that describe areas of social interaction as stimulus for automatic thoughts. This sixteen-year-old patient gave CRT responses as follows:

> I take two weeks off from work. When I come back, a person in another department says she didn't even know I was gone. My first thought is "I am not very important to her."
>
> I make an error in my work and it is called to my attention. My first thought is "I'm stupid."
>
> When I consider the way my family treats me, I think to myself . . . "I don't have a real family."
>
> When I am asked to do a task I have never done before, I usually think . . . "I am not going to do it right."
>
> I've been trying to get a date for the past three weekends and have not been successful. I think to myself . . . "Nobody likes me."

These responses were examined in individual therapy with her cognitive therapist. She was gradually able to explore alternatives and to identify her characteristic tendency to "be negative" and to "jump to conclusions." This learning was extended by a homework assignment to monitor and test automatic thoughts from a family therapy session that week.

A cognitive technique which we have found to be very useful is making a list of the pros and cons of particular choices. With practice, teenagers quickly learn this approach to solving problems. Many adolescents gain a sense of competence and demonstrate more mature, responsible behavior when they employ this new way of thinking. This method is frequently used in individual, family, and group therapy sessions to focus and improve the adolescent's decision-making abilities.

The therapeutic milieu also can provide the opportunity for examining the evidence and establishing the validity or utility of particular perceptions of events. A number of ward activities, including music, poetry, and popular media, can provide clues about teenagers' perceptions of themselves, the world around them, and the future. Other sources of cognitive material include group therapy, ward meetings, and recreational and exercise classes. A staff trained to listen for cognitive processes can provide invaluable data from their multiple interactions with patients in these activities. There are also numerous opportunities in the milieu for carrying out homework assignments, and for rehearsal of new approaches to interpersonal situations.

A fourteen-year-old boy's attendance at gym classes provides an illustration of the use of the general ward milieu. After his first visit to the gym, he had reported "I'll never go again, I'm no good at that sort of thing, everybody will make fun of me." He was a painfully shy, depressed, and isolated young man. The recreational instructor was able to identify the patient's anxiety and withdrawal and offered to talk with him. The patient reported the above thoughts, after which the instructor reassured him that insecurities about athletic skills were very common and that individualized instruction might help him improve his skills and his attitudes about himself. The instructor also suggested that the automatic thoughts could be discussed with the patient's cognitive therapist. This led to further exploration of the patient's thoughts about his physical abilities and to significant therapeutic work on self-image. Several assignments to try new activities and record thoughts and feelings during these activities continued the cognitive therapy in the milieu.

Psychoeducational Techniques

Our adolescent unit places a strong emphasis on learning, both in ward psychoeducational programs and in a full-time school that is staffed by teachers trained in dealing with emotionally disturbed adolescents. Didactic presentations include programs on communication, assertiveness training, sex education, and drug education. We have found an extremely high frequency of problems in these areas among hospitalized adolescents. These problems often are based on lack of experience or misinformation.

The school program is an integral part of the adolescent milieu. The majority of adolescent psychiatric patients have serious academic problems, including learning disabilities, academic failure, and behavioral problems such as truancy or poor study skills. Many of these teenagers develop negative expectations of their success in other areas based on this experience. The special education school program can provide an opportunity to challenge these assumptions and nurture self-esteem.

The assignment of homework is also an integral part of the treatment program. Hospitalized teenagers have homework assignments from both their school classes and their therapy. At times the assignments are closely intertwined, but usually the school work is seen as a separate activity. Cognitive therapy homework includes such procedures as the DRDT, graded task assignments, cognitive rehearsal, and multiple experiments to test out hypotheses. Attitudes toward homework vary greatly, and often reflect past success or frustration with schoolwork. Ability to complete a task may be impaired for reasons such as learning disabilities or motivation problems secondary to depression. However, assignments that are individualized, are relevant, and have a reasonable likelihood of positive outcome are the most effective.

Pharmacotherapy

Psychotropic medications such as neuroleptics, antidepressants, stimulants, and lithium often are indicated in the treatment of psychiatric disorders in adolescents. Issues related to combined cognitive therapy and pharmacotherapy are reviewed elsewhere in this volume. Special considerations in using pharmacologic agents with teenagers include the impact on developing body image and self-concept and the effect of drug treatment on family attitudes and expectations.

Education about risks, benefits, side effects, and mechanism of action of medications can be extremely helpful to teenagers and their families. Except in extreme circumstances, it is advisable that an adolescent be an equal and voluntary partner in making the decision to use medication. It is important to assess regularly the adolescent's perception of the process of taking medication, as these attitudes fluctuate widely. Noncompliance may be the first indication of a negative reaction. Automatic thoughts such as "this drug will help me feel better" or "if I get better my mother will credit the drug" have obvious treatment implications.

Staff Education

The introduction of a cognitive behavioral model to our adolescent inpatient unit led to varied staff reactions. Some eagerly accepted this new technique and found it to be highly compatible with their attitudes about effective therapy. Others were wary and thought that this approach to therapy might be "dangerous and disruptive." The collaborative emphasis was disturbing to some staff members, who believed that this would encourage a massive rebellion of the patients. A few incorrectly viewed the therapy as being based on intellectualization without affective expression.

Intensive therapist and staff training programs, regular supervision, and open staff discussions were needed to change these perceptions and increase acceptance of the model. Our previous experience in introducing research and other special treatment programs to inpatient units indicated that some ward staff prefer to keep the status quo and that any suggested change is likely to cause considerable anxiety. However, staff misunderstandings, anxiety, and behavioral acting out usually can be avoided or modified by a careful and reasoned educational effort. It is probably unrealistic to expect that all staff members in a complex milieu will ascribe fully to the cognitive model. Personality attributes and training background have a large effect on what treatment techniques are found useful. However, it is essential that the entire staff have an understanding of the basic principles of the cognitive behavioral approach and agree to work together with the individual, group, and family cognitive therapists to provide an integrated and cohesive treatment program.

Summary

A cognitive-behavioral approach for inpatient treatment of adolescents has been described. In our opinion this model has several advantageous characteristics that facilitate therapy with this difficult group of patients. The collaborative-empirical working relationship helps to reduce oppositional behavior and destructive acting out and to promote learning. The treatment setting can address the need for the hospitalized teenager to identify and change distorted and immature cognitions and resultant behaviors. At the same time, normal adolescent cognitive development can be facilitated through psychotherapeutic encounters and other multiple learning experiences in the milieu, peer group, family, and school. An expanded sense of self-efficacy is supported by success in these activities.

We have found that standard cognitive therapy techniques developed for outpatient therapy can be used successfully in hospitalized patients. However, other procedures such as room reflect, a behaviorally oriented activity schedule, psychoeducational programs, and use of the milieu as a therapeutic agent also can add to the therapeutic experience. An intensive treatment program utilizing cognitive theory and techniques can offer a powerful mechanism for change. No controlled research has been completed on comparative treatment outcome in adolescent inpatient units that use a cognitive-behavioral model. We are impressed with the utility of this approach and believe that it deserves further development as a treatment for the seriously disturbed teenager.

References

Anthony, E. J. (1982). Normal adolescent development from a cognitive viewpoint. *Journal of the American Academy of Child Psychiatry, 21*, 318–327.
Bandura, A. (1977). Self-efficacy: Toward a unifying theory of behavioral change. *Psychological Review, 84*, 191–215.

Beck, A. T., Rush, A. J., Shaw, B. F., & Emery, G. (1979). *Cognitive therapy of depression.* New York: Guilford Press.

Elkind, D. (1967). Egocentrism in adolescence. *Child Development, 38,* 1025–1034.

Gittelson, M. (1948). Character synthesis: The psychotherapeutic problem of adolescence. *American Journal of Orthopsychiatry, 18,* 422–431.

Guidano, V. F., & Liotti, G. (1983). *Cognitive processes and emotional disorders.* New York: Guilford Press.

Kahn, D. G., & Boyer, D. N. (1980). Inpatient hospital treatment of adolescents. *Psychiatric Clinics of North America, 3,* 513–545.

Meeks, J. E. (1980). *The fragile alliance.* Malabar, Florida: Robert E. Kreiger Publishing.

Offer, D., Ostrov, E., & Howard, K. I. (1981). *The adolescent: A psychological self-portrait.* New York: Basic Books.

Petersen, A. C., & Offer, D. (1979). Adolescent development: Sixteen to nineteen years. In *Basic handbook of child psychiatry,* J. D. Noshpitz (Ed.), (pp. 213–233). New York: Basic Books.

Watkins, J. T., & Rush, A. J. (1983). Cognitive response test. *Cognitive Therapy and Research, 7,* 425–435.

Weissman, A. N. (1979). The dysfunctional attitude scale: A validation study. *Dissertation Abstracts International, 40,* 1389–1390b.

Wright, J. H., & Beck, A. T. (1983). Cognitive therapy of depression: Theory and practice. *Hospital and Community Psychiatry, 34,* 1119–1127.

Chapter 5

PROBLEM-SOLVING TRAINING

A Cognitive Group Therapy Modality

Erich Coché

The ability to solve interpersonal problems is closely related to effective daily living. In fact, some authors (e.g., Zigler & Phillips, 1961) have regarded this ability as a major criterion for mental health. Spivack and associates (1976) were able repeatedly to document the close link between interpersonal problem-solving skills and emotional health.

In response to the research done by Spivack and his group, the research division at Friends Hospital in Philadelphia began in 1973 to develop a training strategy designed to increase the problem-solving skills of psychiatric patients: the Problem-Solving Training (PST).[1] In the ensuing research projects a large number of patients with varying diagnoses took part in the training, which is usually conducted in groups and takes the participants through a series of six steps that will be described in detail in this chapter.

Some of the roots of PST can be traced back to the brainstorming approaches of the 1930s (Osborn, 1963). In fact, industrial psychologists and managers have long been concerned with methods of problem solving and their refinement. However, most of the problems they focus on are impersonal, and as we now know from the studies by Spivack and Shure (1974), impersonal and interpersonal problem-solving skills are somewhat different and only moderately correlated.

---

[1]The research that led to the development and evaluation of the PST procedure was supported by a grant from the Wyomissing Foundation; this contribution is gratefully acknowledged here.

Of course, the concomitant development of cognitive-behavioral therapy (CBT) also shaped the progress of PST research. Closer attention was paid to patients' cognitions, their internal evaluative statements, their openness to alternatives, the realism or irrationality of their self-statements. Aside from attention to cognitions, the firm belief in the intimate connection between cognition and emotion and the alterability of one through the other was shared by PST and CBT advocates alike. Thus, PST became a cognitive-therapeutic approach among others.

Though our PST approach as developed at Friends Hospital was started without knowledge of the trailblazing paper by D'Zurilla and Goldfried (1971), many of the ideas presented in it are put into practice in the PST method. Likewise, the program described by Siegel and Spivack (1976) is very similar in principle, though there are some major differences in their design of the individual problem-solving steps.

Spivack et al. (1976) and Mahoney & Arnkoff (1978) present reviews of the various problem-solving therapy approaches tried so far. A more extensive review is given by Kämmerer (1983). Because of the availability of these reviews this chapter will focus on the actual conduct of PST, some of the possible pitfalls, and some methods to enhance its usefulness in the psychiatric inpatient setting.

THE BASIC PROCEDURE

Screening of Prospective Members

The group usually is composed of 4 to 10 participants. In the course of our studies PST groups have been conducted with patients having a wide variety of psychiatric disorders. There are some data (Coché & Flick, 1975; Coché, Cooper, & Petermann, 1984) indicating that some types of patients have a better chance of benefiting from the experience than others. Therefore, we recommend the following restrictions in screening.

First, there ought to be a reasonable degree of intellectual capability. The criterion used was whether or not the patient was capable of participating in the pretesting necessary for the research groups. Anyone who did not understand the instructions for the tests used here (e.g., the Minimult) was considered inappropriate for the group. This criterion has served us well; it kept people out of the groups who would have been disruptive because of their limitations in intellectual abilities.

Second, there are some demands in respect to the participants' mnestic abilities. Patients with serious memory disturbances do not profit from PST. For this reason we routinely excluded patients who were scheduled for electroconvulsive treatment and patients with serious brain pathology. A moderate degree of memory loss, as is common in geriatric patients has not been found to be a hindrance as long as it is dealt with appropriately (Wondolowski, 1978).

Third, in the interest of a cooperatively working group it is advisable to keep out those patients who would by their disruptive or otherwise antisocial behaviors undermine the group's progress. Naturally, we have had our share of those patients whom most therapists would rather not have in their groups because they are difficult; but these usually did profit from the experience, and the efforts necessary on the part of the group leader were worth it. However, there were a few who were simply not appropriate. Usually, they exhibited their undesirable behaviors already during pretesting, which therefore kept these patients out. Only very few did indeed come to the group and seriously disrupt things. How we dealt with that will be discussed later in this chapter.

Finally, participation always should be voluntary. Therapeutic efforts that are forced on a patient are rarely successful and often unethical as well. Prospective group members should therefore be informed of the purposes and techniques of the training, and their consent should be obtained before the start.

All of this points out the value of a pretraining screening. As long as we conducted our groups within a research framework, we needed to see the participants for their pretesting and obtain their consent to participate. Yet even when not conducting research, we either gave some screening tests like the Minimult or conducted an interview to ensure that new members met the above criteria and to obtain their informed consent. During this interview we usually tell the participants that the group will meet for eight sessions, and we explain in general terms what the group does. If prospective members are afraid of "group therapy" because they expect hard confrontations, as they may have seen on television, they are reassured that these groups are different and their cognitive emphasis is pointed out. We also usually tell the prospective participants that these groups have been shown to be successful with many types of clients. If the group is conducted for research purposes, members are apprised of that fact.

Opening the First Session

We usually begin by stating that the purpose of the group is to help people get some more experience in interpersonal problem solving; for that reason we would like the members of the group to bring up problems for discussion, and the group will then try to come up with as many possible solutions as can be found. We emphasize that all solutions are welcome and that only when no one can think of any new ones will their usefulness be discussed. We also explain that we will keep a log of all the problems and solutions and will read from the log when needed to refresh people's memories. (We have on occasion used a blackboard, which was found to be slightly disruptive and uncomfortable to some leaders and patients but definitely necessary in some, especially the geriatric groups.) The log is of course necessary in order to keep track of all the solutions suggested in step 3. It is kept by the leader or co-leader and is considered group property. (More about the log is presented later in this chapter.) After this relatively brief introduction we are ready to begin the program by asking for the first problem to be worked on.

Duration of the Group

Originally we planned to run our groups for 4 weeks with about two or three sessions per week. Because of the fast turnover at Friends Hospital, with a median length of stay in 1976 of around 25 days, we needed to operate more quickly. We therefore ran 2-week groups with four sessions in each week. This format has worked well for us. Extending the number of sessions has not been feasible; the repetitive structure can make the process boring if it is extended for too long. A shorter series of sessions was tried by Zelazowski (1976) and was found to be less effective. Kunz (1976) also found that hospitalized patients who participated in less than seven sessions did not derive the desired benefits from the program.

Sixty to ninety minutes has been found to be the optimal length for a training group session. Groups lasting less than an hour have been found to be less successful in teaching the skills we try to attain.

Step 1: Bringing up a Problem

The group experience itself begins with a request by the leader for any member to present a problem, either personal or practical. Usually, the first few sessions are concerned with general problems involving situations on the halls, with aides or doctors, or with hospital activities, such as: "They play the radio too loud on my unit; what can be done about it?" Over time the group members become more relaxed and willing to present more personal or emotional problems to the group for consideration. In other groups, one person sets the tone by starting out with a highly personal problem such as: "Recently I've lost interest in having sex with my wife; what can I do?" This can then either inspire the group to continue at that level or it can make the patients uneasy and have the effect that people shy away from personal issues for a while.

The group leader does not ask a particular group member for a problem or a solution, but other group members at times exert some group pressure to encourage a silent co-member to present a problem.

There is one situation in which the leader is the one to bring up a problem: if the group has a problem in its own dynamics that keeps it from working effectively, the leader can raise this as an issue to be worked on. Difficult group situations, such as a monopolizing member, a "yes-but" player, or complaints of some members that they are bored or that the group is too quiet can then be dealt with in an open yet nonjudgmental way.

Step 2: Clarifying the Problem and Information Gathering

Frequently, patients are unable to pose a problem in a clear, concise manner, which can cause much confusion among the other members. This is the time when the most is required of the leader's interpersonal skill. By encouraging the patient to restate the problem and by asking specific questions, one tries to clear up any existing confusion as to the problem on the floor. Restating the problem and encouraging the group to seek more information are necessary parts of this step.

Asking the person who presented the problem for more information is very important. It teaches information seeking as a basic part of problem-solving skills and it prevents people from rushing in with suggestions that might sound silly, like telling a widowed patient to "talk it over with your husband."

The danger in this step lies in the fact that many patients try to use this part of the process as an opportunity to tell their life stories. Some get so involved that they only want to use the group as a sounding board for their complaints but not as a forum to work on effective solutions. Here the leader has to stop lengthy stories and help the group to return to the problem, either by rephrasing it or by restating the purpose of the group.

Of course, it can be argued that an outpouring of complaints to an attentive group is cathartic and thus helpful to the patient. That is certainly a logical possibility, but in our experience the opposite has more often been true: patients who tell their life stories at great length take the group's polite silence as a confirmation of their preshaped opinions and come away with no fresh solution and no behavior change respective to the problem they brought up.

Step 3: Presenting Solutions

The reduced capacity of the patients to solve interpersonal problems effectively is often due to a failure to search for alternative solutions to a problem. Many patients tend to respond to problems with a pet solution that they use over and over without much regard to its applicability and without the realization that alternatives exist. The search for alternatives is therefore a central aspect of the PST program.

After the problem has been presented and clarified, the leader asks for possible solutions from the group. The major rules for this phase—which is explained to all members right from the start—is that all criticism to the alternatives discussed has to be postponed until the group has moved on to step 4. As solutions are verbalized, a log is kept by one of the leaders, recording all problems and solutions presented during the session (including which member offered the problem or solution). The log serves as a reference to remind the group which solutions already have been suggested and to aid the members in further exploration of other possible alternative means. The log also serves as a reinforcer: having the solution written down underscores its acceptance and appreciation. Members can at any time ask the logkeeper to reread all the suggestions made so far.

During this brainstorming phase of PST frequent social reinforcement is given for presenting as many solutions as possible. The leader is not concerned with the content of the solutions—no value judgments or criticisms as to the appropriateness of the suggestions are made—but the mere giving of alternatives is rewarded by thanks, smiles, and entering the solution into the log.

Belschner (1976) stresses the importance of reinforcement for giving solutions during this phase. Going back to Osborn's (1963) work, he proposes to make use of the questions and "manipulative verbs" developed by Osborn. Although these techniques can indeed be very helpful in generating new solutions, we concluded that the mental flexibility and high level of abstraction needed for their application was not present in many of our patients. We thus decided merely to instruct the group to produce suggestions as best as it can without giving further help.

The leader makes no suggestions. This may at times be difficult, when it appears that the group is overlooking the most obvious solutions. We have found, however, that this kind of restraint is necessary lest the group develops a dependency on the leader, which could become a serious handicap as the sessions continue. Often a group finds the solution that was on the leader's mind by itself given enough time and support. Similarly, some group members come close to an idea and put it out tentatively but will develop it only if given enough encouragement. Not infrequently, a patient will make a statement or ask a question that bears in it the seeds of a solution, which, however, is not stated as such. It is up to the leader to help the patient to see the potential for a solution in that contribution. At times this requires quite some skill on the part of the leader who wants to help the patient; more often nothing else is needed but a simple question like: "Do you see a possible solution in what you just said?"

While solutions are being presented, the leader may on occasion restate the problem in order to maintain clarity in the discussion and keep the solutions from wandering away from the problem at hand. Referring the patients back to the present problem also avoids having the group present solutions that are not relevant to the specific problem it is working on.

During this phase some brief returns to step 2 may at times be necessary: In order to develop a particular solution more information may be needed than is available. Simple factual questions are usually sufficient to obtain the necessary data; some patients will, however, again misuse these brief returns to step 2 to tell the group lengthy stories and thus keep it from searching for more solutions. The leader may have to intervene here and gently bring the group back to its task.

The group continues to provide alternative solutions until it is apparent that the members have exhausted their resources for that particular problem. This determination usually is made by the leader; at times the group members will voice a desire to go on to the next step.

Step 4: Discussion of Feasibility

The transition from step 3 to step 4 is a crucial point. To keep the brainstorming phase free of criticism, it is necessary to make a definite announcement that the group has now reached the fourth stage and is therefore allowed to examine the suggestions that have been made and entered into the log. Before we do this we usually end step 3 by commenting favorably on the large number of ideas that were generated, if this was indeed the case. We then announce that it is time to now take a look at all these ideas and see which ones are likely to work. For this we usually reread the problem and the solutions from the log. The group is then asked to give opinions on which solution they believe is most likely to succeed. If no one begins the discussion spontaneously, the person who brought up the problem initially can be singled out to give the first opinion.

To give the discussion a focus and to prevent some patients from getting into a "yes-but" frame of mind, we encourage the group to stick to two major issues during this phase: Which idea is most likely to be successful and what is the cost likely to be if I use one solution rather than another? Cost is discussed in terms of money, hard work, pain, disturbed relationships, and similar concepts.

During a discussion of the likelihood of success it is at times necessary to remind people, especially those who are trying too hard to foist their pet solutions onto others, that what is likely to work for one person may not work for others. This also makes it much easier for the participants to live with the fact that their favorite suggestion may have been rejected by others. This way, they will not get discouraged from continuing their efforts to find creative solutions for future problems raised in the group.

There are some occasions in which a patient decides that a certain solution is worth being tried out. However, in actually implementing it, there again may be a number of options. If this is the case, the leader can suggest that the implementation itself be raised as the next problem for the group to work on. This idea has been described by other authors in the field (e.g., Wickelgren, 1974) who in fact suggest separate steps of (a) generating broad strategies, (b) choosing among these, and (c) generating ideas of implementation. A split-off like that appeared to us too complex to teach to our patients, especially since it happens only rarely; instead we prefer merely to raise the general strategy from one solution to the level of a new problem, which is then worked on in the usual manner. When it does happen, it presents an opportunity to teach the clients that we cannot always resolve a problem by running through our procedure just once but that two or even more rounds may be necessary.

It also frequently happens that new solutions arise during the discussion phase. When this occurs, the new suggestion is acknowledged and entered into the log. It is then discussed as to its feasibility just as the others were, but the leader still makes efforts to keep solutions and criticism apart as separate steps.

Step 5: Role-Playing

This phase has been added to the PST program to help patients transfer what they have learned cognitively to the real-life problem situations they have to deal with. The leader usually makes the judgment as to whether a particular problem and maybe one or two of the proposed solutions lend themselves to role playing in the group. The play is usually set up by asking for volunteers. The leaders can "get into the act" too. If one of them, for instance, plays the role of the patient with the problem, it provides an opportunity of teaching through modeling. At times we let the group member play the role of the "opponent" with whom something has to be worked out. This can be a real eye-opener: it can give the patient some idea of how the other one feels and can thus provide additional strategies in dealing with the other person.

Most of the time we let the participants play themselves in enacting a suggested solution. This often allows them to practice a behavior never used before and gives them a feeling of mastery before the real-life situation occurs.

There is likely to be some resistance to the role-playing idea when it is first brought up. This can be much reduced by explaining to the group what the advantages are, by a willingness of the leader to participate too, and by starting out with an easy-to-play situation. After the first hurdle is taken, group members usually like the technique and go along with it enthusiastically. It gives them a chance actually to see their solution ideas at work, which acts as a further reinforcer.

Of course, this step is optional. Many problems and solutions do not lend themselves to role-playing, and using this technique when it is not called for can act as a deterrent to further attempts at role-playing.

Step 6: Reporting Back to the Group

Many problems raised by the members deal directly with issues that have arisen within the immediate environment (e.g., hospital or family). In these cases we encourage the members to report back to the group in one of the following sessions on how the solution worked out. Often we start a new session (except the first one, of course) by asking around if anyone used any suggested alternatives from a previous session. This procedure again reinforces the real-life quality of the work done in the group. It also rewards the giving of solutions and thus stimulates the group to do more of that. Finally, it teaches the group members that checking out the actual workings of a solution is an important step in problem solving.

At times a group member will report that a solution that was tried did not succeed. We usually accept this as a challenge to the group to deal with the problem again and come up with a new set of alternatives.

The Log

For the log we use simple lined paper with or without a clipboard. First we enter the date and ordinal number of the session. Then we enter the problem the way it was stated after the group had gained clarity of what the problem was. We also note who brought up the problem. After that we write down all the solutions produced. Even if a suggested alternative is merely a variation of a prior one, it deserves to be entered. Here too we note the name of the person who brought up the suggestion.

The log is the property of the group. There is nothing secret or holy about it. Any group member who wishes to see it can do so. At times we have given copies of all of the proposed ideas to the person who wanted help with a problem. This then aided the member in studying them some more and in choosing among them.

The Wall Display

To help people to remember the procedure and which step they are on we have at times made use of a simple poster on the wall which reads as follows:

Steps in Problem Solving

1. Bringing up a problem.
2. Clarifying the problem, gathering information.
3. Bringing up solutions.
   Remember: No criticism.
4. Weighing the solutions.
   How likely is it to work?
   What are the costs involved?

This poster has been especially valuable in working with elderly patients. It also makes it easier to tell the group if it is skipping a phase.

Example

The following is an example of a problem presented in one of our PST group sessions:

The problem was presented by a middle-aged, hospitalized, depressed female patient who was unhappy about her medication. She described some of the effects it had on her and expressed a strong dislike for being "forced" to take the medication. The leader then asked the patient to pose the problem to the group for their suggestions, thereby encouraging her to clarify the problem and to help the group focus their attention on the next step of presenting the patient with some alternatives. The problem, after clarification, was stated and entered into the log as: "What can you do when your medication is bothering you and you dislike taking it?" The leader then asked the group to think of solutions, and several were verbalized and entered into the log in this way:

a. You can refuse to take your medication.
b. Talk to your doctor about your feelings.
c. Have patience and realize that it takes a little while to get used to drugs.
d. You can pray to God that the nurse may forget to give it to you.
e. Ask the doctor if there is another drug you can take that may have fewer side effects. (This is a variant of b.)

All of these ideas were entered into the log together with the name of the person who suggested them. When the group felt it had exhausted its supply of solutions, the leader began the discussion of the feasibility or practicality of each solution. This group decided to combine two solutions; they felt both talking to your doctor about your feelings and fears and asking for a different medication would be the most desirable solution.

In the next step several patients volunteered to enact the problem and the preferred solution. The patient who posed the problem assumed the role of herself; another one played the physician.

The final step occurred a few days later when the patient reported back to the group about the success of the technique she used.

COPING WITH SPECIAL SITUATIONS

The Role of the Leader

The group leader's main function is to maintain the structure of the group by intermittently reminding the group of its goal to learn to solve problems and to guide the group through the various necessary steps.

The leader at times has to interrupt an ongoing process in order to prevent the group from skipping a step. It is important that this be done with a great deal of tact in order not to discourage people from participation.

We have had a variety of leaders for our groups in the last few years. Many of them were young college graduates or graduate students working with us as research assistants. They worked either alone or in two-person teams. Usually they felt more comfortable in the latter situation, which also allowed them to split up the dual function of conducting the group and keeping the log.

To be an effective leader one has to have the usual therapist qualities, e.g., those described by Traux and Carkhuff (1967). We watch out for these in selecting our prospective leaders. Beyond that, we also train them, usually by having them read some of the literature in cognitive behavior modification and by having them work as co-leaders in a group with an experienced leader.

Like most other therapeutic endeavors, PST challenges the patient to change some of his/her behaviors. Yet change is never easy. Even though a patient might be unhappy and might know that a certain behavior is counterproductive, the idea of changing it is likely to be threatening. Thus, resistance is bound to occur in any one of a multitude of ways. It is in dealing with such resistances and similar events that the therapeutic skills of the leader become most essential.

The basic procedure of PST is relatively easily learned and gives novice therapists a handy structure to impose on their groups to everyone's benefit. Yet the simplicity is deceptive: Things do go wrong, resistance appears, and the effectiveness of the whole group is in jeopardy if these events are handled poorly.

To illustrate the point, one of our co-workers (Zelazowski, 1976) conducted an experiment in which he taught the PST procedure to a number of patients who then, under his supervision, conducted PST groups for other patients. The results were mixed: As long as things were going smoothly, the patient-trainers did a fine job; they felt that they were improving their own problem-solving skills, and the researcher could just watch the action. However, nearly every time resistance arose and things become difficult, attendance dropped, and patients complained, the patient trainers began to feel worried and overwhelmed and the researcher-supervisor had to intervene a great deal. Real therapeutic skills were needed to lead the group out of the crisis.

Within-Group Issues

The PST technique has a favorite solution to its own problems built right into it. When a difficulty arises in the group, the trainer has the privilege of raising it as a problem to be discussed and to be worked on. It is our practice to give here-and-now group problems preference over problems dealing with issues outside the group. This basic strategy allows for an effective handling of most problems that arise within a group. The group is encouraged to own the problem and to work toward its solution by inventing alternative means and by evaluating their pros and cons. In so doing, the group becomes less dependent on the leader. Even though this may arouse some anxiety at first, the payoff is a sense of accomplishment and optimism, a belief that difficulties can be overcome when handled in the right spirit. In addition, the members of a group who successfully face and resolve their own intragroup problems are more likely to be willing to face their own personal problems with a positive attitude.

In one of our PST groups, George, a forty-two-year-old drug-dependent salesman, was frequently heard making disparaging remarks about women in general and about the female group participants in particular. One day he was late for the session, and while waiting for the group to begin, several of the women complained about his sexist attitudes and insults. The leader was uncomfortable with the discussion and suggested that rather than talk about an absent member the group might choose to work on this as a problem worth solving. Much to his surprise the group welcomed the idea and started working on it as soon as George arrived. Because it was presented in a tactful way, George was able to hear the issue, participate in the discussion on clarification, and even contribute two of the six solutions to the problem of how he could stop antagonizing women with his remarks. Although it may have altered George's basic stance toward women only slightly, it helped him to become more aware of his effect on them and of alternate ways of behaving.

In institutional groups (e.g., schools, hospitals, camps, etc.) it is also wise, when one has a choice, to give preference to in-house problems over external or noninstitutional problems. The greater immediacy provides additional sources of reinforcement: If a participant can come back a few days later and tell the group about solutions that were tried out, it is usually an event that encourages the group, especially those members who suggested the means that ultimately were chosen, even if they may not have succeeded completely. Furthermore, working out problems patients have in their immediate environment may make them more receptive to other therapeutic programs offered by the institution.

When to Delve and When Not

One issue that always requires judgment on the part of the trainer is the question of how long to dwell on one particular step of the procedure, especially step 2. Many patients come into the groups with the expectation that this is a therapy group in which one "pours one's heart out" and discusses the ramifications and antecedents of a problem at great length. In PST such lengthy discussions usually represent not merely a misunderstanding but a resistance to the technique itself, which is, after all, not focused on past experiences and free associations.

Most of these diversions occur at step 2, when the group indeed has to gather some information in order to deal appropriately with the problem. Many fine solutions will have to be discarded if the group does not get sufficient information about the circumstances of the problem at hand. Yet if too much time is spent on information giving, the group becomes bored with the problem before it even reaches step 3. A good yardstick for the leader to use is to ask oneself whether the verbalizations produced by the patient are necessary in order to generate adequate solutions. If not, it may be wise either to ask the participant what this has to do with solving the dilemma or encourage the group to move on to step 3 and bring forth some alternatives. An alternative approach is to ask the group as a whole if the information is sufficient to solve the problem.

Another favorite spot for excursions from the PST procedure is step 4. The patient who raised the problem is encouraged to state reasons for liking or disliking a particular solution, but long monologues must be discouraged. Most of the time it suffices to state one's feelings briefly about each one of the solutions brought up, what one believes its likelihood for success is, and what price one has to pay to obtain the desired goal.

The leader thus has to be watchful, especially with a group that likes to avoid working by merely talking a lot. There is some latitude between two extremes: On the one end is the habit of letting the group go off on tangents and talk for as long as it wants to. This avenue may be very enjoyable, and because of the warm friendly spirit that goes with it, it also may have therapeutic effects, but it misses the task of PST. On the other side is the stubborn insistance on crisp and brief verbalizations in which little time is spent on each individual step and a considerable number of problems get dealt with in each session. Though trainers will develop their own styles, which are likely to lean to one side or the other, each of the extremes mentioned here is to be avoided. In one, the group becomes too unstructured, misses the task or gets bored; in the other, some important elements of the technique are short-shrifted, and some creative solutions, which are most likely to arise if the atmosphere is relaxed, may never come up at all.

"Yes, But"

Eric Berne (1964) described a game that he calls "why don't you—yes, but," in which one person makes suggestions and the other counters each one with an apparent agreement at first and then with reasons why it would not work. The latter person, the yes-but player, is potentially the most frustrating person a PST leader can find in a group. People who are really good at this game also can be very discouraging to the others in the group. Therefore, the yes-but player deserves particular attention.

Spivack et al. (1976) mention how people have specific deficiencies in their interpersonal cognitive problem-solving (ICPS) skills that can be corrected by PST. The specific deficit of the yes-but player is a tendency to reject solutions before their potential usefulness has been fully examined. There may be a payoff in the rejecting activity that may be more interpersonal than cognitive in nature, consisting mostly in a feeling of superiority as described by Berne (1964), but the fact remains that a person who frequently uses yes-but may indeed have a serious disturbance in problem-solving abilities. This person may get repeatedly into difficult situations with no alternatives for getting out because all solutions have been rejected without a thorough studying of their feasibility.

The general approach of the leader to the yes-but–playing member is one of "benign neglect." In behavioral terms, the game constitutes a behavior the leader would like to extinguish. Not paying much attention to it often achieves the desired effect. Furthermore, a strict adherence to the PST procedure means going ahead with the plan undaunted by the yes-but behavior. If it occurs during step 3, the patient is courteously—if necessary, repeatedly—requested to withhold all criticism until step 4. Meanwhile all the solutions suggested by the membership are faithfully written down. This provides reinforcement for those who suggest alternatives. Such encouragement is important because the yes-but player can have a serious discouraging effect on the rest of the group, who could easily feel that their efforts are futile since no idea they bring up meets with acceptance.

If the yes-but activity occurs during the step 4, it constitutes a slightly different problem. This, after all, is the appropriate time to address the likelihood of success for the given solutions. The member who raised the problem, and then finds some reason that each suggested alternative would not succeed, is—on the surface at least—doing the right thing. Unfortunately, this person also comes across as discouraging or annoying or both.

Very often the other group members themselves will counteract such activities; frequently they will point out that a particular solution worked for them. If they do not do this, the leader might do well to stress to the whole group that any given solution may work well for some people but not for others; in other words, even though this one may not be successful for Mr. X, that should not stop us from paying attention to it because it may be just right for other people in the group. The leader could even ask if there is anyone in the group who had a personal experience with this or a similar technique of dealing with the problem at hand.

The Monopolizer

A very common type of member is the one who deals with social anxiety by talking incessantly. In the PST group such a person may come across as overbearing, having all kinds of suggestions for everybody without allowing time or consideration for other people to bring up theirs. The group is likely to get quite irritated with this person, sometimes to the point where a few members are ready to leave the group on account of the talkative one. Frequently, they are too intimidated by this member to speak up directly, but they will let the leader know, usually after or between sessions.

Over the years we have developed a number of strategies to deal with the issue of a monopolizing member. In some of these we look on this as a group problem and let the group work on it; in others we prefer to think of it as something the leader can more effectively handle directly.

The main strategy is, of course, to make it a group issue and bring it up as a problem to be worked on. That is particularly appropriate where several members have already complained about this person. Again, the trainer has decided that the group owns the problem and therefore should be working on it. This is likely to work quite well as long as the group is not too intimidated by the monopolizer and as long as this patient is willing to listen to what the group has to say without becoming too defensive. Some intervention from the leader to prevent scapegoating may be necessary at this point.

An alternative strategy is to have a frank discussion between the trainer and the monopolizing member between sessions. Often such a talk about this member's behavior can be quite successful in reducing its frequency without causing too much anxiety. One of the main problems of letting the group handle the problem is that the monopolizer may feel insulted by the group's intervention and may decide to sulk, i.e., shut up completely but in a very theatrical manner, thus continuing to keep the group from working effectively.

Another technique that can be used in conjunction with talking to the patient between sessions is one in which the leader sits next to the index member and explains that whenever he talks too much, the trainer will gently place one hand on his/her arm as a sign that it is time to slow down. This has to be done after an initial explanation and with some caution because it could potentially reinforce the undesired behavior if the patient in question has a strong need for physical touch. When talking to the patient either between sessions or during a general discussion of this behavior, it is advisable also to point out the positive aspects of the high verbal activity level. Because of it the patient often gets the group going, provides a multitude of ideas for solving problems in a constructive way, and examines the solutions raised. The member is also showing an interest in the group and often a good deal of concern for other people by trying to help them as best as possible. Pointing out these positive aspects of monopolizing behavior not only makes negative feedback more acceptable but also sets the record straight and shows that there are many sides to one and the same behavior.

In extreme cases where despite all efforts the monopolizing activity cannot be stopped, especially if it is nonconstructive and tangential talk rather than suggesting alternatives, it may be necessary to discharge this member from the group. This is something that should be used only as a last-resort device and only after all other techniques have been exhausted. In our experience this has never been necessary with someone who was merely monopolizing a group. We had to do it in only two cases when working with psychiatric patients, where these persons were not only monopolizing but also floridly psychotic in their verbalizations.

Problems with Staff in Institutional Settings

In psychiatric and similar institutions many of the problems brought up by patients center around staff members or other patients who are not present in the group—a nurse on the hall, an occupational therapist, or a particular physician. In these situations it is most important to handle the problem with tact lest the group meeting deteriorate into a gripe session. At times the patient brings up the problem in a vague manner that requires some work on the part of the leader to help the patient to redefine the issue in such a way that it becomes a workable problem. If the patient comes with a vague or paranoid complaint like "Dr. Smith hates me because he hates Italians," it is necessary to help the patient "own" the problem. If it appears that the patient wants only to gripe and not seriously work on the problem, it may be advisable merely to tell the patient to work on this with the doctor in question and not take up group time with it.

In most cases it is possible to redefine a problem in such a way that the patient does indeed accept and own it and then works on it in the usual manner. The following is an example from one of our PST groups: A woman patient complained that whenever she talked with her physician he appeared to be extremely distractable. He would have his sessions with her out in the hallway where other people would walk by whom he would greet in his usual, friendly manner while at the same time attempting to maintain a discussion with her. On other occasions he would stare out the window and have his eyes fixed on a lively group of squirrels in front of the window. The patient felt this distractability to be an insult to her and that it raised many doubts whether this physician was listening to her at all. Because the patient saw her own personal involvement in this problem, especially where her self-esteem and her doubts about being listened to came into play, we decided that this was an appropriate issue to work on for the whole group. The group very quickly came up with about six solutions, many of which were a variant on the main idea of bringing this up as a problem directly with the physician in question. In step 4 the patient agreed that talking directly to her physician would probably be most effective. However, she had some hesitation about it because she felt intimidated by him. With some encouragement from the leaders she was able to role-play this situation. One group member played the role of the distractable physician; the patient played herself. After three attempts she had indeed developed an effective way of talking to the physician. In a subsequent session she came back to the group with her report that she had indeed used this solution and she felt that the problem had been solved satisfactorily.

Sometimes patients bring up a problem not in order to work on a solution but rather to induce the group leader/therapist to take some kind of action, to fix something in the patient's environment. Usually the member wants immediate action and wants to retain a rather passive role in this. It is important for the leader to stress at these points that that is not the purpose of the group. The group has been formed to teach participants how to solve problems themselves, and therefore letting the leader work out a member's problem is not helpful for that member nor for anyone else in the group.

Boredom

It happens on occasion that group members, particularly after six to eight sessions of PST, will tell the leader that they are bored. At times the leader may find out from a member who has been absent that boredom was the reason for the absence. In these cases, it is again most appropriate to raise this as a group problem. This is most important because it conveys the message that the leader is not there to entertain the patients and that the group has to take responsibility for its own process. Furthermore, when the group discusses the problem of boredom, it gives a great deal of very helpful feedback to the leader. It usually turns out that the group has been spending too much time on one particular step in the process. If too much time is spent on information gathering as part of step 2 or on discussing the feasibility of the solutions in step 4, the group handles fewer and fewer problems per session and is likely to get bored. It also has been found that groups who use an appropriate amount of role playing have fewer problems with boredom. Role playing livens up the sessions and can at times get members involved who have so far been "sitting on the sidelines."

At times the leader might sense boredom although no one in the group has complained of it. In such situations it may be a good idea to discuss it with the co-leader, if there is one, or with a supervisor. On occasion it may turn out to be a projection of one's own boredom. In such cases the group leader may have been doing problem solving for too long; solutions might be to provide some variety in the trainer's own professional life or merely to have him go on a vacation.

Dropouts

In any form of group psychotherapy or training there are occasions on which certain members will not appear for the group. There are a number of ways of dealing with that; one would be to disregard it and continue the group as usual. Another would be to treat this as a group problem and allow the group to work on it. This is particularly advisable where the dropout or absenteeism rate is rather high. It also appears to be good practice to have a talk with the absent member between sessions if possible. Particularly in an institutional setting it is easy to walk over to the patient's residence hall and have a talk there. In this talk the leader obtains good feedback about the group and about things or people that displease the absent member. Very often he is annoyed with a certain atmosphere or with particular people in the group. In many cases it suffices to encourage this member to bring up the problem as a group problem. Having received this type of permission from the group leader often gives the member enough encouragement to actually tackle the problem in the group.

Psychotic Problems and Solutions

Every once in a while a patient will raise a problem that is definitely psychotic in nature. Its content may be bizarre or it is phrased in a manner that renders it unintelligible. In some cases the patient—with some help from others—can rephrase the problem in such a way that the group can understand it. In other cases the leader may need to assist the patient in rephrasing the problem in such a way that it becomes a worthwhile problem to work on. Some attempt at doing this is desirable in any case. At times the group as a whole may be able to help in the rephrasing of the problem. Only on some rare occasion would it be impossible to find a meaningful problem in the patient's utterings, in which case it may be necessary to tell the patient that the group really cannot find a problem that it can work on in his verbalizations. Sometimes the patient may be able to suggest a different problem, but on some occasions the group may have to go to something else. A great deal of consideration for the patient is necessary at that point in order not to discourage the patient from ever bringing up problems again.

Bizarre solutions present less of a problem to the leader than bizarre problems. All solutions are welcome, and therefore even the most bizarre solutions are faithfully written down in the log. They are then discussed in stage 4, at which time the patient usually learns that bizarre solutions are not likely to be successful.

Some attention needs to be paid to the learning that occurs in this process. If the psychotic solution is accepted as a matter of course and discussed appropriately, it is usually not rewarded to the point where the patient would henceforth come up with more psychotic solutions. In most cases the patient learns that this type of solution is not likely to be successful and will therefore come up with fewer solutions of this kind. There are some cases, however, in which participants feel amply rewarded for bringing up absurd suggestions by the friendly, supportive atmosphere in the group. In these cases a strategy of neglect on the part of the leader may be more likely to extinguish this type of behavior. If there is some indication that a patient is "putting on" his craziness in order to get a rise out of the leader or in order to undermine the process, it may be necessary to raise this as a group problem and allow the group to work on it. To be creative and come up with really novel solutions, a certan amount of zaniness is in fact desirable. Therefore, it is wise to hold back with a judgment that a soltuion is "bizarre." At times some apparently crazy ideas have the nucleus for an excellent solution in them.

Illegal or Delinquent Solutions

A variant of the bizarre solution is the criminal solution. Patients may very well suggest ideas to handle the problem that are definitely against the law. These suggestions are no cause for alarm. Step 4 usually takes care of them. If the group pays attention to the price involved in the carrying out of a suggestion, it will quickly find that the price for this type of solution is likely to be imprisonment, which is usually a rather high price to pay for something a person wants. Our research data have shown, in fact, that sociopathic tendencies of the patients decrease after 2 weeks of treatment through the use of PST groups as evidenced by differences in pre- and post-test scores on Scale 4 of the Minimult (Coché & Douglas, 1977).

Research Findings

The first study using the PST approach (Coché and Flick, 1975) reported on a series of PST groups that had been compared with playreading groups (the placebo condition) and a no-group control sample. In three separate analyses of variance it was found that time (hospitalization) alone improved the patients' functioning on the criterion tests of problem solving but that PST advanced the improvement significantly. The outcome measure in this case was the MEPS (Platt & Spivack, 1972), a test specifically geared at assessing interpersonal problem-solving skills.

In a second study (Coché & Douglas, 1977) we compared people in PST, playreading, and control groups on outcome measures that went beyond the assessment of problem-solving skills. In this case it was found that PST groups were more successful than the other two conditions in improving the participants' impulse control, self-esteem, and feelings of competence. The playreading group was as helpful as PST in reducing depression and general psychopathology. Both group conditions were superior to the control conditions in a large number of outcome measures.

In a third study (Coché, Cooper, & Petermann, 1984), patients were randomly assigned to either a brief interactive group therapy or a PST group. Results of this study showed no general superiority of one approach over the other, and men and women appeared to make the same gains. However, there was a significant interaction between gender and group modality: women gained more from group therapy and men more from PST. It appears that the men were more comfortable with the systematic, rational approach to problem solving in the PST condition, whereas the women enjoyed the group therapeutic approach more which, after all, stressed interpersonal exchange and the expression of feelings, domains in which women have traditionally been more encouraged than men.

Variations of the PST technique were tried by Kunz (1976) and Zelazowski (1976), whereas Wondolowski (1978) and Kunz et al. (1977) tried PST with special inpatient populations (geriatric and alcoholic patients).

Altogether, the findings of the research so far have been very encouraging, showing that PST can be a valuable short-term group-therapy adjunct to the treatment regimen applied in a hospital setting, that it can increase the self-confidence of the participants, can reduce depressions, and can contribute to the better functioning of the institution too.

Acknowledgments

The author wants to thank Ms. Anne Flick, Dr. Gary D. Kunz, and Ms. Barbara Polikoff for their assistance in formulating some of the thoughts in this chapter.

References

Belschner, W. (1976). Kreativitätstraining als transferiorientierte Behandlungstechnik. *Bildung und Erziehung, 29*, 216–228.
Berne, E. (1964). *Games people play.* New York: Grove Press.
Coché, E., Cooper, J. B., & Petermann, K. J. (1984). Differential outcomes of cognitive and interactional group therapies. *Small Group Behavior, 15*, 497–509.
Coché, E., & Douglas, A. A. (1977). Therapeutic effects of problem-solving training and play-reading groups. *Journal of Clinical Psychology, 33*, 820–827.
Coché, E., & Flick, A. (1975). Problem-solving training groups for hospitalized psychiatric patients. *Journal of Psychology, 91*, 19–29.
D'Zurilla, T. J., & Goldfried, M. R. (1971). Problem solving and behavior modification. *Journal of Abnormal Psychology, 78*, 107–126.
Kämmerer, A. (1983). *Die therapeutische Strategie Problemlösen.* Münster, Germany: Aschendorff.
Kunz, G. (1976). *Interpersonal problem-solving training: A structured group intervention as therapy for hospitalized psychiatric patients.* Doctoral dissertation, Temple University, Philadelphia.
Kunz, G., Coché, E., Hamme, P., & Korbor, W. (1977). Problem-solving training: A structured therapeutic modality for new drug and alcohol admissions. In *Addiction, research and treatment: Converging trends,* E. L. Gottheil, A. T. McLellen, K. A. Druley, & A. I. Alterman (Eds.). New York: Pergamon Press.
Mahoney, M. J., & Arnkoff, D. (1978). Cognitive and self-control therapies. In *Handbook of psychotherapy and behavior change: An empirical analysis* (2nd ed.), S. L. Garfield & A. E. Bergin (Eds.). New York: Wiley.
Osborn, A. F. (1963). *Applied imagination: Principles and procedures of creative problem-solving* (3rd ed.). New York: Scribner's.
Platt, J. J. & Spivack, G. (1972). Problem-solving thinking of psychiatric patients. *Journal of Consulting and Clinical Psychology, 39*, 148–151.
Siegel, J. M., & Spivack, G. (1976). A new therapy program for chronic patients. *Behavior Therapy, 7*, 129–130.
Spivack, G., Platt, J. J., & Shure, M. B. (1976). *The problem-solving approach to adjustment.* San Francisco: Jossey-Bass.
Spivack, G., & Shure, M. (1974). *Social adjustment of young children.* San Francisco: Jossey-Bass.
Traux, C. B., & Carkhuff, R. R. (1967). *Toward effective counseling and psychotherapy: Training and practice.* Chicago: Aldine-Atherton.
Wickelgren, W. A. (1974). *How to solve problems.* San Francisco: W. H. Freeman.
Wondolowski, M. (1978). *Interpersonal problem-solving training groups for hospitalized aged psychiatric patients.* Unpublished doctoral dissertation, Temple University, Philadelphia.
Zelazowski, R. R. (1976). *Hospitalized psychiatric patients as co-leaders of problem-solving training groups. A pilot study.* Unpublished master's thesis, West Chester State College, West Chester, PA.
Zigler, E., & Phillips, L. (1961). Psychiatric diagnosis and symptomatology. *Journal of Abnormal and Social Psychology, 63*, 69–75.

Chapter 6

COGNITIVE THERAPY WITH THE YOUNG ADULT CHRONIC PATIENT

Vincent B. Greenwood

Recently, there has been an effort to extend the application of cognitive therapy to different patient populations (Emery, Hollon, & Bedrosian, 1981). In that spirit, I should like to share my experiences and observations in applying group cognitive therapy to a very difficult patient population, the young adult chronic patient. To my knowledge, this is the first attempt to apply cognitive group therapy to this patient population.

Patient Population

Since the advent of deinstitutionalization, a difficult patient group has emerged, known as the young adult chronic or "revolving door" patient. These are patients, mostly in their twenties and thirties, with serious psychiatric disabilities. They are the first generation of mental patients forced to cope with the stresses and demands of community living (Pepper, Kirshner, & Ryglewicz, 1981). They do not cope well and consequently become perpetual or recurrent clients of mental health systems, social service agencies, and frequently the legal-penal system. They pose treatment and service delivery system dilemmas that are significantly different from those posed by earlier generations of the severely mentally disabled.

The great majority of these patients carry an Axis I diagnosis of schizophrenia. In addition, many display severe borderline pathology. Although their symptom pictures vary greatly, there is considerable similarity in their functional characteristics. All of these patients display severe difficulties in social functioning. They have few social or vocational skills and no natural support systems. Thus, what is an everyday problem in living for us becomes a crisis for them. When under such stress, they show serious disorders in reality testing, affect modulation, and impulse control, exhibiting both aggressive and self-destructive behavior (Schwartz & Goldfinger, 1981).

Perhaps the most problematic characteristic of these patients is their lack of involvement in treatment. They do not define themselves as mental patients. They typically are brought to the hospital against their will and often feel victimized by the mental health system. Their hospitalizations are often stormy, and they end up rejecting treatment—vehemently or passively. The burden, consequently, rests with the mental health system to design treatments that will be responsive to this new class of psychiatric "untouchables."

In attempting to tailor cognitive therapy to this patient group, I have observed different stages over the course of psychotherapy. (I am defining *stage* as a set of therapist operations designed to effect reliable changes in the patient.) Detailing treatment in stages seems particularly useful with this patient population, who are notorious for their lack of involvement with and adherence to psychotherapeutic approaches.

Anthony, a leader in the development and evaluation of rehabilitation treatment packages for the severely psychiatrically disabled, has recently proposed an innovative outcome evaluation model that incorporates specific stages of involvement and understanding (Anthony, 1980). In this model, it is crucial that evaluators assess the extent to which patients become involved with and understand treatment before attempting to evaluate outcome. Likewise, clinicians working with this patient group need to address specifically these issues of involvement and understanding. It would be unfortunate to reject a particular treatment modality merely because the patient has not been sufficiently "exposed" to the essential ingredients of the treatment. It would be equally unfortunate if practitioners did not make modifications in a particular treatment approach to ensure that patients are exposed to the more potent aspects of the treatment.

Thus, the straightforward application of cognitive therapy, as, for example, outlined in the *Cognitive Therapy of Depression* (Beck, Rush, Shaw, & Emery, 1979) rests on a number of assumptions that are invalid with the young chronic patient. Engaging the patient in a collaborative analysis and treatment of his problematic behavior and cognitive distortions rests on the following premises:

1. The patient is motivated to seek treatment.
2. The patient acknowledges he/she has a psychological problem (i.e., patient has a minimal degree of insight).
3. The patient has the belief that it is acceptable to self-disclose.
4. The patient is capable of attending to and understanding the treatment that is being offered.

5. The patient is capable of acquiring some of the fundamental skills that are the focus of cognitive therapy (e.g., introspection, disputational skills, an empirical problem-solving style) (Beck et al., 1979).

The above-noted qualities typically are present at the outset of treatment with those suffering affective or anxiety-based disorders. With psychotic patients, they are not present. Consequently, the cognitive therapist who is unwilling actively to seek appropriate modifications will be frustrated in his attempts to administer the armamentarium of behavioral and cognitive change strategies.

STAGES OF TREATMENT

Three stages of group cognitive therapy with the young chronic patient have been abstracted. The first stage has an explicit agenda of securing the patient's involvement in treatment. The second stage tries to facilitate the patient's understanding of the cognitive therapy treatment process—what Beck et al. (1979) and others have termed the "socialization" stage. The third stage involves the application of specific cognitive and behavioral change strategies with the primary goal of helping patients change their maladaptive perceptions and ideas.

These stages, as just described, are generic stages that probably would be utilized in the treatment of almost any clinical disorder. When compared with the course of therapy for neurotic disorders, however, significant differences arise with regard to the timing, effort, and techniques involved in consummating each stage.

THERAPY GUIDELINES

The major guideline for therapists in conducting this kind of group is to develop a sophisticated appreciation of the cognitive viewpoint (Beck, 1976) so that group phenomena and change strategies can be conceptualized in cognitive terms. It would be useful at this point to reiterate and highlight the distinction made by Glass and Arnkoff (1981) and others between therapy process and therapy procedure. Therapy process refers to the model of change that underlies a course of therapy, whereas therapy procedures refer to specific techniques used to bring about change. The cognitive therapist will find this distinction particularly useful with this patient group. Given the "multimodal" nature of pathology in these patients, it is important for the therapist to delineate an internally consistent view of the therapy process. This will allow the therapist to experiment with a wide range of techniques in an orderly and coherent fashion. Perhaps more so than with other disorders, therapists must "think cognitive" and yet operate in a multimodal fashion in order to exploit opportunities for constructive change.

Another guideline in the group treatment of these patients is the desirability of multiple therapists. There are a number of reasons for this recommendation. The psychological makeup of the patients is best apprehended by both a group-process and a problem-oriented focus. Patients become more keenly aware of their distorted perceptions and unrealistic premises when they arise in the group process. When such distortions are triggered, a vigorous, directive, and often didactic approach is required to help patients disengage from, and then critically evaluate, their cognitive distortions. The use of co-therapists provides a division of therapeutic attention and labor that helps ensure that distortions are first attended to and then challenged. In addition, given the attentional difficulties and volatile interpersonal styles of many of these patients, management of the group (e.g., gate-keeping functions, limit-setting, etc.) could overwhelm a single therapist. Finally, some of the most useful techniques, such as modeling and role playing, require the presence of at least two therapists.

The outline of treatment strategies for the cognitive group therapy of psychotics are elaborated to include (a) the goal of the stage; (b) the guiding principles or basic schemata in the therapist's mind that guide his behavior; (c) process criteria—specifically, the cognitive change or shift desired in patients—that enable the therapist to judge when the stage is completed; and (d) specific techniques found useful.

The group itself consisted of eight patients recruited from a ward for young adult chronic patients at a large public psychiatric hospital. Two therapists conducted the group. With a maximum of eight patients at any one time, the group met once weekly for 10 months. Turnover in the group was minimal, with a total of 12 patients involved during the life of the group. The therapists were supervised on a weekly basis by the director of training at the Center for Cognitive Therapy in Philadelphia.

STAGE I: INVOLVEMENT

The first stage of therapy aims to secure the patient's involvement in treatment. In order to underline the need for this state, I would like to portray the quality of the resistance that these patients revealed when anticipating involvement in group treatment. Comments from the first few sessions reveal concerns more intense and of a different degree than the usual neurotic fears regarding involvement in groups.

"When I talk, I feel obsolete."

"I can't sit in the same group with these people, since they are sinful."

"If I reveal my problems, others will catch them."

Almost all of patients indicated that they would suffer serious harm, or inflict serious harm, by becoming involved in group treatment. Such concerns include but go beyond the approval and performance anxiety preoccupations of neurotics. Concerns over fusion, disintegration of one's identity, persecution, and loss of control were aroused by the invitation to group treatment.

Given the intensity and interpersonal nature of these anxieties, the guiding principle at the outset of treatment was to create a trusting emotional climate in the group by achieving strong patient-therapist rapport. While acknowledging that the establishment of a warm and genuine patient-therapist relationship is a time-tested treatment principle applicable to almost all disorders, it is particularly salient for this patient group.

Initially, the group itself must acquire motivating properties for the patient. These patients, unlike neurotics, do not identify problems in their social lives that they feel motivated to solve. Both the primitive nature of their prominent defense mechanisms and the apathy and despair that dominate the conscious lives of these patients emphasize the need to make the group experience itself gratifying. These patients seem unable to perceive a better way to live their lives. Until such hope is instilled, the group needs to be a haven of interpersonal nourishment.

Although I agree with Ellis (1959) that the realization of a warm and genuine patient-therapist relationship characterized by unconditional positive regard is not a necessary condition in working effectively with neurotics, it appears to be a necessary, although by no means sufficient, condition for change with this severely disabled group. When patients link their heightened involvement in the therapy process with their liking for the therapist, it is fair to assume that the realization of the core facilitative interpersonal conditions can ameliorate significantly the often-noted motivational and attentional problems of these patients.

The cognitive shift desired in patients during this stage would be from rejection to acceptance, from "I can't tolerate this group . . . it is irrelevant . . . I don't need it" to "This is a relatively safe place where I can get help for some of my problems."

To establish rapport and secure the patient's involvement in treatment, the therapist needs to seek behaviors consonant with the core facilitative conditions of respect, genuineness, and empathy as originally highlighted by Rogers (1957). These strategies are advocated after having observed that they lead to change in the patient's cognitions of involvement in treatment and not because they represent necessary and sufficient conditions of change.

The following are some of the guidelines and specific therapist behaviors found particularly beneficial with psychotic patients.

Two guidelines are advocated in the expression of empathy at the beginning of treatment: (a) err on the side of ensuring that the patient feels understood, rather than articulating beliefs or implicit attitudes that are out of his awareness; and (b) when the therapist's comments go beyond what the patient is immediately expressing and experiencing, they always should be in the service of reducing, rather than increasing, the patient's anxiety.

I have found therapist self-disclosure to be a potent intervention in cutting through patient denial. Particularly when therapists reveal they have problems similar to patients' (e.g., communicating with others, feeling put down, loneliness), a very open discussion of these issues often ensues. After such a discussion it is much easier to illuminate the cognitions that contributed to the denial (e.g., "If I admit my difficulties, people will think I'm homosexual").

Therapist self-disclosure in the initial stage of treatment should convey the cognitive view, provide structure, and invite—rather than demand—participation. An illustration:

> When I'm in groups, I often get scared. I worry that I will appear foolish. If I tell people some of the things I am thinking, they may not like or respect me. I'd like to know if others have this fear also. But first, let me say I try to fight off this fear by reminding myself people are usually more understanding and sympathetic. Also, when I force myself to speak up, I often find others have similar problems and can be quite helpful to me.

Communicating understanding and tolerance for the patient's self-defeating behavior also seems to be essential for future collaboration. An immediate or zealous focus on change automatically can elicit severe resistance to, if not actual flight from, the group.

Other interviewing guidelines that would be suggested at the beginning of treatment include reinforcing reality testing, supporting ambiguous defenses of the patient, keeping comments brief and directive (avoid open-ended interpretations), and accentuating friendly nonverbal behavior, such as shaking hands.

Because psychotic patients often can bring such intense resistance to therapy, it is somewhat surprising that such patients exhibit a good deal of cognitive and behavioral change regarding their involvement in group treatment after a relatively brief period of time. After eight sessions attendance was stable. As for the patient's involvement in treatment, the following comments provide anecdotal evidence of a cognitive shift:

"People in here don't look so mean anymore."
"This group is like a family."
"I wish we could meet more often."
"You can really talk about anything in here."

What accounts for such dramatic behavior change? The following quotation from Beels (1980), a leading spokesman in the treatment of this patient group, captures the poignant experience of such patients at the outset of treatment and provides some understanding as to why patients can change their group behavior significantly in a brief period of time.

> In the psychotic state, and to some degree after it has subsided, a person's experience of initiative, distance and exchange has changed. Schizophrenics often feel great anxiety at the simplest initiatives. Their difficulty in carrying out greetings and negotiations with strangers is famous and the

reason why evidences of thought disorder are especially present in the psychiatric interview. There is difficulty over control with social distance. Feelings of pursuit and rejection may overwhelm the patient in situations where for the most of us there is merely the problem of encouraging someone or putting someone off. What is manners for us, is for him an operatic nightmare. (p. 10)

Once psychotic patients perceive the therapist as someone they can rely on to respond sensitively to and guide their awkward and anxiety-laden attempts to communicate with others, they seem willing to risk much greater involvement in the therapy process.

Stage II: Understanding

The next objective is to facilitate the patient's understanding of the cognitive therapy process and to create a working alliance focused on how problems can be solved. Again, it would be unwarranted to assume that these patients possess insight into the cognitive therapy process. Doses of time and creativity are required to impart this understanding.

Recently (Gardner, 1980; Heitler, 1976; Lorion, 1974), there has been empirical support for the unfortunate clinical observation that low-income, poor-prognosis patients tend to have very little idea of what psychotherapy is, how it can help them, and how they can involve themselves in the therapy process. The skills required to become meaningfully engaged in the therapy process very often are lacking. In stage I, it was not that patients did not possess the skills to become involved in group treatment, rather that they had "negative" cognitions regarding such involvement. In this next stage, it is not that patients had negative cognitions about the therapy process, rather that they had very few cognitions at all.

In the second stage of treatment, the therapist must become much more directive and didactic. However, as he is trying to bring to life the cognitive viewpoint—specifically, that people create their own feelings and determine their own behavior by the way they think and perceive—he quickly collides with one of the cardinal features of this patient group; namely, their ingrained projective defenses. At this stage, patients acknowledge that they have serious problems in living and suffer from some searing emotional states. The cause of their suffering, however, does not reside in their maladaptive thinking but somewhere "out there," in the real or imagined environment. The notion that people can control their own destiny is a radical notion for neurotics and normals. For psychotics, it is revolutionary.

The guiding principles in the therapy during stage II are, first, to convey the central role of thinking on the person's affect and behavior, and second, to encourage self-attributions of internal causation. In each session, after important interchanges or role-playing exercises, care would be taken to highlight the cognitive underpinnings (e.g., "If you think _____, then you'll feel/behave _____; whereas, if you think _____, then you'll feel/behave _____"). The cognitive shift desired in patients during this stage is from mystification (e.g., "I don't understand what therapy is") and helplessness (e.g., "He, she, it or they are causing my suffering") to understanding and control (e.g., "I can reduce my suffering and achieve my goals by changing the way I think about and interpret life experiences").

Before listing some of the specific techniques we found to be more useful in the socialization process, I would like to abstract a broad strategic principle that applies throughout the course of treatment but which is particularly noteworthy in this stage: *Employ techniques that take into account the attentional difficulties of these patients.* Of the broad range of cognitive deficits in this patient group, the most problematic is their inability to attend and to filter out irrelevant stimuli in their environment. It is therefore important to use strategies that capture the patient's attention and involve him/her actively. This is particularly true in the group situation, where it is difficult to monitor and solicit constantly each patient's attention throughout the session.

To convey the cognitive view, one of the most helpful techniques was modeling. One teaching technique was for the therapists to plan "skits" to demonstrate the essential role of cognitions in determining one's reactions to an event. We would, for example, act out the same scene—waiting for a friend who was late—a number of times, modeling self-talk indicative of anger, self-disparagement, or indifference. After the skit, we would highlight the cognitive viewpoint by comparing various concrete reactions.

The ABC model (Ellis, 1962), because of its simplicity, proved to be an effective vehicle to teach the cognitive view. One strategy that mobilized group members' attention would involve the therapist clearly labeling the *A* (activating event) and *C* (emotional consequence) components of an emotional episode, and then asking all group members to figure out possible self-statements *(B)* that would have led to the emotional consequence *(C)*.

An important objective during this stage of treatment was to help patients disengage from the self-defeating automatic perceptions and reactions that occurred in the group. Therapists would offer a model on how to disengage by constantly "collecting data" regarding how patients were reacting to one another and to the therapists and by probing for the implicit assumptions that are fueling such reactions (e.g., "Mary, you look crushed when I cut you off. What are you thinking and feeling right now?").

"Checking it out" soon becomes part of the group culture as indicated in the following comments by patients:

"I'd like to know when others are reading my mind."
"Why are people always looking at me in here?"
"You must think I'm a sissy now that you know I was molested as a child."

After approximately 12 sessions, a majority of patients in the group were demonstrating a rudimentary understanding of the cognitive model by initiating attempts to analyze problems in terms of self-statements. I also was heartened by reports from other staff members that this behavior was generalizing beyond the cognitive therapy group.

STAGE III: COGNITIVE RESTRUCTURING

It was at this point that I believed it was time to introduce cognitive and behavior change strategies, specifically designed to alter the maladaptive thinking of group members, with some confidence that such strategies would not be met with confusion or resistance.

The cognitive shift desired in patients during this stage is difficult to capsulize or parsimoniously summarize as I have tried to do in stages I and II. The range of information-processing distortions and of dysfunctional underlying assumptions is much greater than in other disorders. I will, however, list some of the most common information-processing distortions that occurred in the group, with examples of some of the basic assumptions or core beliefs that accompanied these distortions.

1. *Selective abstraction and arbitrary inference.* These distortions usually occur simultaneously and refer to the process whereby the patient first focuses on a particular detail in the environment and then draws a conclusion that is unwarranted if he were to consider other relevant data. In depression, this type of dysfunctional thinking usually takes the form of a disparaging personalization. In the group there was a more ominous theme. Patients were vigilantly scanning the environment for "clues" to support hypotheses concerning danger and threat. A major primary assumption that fuels this style of thinking is that everything has meaning; or specifically, that people constantly are sending messages of hatred to me.

2. *Dichotomous—that is, all-or-none thinking.* This refers to the tendency to think in absolute terms. This characteristic, which many contemporary theorists label "splitting," is a thinking pattern that is well ingrained with this group. It is seen vividly when patients describe themselves or significant others in their life. They frequently describe themselves and others as all good and powerful, or as all evil and utterly ineffectual. Some of the primary assumptions that underlie this thinking pattern include "if part of me is bad, all of me is bad" and "If you do not love me, you hate me."

3. *Magnification—that is, catastrophizing.* This refers to the tendencies to exaggerate or overestimate the meaning of a particular event or its future negative consequences. This cognitive predisposition represents one of the most devastating components of schizophrenic illness. This pattern frequently is elicited when such patients take tentative steps to face themselves and their limitations more realistically, or when they begin to take some initiative in overcoming their withdrawal tendencies. Such steps take on what appears to

be a life-and-death struggle. The predominant underlying assumption accompanying the catastrophizing response is that psychological and behavioral risk taking results in annihilation.

4. *Faulty Attribution.* This is the process whereby the patient severely underestimates or overestimates the extent to which he/she can control his/her behavior, the behavior of others, and events in the world. The basic assumptions here seem to be "I have no control over my thoughts, feelings, or behavior. Voices, demons, and so forth have control. If I wish something, it will happen."

Because the pathology in the new chronic patient is so severe and in some respects intractable, it is essential for the cognitive therapist to develop a realistic framework to gauge change. It quickly was discovered that certain constraints and qualifications had to be added to those cognitive change principles proved effective with other patient groups. These qualifications can be translated into the following strategic principle: *The focus of cognitive restructuring strategies should not be on the central characteristics of the patient's thought disorder.*

This principle dictates trying to avoid interactions that require the patient to overcome some of the cardinal features of his disability. Thus, strategies that are contingent on the patient's ability to introspect, to make subtle semantic distinctions, to employ an empirical problem-solving style, to generate and sustain a continuous cognitive horizon of alternative hypotheses, or to challenge delusional thinking dispassionately are unlikely to succeed. It is unclear at present whether such deficits are absolutely refractory to change or whether they might be ameliorated in a later stage of treatment. It is evident that socialization to the cognitive therapy model itself is not sufficient to produce change in these areas.

One implication of this viewpoint is to focus on the patient's distortion of events and interactions rather than on his/her underlying beliefs and premises. Given the very real impoverished existence of most of these patients, the more "elegant" cognitive therapy goal of getting the patient to challenge irrational premises regarding personal worth or achievement is unrealistic. Distinctions between "awful" as opposed to "quite frustrating" circumstances have little meaning for this group. What does appear to have a great deal of meaning is to demonstrate that, although mired in a truly sorry stage of affairs, they do distort events in a way that reinforces their avoidance tendencies and sense of worthlessness.

Once patients in the group reduced their reliance on the defenses of denail and projection, they revealed that they rather consistently overreacted to interpersonal stimuli in a negative fashion. Things really are not as miserable or threatening as they construe them. Thus, a good deal of time is spent helping patients discriminate between what Whalen, DiGiuseppe, and Wessler (1980) have termed "confirmable" reality and "perceived" (i.e., distorted) reality. The following examples illustrate this point.

KATHY: When you said patients on the ward bothered you, I guess you meant me.
ROBERT: No, not you Kathy, I was talking about . . .
KATHY: That's a relief.
THERAPIST: Kathy, I notice when someone mentions something negative, you often assume you're to blame.

CHARLES: I stopped the conversation because I knew Deloris was bored with me and didn't want to talk.
THERAPIST: Is that true?
DELORIS: Not really. I was preoccupied with something else. . . . I sort of wish we had talked longer.
THERAPIST: Charles, when a conversation doesn't go well you assume it's because there's something wrong with you and you end it.

The above examples reflect how these patients have deep-rooted premises that greatly contribute to their avoidance of others. The desired outcome of such interventions is slowing down the patient's automatic responses to interpersonal stimuli and introducing into their consciousness alternative, more realistic ways of interpreting events.

Another effective intervention during this stage was stress inoculation training (Meichenbaum, 1977), using modeling and role playing as a teaching medium. First, therapists would articulate some of the distortions and irrational assumptions triggered when faced with a stressful encounter (e.g., approaching someone to initiate a conversation). Therapists would then model coping self-statements before, during, and after the encounter. Patients were then asked to role-play the same social situations using the coping self-statements.

The strategic principle applies to delusional thinking. Our attempts to encourage patients to re-evaluate aspects of their delusional system typically result in increased guardedness. Jacobs (1980) recently has introduced the distinction between thinking and knowing. Thinking is characterized as an endless dialogue we constantly carry on with ourselves in solitude. Thinking is governed by reason. Knowing, on the other hand, is more of an awareness of truths, such as knowing one is a man or woman. Jacobs contends that knowing cannot be directly altered by thinking or metathinking (i.e., thinking about thinking). It is likewise our clinical experience that delusional thinking, particularly grandiose delusions of self, are never fully surrendered. The patient's delusional interpretations of self and others often recede when the patient is functioning well. However, they typically re-emerge when the patient is under stress.

The implication of this view for the cognitive therapist is that waging a frontal cognitive assault on what appears to be a chronic, if fluctuating, intrinsic impairment is unlikely to succeed. When delusional material is presented, attempts are made to translate it into consensually validated interpersonal or intrapersonal concerns (e.g., "Sam, it seems like you can't accept yourself as someone who gets angry," rather than "Sam, what evidence do you have that a demon is possessing you?").

Conclusion

A stage theory of group cognitive therapy with the young adult chronic patient has been presented. I am very encouraged regarding the potential of group cognitive therapy with this patient group. With it, cognitive therapy appears to possess a number of advantages over traditional psychotherapy.

1. Because cognitive therapy emanates from a clearcut theory of human functioning and behavior change and offers specific strategies for change, a greater isomorphism between psychotherapy process and procedure is achieved. Conceptualizing severe psychopathology in cognitive terms—specifically, detailing information-processing distortions and concomitant underlying assumptions—allows for a more precise clarity and concreteness in the actual practice of cognitive therapy, which are essential dimensions in the treatment of this patient group. Payoffs include not only more vivid learning experiences in therapy but also laying the groundwork for the application of skills learned in therapy without the guidance of therapist.

2. Cognitive therapy has the technical advantage of flexibility as well as precision. Given the extreme variability of the symptom picture, and cognitive and behavioral deficits of the young chronic patient, it is noteworthy that cognitive therapy passes the test of utility in that it can be applied by people in the field working with this patient population. It thus avoids the pitfalls of methodologically sound, but to date clinically irrelevant, discrete social skills approaches (Wallace, Nelson, & Liberman, 1979) and the documented (Mosher & Keith, 1980) inadequacy of traditional therapy approaches.

3. The structure of cognitive therapy—specifically, the emphasis on collaboration and on the powerful role of cognitions in influencing behavior—is an antidote to two of the most problematic features of this patient group: their lack of self-reliance and their tendency to disown and project responsibility for their behavior. Cognitive therapy stands in stark contrast to analytic and object-relations approaches, which, because of their conceptual ambiguity and emphasis on transference, appear to exacerbate these tendencies. Unlike these approaches, the cognitive view does not hold that ingrained ways of thinking and perceiving will wither away as the vicissitudes of the patient-therapist relationship are worked out. Rather, an active and directive approach that provides repeated learning experiences to supplant distorted thinking and perceiving—the hallmark of cognitive therapy—is deemed necessary to produce change in this patient group. It also is hypothesized that group treatment holds unique advantages for this patient group.

4. Some of the basic dysfunctional assumptions of this patient group are

so powerful that it may not be possible to dispute them without the immediate raw data provided by the group interaction as disconfirming evidence. Psychotic patients are not aware of believing they are fused, persecuted, and so forth. Rather, they experience these states directly and acutely with others. It is necessary to create some uncertainty in the experiencing of these feelings and perceptions before illuminating the dysfunctional underlying assumptions.

5. There is mounting evidence (e.g., Brown, Birley, & Wing, 1972; Leff, Hirsh, & Gaind, 1973) that the most potent triggers to psychotic behavior are interpersonal. It is possible that the most effective learning and best opportunities to modify perceptions and maladaptive assumptions can take place in the emotionally charged atmosphere built into the group treatment format. Learning experiences can be linked to one of the most crippling handicaps of this patient group; namely, their difficulty in forming interpersonal relationships.

Summary

The purpose of this chapter was to report on the application of a group cognitive therapy approach with the young adult chronic patient. Given the impoverished state of the psychotherapy art with this patient group, the intention was to experiment with a range of cognitive therapy strategies and then observe the results. In that spirit, this chapter focused on modifications in the cognitive therapy approach found useful with this patient group. Observations were presented in the context of a stage theory that emphasized the need to secure the patient's involvement with and socialization to the treatment process. It is our hope that the speculative clinical observations presented will motivate others to attempt more rigorous study of the application of cognitive therapy to this difficult patient group.

Acknowledgments

The author is grateful to Arthur Freeman, director of training at the Center for Cognitive Therapy in Philadelphia, for his support and helpful discussion of some of the issues raised in this manuscript.

References

Anthony, W. A. (1980). A client outcome planning model for assessing psychiatric rehabilitation interventions. Working paper for NIMH-sponsored conference on Outcome Research with the Severely Mentally Disabled, Portsmouth, NH.

Beck, A. T. (1976). *Cognitive therapy and the emotional disorders.* New York: International Universities Press.

Beck, A. T., Rush, A. J., Shaw, B. F., & Emery, G. (1979). *Cognitive therapy of depression: A treatment manual.* New York: Guilford Press.

Beels, C. (1980). The measurement of social support in schizophrenia. Unpublished manuscript, Columbia University.

Brown, G., Birley, J. L., & Wing, J. K. (1972). Influence of family life on the course of schizophrenia. *British Journal of Psychiatry, 121,* 241–258.

Ellis, A. (1959). Requisite conditions for basic personality change. *Journal of Consulting Psychology, 23,* 538–540.

Ellis, A. (1962). *Reason and emotion in psychotherapy.* New York: Lyle Stuart.

Emery, G., Hollon, S. D., & Bedrosian, R. D. (1981). *New directions in cognitive therapy—a casebook.* New York: Guilford Press.

Gardner, L. H. (1980). Racial, ethnic and social class considerations in psychotherapy supervision. In *Psychotherapy supervision: Theory, research and practice,* A. K. Hess (Ed.), (pp. 538–598). New York: John Wiley.

Glass, C. R., & Arnkoff, D. B. (1981). Thinking it through: Selected issues in cognitive assessment and therapy. In *Advances in cognitive-behavioral research and therapy,* (Vol. 1), P. C. Kendall (Ed.), (pp. 539–596). New York: Academic Press.

Heitler, J. B. (1976). Preparatory techniques in initiating expressive psychotherapy with lower-class, unsophisticated patients. *Psychological Bulletin, 83,* 339–352.

Jacobs, L. I. (1980). A cognitive approach to persistent delusions. *American Journal of Psychotherapy, 4,* 556–563.

Leff, J. P., Hirsh, S. R., & Gaind, C. L. (1973). Life events and maintenance therapy in schizophrenic relapse. *British Journal of Psychiatry, 123,* 659–660.

Lorion, R. P. (1974). Patients and therapist variables in the treatment of low-income patients. *Psychological Bulletin, 81,* 334–354.

Meichenbaum, D. (1977). *Cognitive-behavior modification: An integrative approach.* New York: Plenum Press.

Mosher, L. R., & Keith, S. J. (1980). Psychosocial treatment: Individual, group, family and community support approaches. *Schizophrenia Bulletin, 6,* 10–43.

Pepper, B., Kirshner, M. C., & Ryglewicz, H. (1981). The young adult chronic patient: Overview of a population. *Hospital and Community Psychiatry, 32,* 463–469.

Rogers, C. R. (1957). The necessary and sufficient conditions of therapeutic personality change. *Journal of Consulting Psychology, 21,* 459–461.

Schwartz, S. R., & Goldfinger, S. M. (1981). The new chronic patient: Clinical characteristics of an emerging subgroup. *Hospital and Community Psychiatry, 32,* 470–474.

Walen, S. R., DiGiuseppe, R., & Wessler, R. L. (1980). *A practitioners guide to rational-emotive therapy.* New York: Oxford University Press.

Wallace, C. J., Nelson, C. J., & Liberman, R. P. (1979). A review and critique of social skills training with schizophrenic patients. *Schizophrenia Bulletin, 5,* 88–121.

Chapter 7

FULLY INTEGRATED IN- AND OUTPATIENT SERVICES IN A PSYCHIATRIC SECTOR

Implementation of a New Model for the Care of Psychiatric Patients Favoring Continuity of Care

Carlo Perris, Karin Rodhe, Astrid Palm, M. Ableson, Siv Hellgren, Carola Lilja, and H. Soderman

The ability to assure continuity of care for every patient is a goal shared by the medical community, and a fundamental tenet of what is currently viewed as good medical care (Becker, Drachman, & Kirscht, 1974). There is, however, much debate as to what this concept implies for actual practice (Bachrach, 1981). Although the concept of continuity of care has been one among the most sought after goals in psychiatric care delivery systems, it seems that it continues to be a goal more than a reality (Granet & Talbott, 1978). While continuity of care is a goal of psychiatric care in Sweden (Socialstyrelsen, 1978; SPRI, 1982), it is unclear whether it refers to a planned coordination of the movement of a patient along the various components of the care delivery system or to continuity by the same care giver (or group of care givers) according to the patient's needs.

In traditional psychiatric settings in Sweden, when the responsibility of outpatient care was reserved to doctors,[1] some degree of continuity could be

---

[1] In Sweden the term *doctor* is reserved for the M.D.

achieved if the doctors working in an outpatient clinic also had responsibility for working in an admission ward. In this case, it was possible for a patient to continue the treatment with the same doctor first as an outpatient and later as an inpatient. However, even under such fortunate circumstances, continuity of care could be broken if the patient had to be moved from one ward to another after admission or from a ward at a general hospital to a ward at a mental hospital. In such cases the relationship with the treating doctor was broken. There was a risk that the transfer could involve changes not only in setting but in theoretical approaches to psychiatric care resulting in a radical change in the patient's treatment program.

There has been an increasing demand for psychiatric consultations from medical doctors, which has led to the development of new organizational models of patient care. These models have been inspired by the principles of sectorization and decentralization and have led to the establishment in Sweden of special outpatient units staffed with personnel recruited from different professional groups, not all of them closely tied with inpatient care. Under such conditions, continuity of care, in the more strict sense of the concept, becomes a utopian concept.

The issue of continuity has been a major concern for those of us in the process of reorganizing the psychiatric services in the County of Vasterbotten, an ongoing process for the past several years (Gottfries, Ivanov, Jacobsson, Lindberg, & Perris, 1978; Jacobsson & Perris, 1973; Perris, 1982; 1983).[2]

At the beginning of the restructuring process, psychiatric facilities were available almost exclusively at Umea, a university town at the southeast corner of the county, and comprised a relatively large (1,200-bed) former State hospital, a University Department of Psychiatry at the General Hospital (56 beds), and a few nursing homes for psychiatric patients. During the years in which the restructuring process has been going on, the main goals have been (a) a decentralization of services, (b) a successive reduction in the utilization of the facilities at the mental hospital and at the nursing homes, and (c) the development of alternative structures in the community for the support of deinstitutionalized patients. Many of these goals have been accomplished, and the results of our efforts have been reported in previous papers (Dahlgren, Gottfries, Perris, & Jacobsson, 1975; Perris, 1978; 1983).

The important steps in this process of reorganization involved the promotion of a more consistent ideological approach to treatment and greater continuity of care. In addition, we have effected the full integration of the mental hosptial and the university department of psychiatry within one care delivery system, and division of the huge catchment area into three psychiatric

---

[2]Vasterbotten is the second most northern county of Sweden, with an area of 55,000 square kilometers and a sparse population of about 250,000 inhabitants, most of whom are concentrated in two towns close to the coast.

sectors, each with wards at both the general hospital and the mental hospital at its disposal (Andersen, Dimitrijevic, Jacobsson, Palm, Perris, Rapp, Smigan, & Strandman 1978; Perris, 1982). Since the senior doctors in charge of those wards worked at both hospitals, some degree of consistency in the treatment policy could be achieved along the whole chain of the care delivery system.

We aspired, however, to a more pronounced continuity in the assistance given to the patients in our area. We will confine our report to further development in the organization of psychiatric care in the Umea sector, serving the town of Umea and its immediate surroundings with a population of about 90,000 inhabitants. The main emphasis will be on the stepwise objectives that we expected would bring us closer to our goal.

DEVELOPMENT OF OUTPATIENT UNITS AND SUBSECTORIZATION

In early 1980, following a general trend in Sweden, two special teams were created that would have the responsibility for most of the outpatient care in the area, the principal exception being those patients who, after being discharged from a ward, were followed up by the professional staff who had had care of them during their stay at the hospital. Each team was composed of one senior psychiatrist, one psychologist, one social worker, one psychiatric nurse, and one clerical worker. Attached to each team was a head nurse in charge of the patients in family care. In addition, junior residents at the department at the general hospital were expected to share their duties between the outpatient units and the wards at the general hospital where the teams were based.

When these outpatient units were established, it was decided that the main sector should be divided into two equivalent subsectors. Since we planned that the activity of the outpatient teams should be mostly outpatient focused, we expected, according to our previous positive experience (Gottfries, Jacobsson, & Perris, 1976; Perris, 1978), that a subsectorization would promote a closer and more consistent liaison with the district health services and the district social welfare units in each subsector.

At that time the admission of the acutely ill could occur at either one of two similar 15-bed wards at the general hospital or at a 17-bed ward at the mental hospital. Since the location of the outpatient units was at the general hospital, it was relatively easy for patients who were seen at an outpatient clinic and found in need of admission to be followed by the staff member who had met the patient in the clinic. Further, this staff member could introduce the patient to the personnel at the ward where the patient was to be admitted. Conversely, the follow-up of patients leaving a ward could be planned with the personnel at the outpatient unit that would become responsible for the care of the patient after discharge. The principle of treatment continuity was much more difficult to follow when a patient had to be admitted to the ward at the mental hospital, located some ten kilometers away, or when a patient was discharged from this ward. Periodic meetings occurred between the personnel at the outpatient units and those from the ward of the mental hospital, but at those occasions it was felt that because of time limitations treatment programs for only a few patients could be discussed. In addition, since our wards consistently operated according to the principle that every admitted patient becomes the responsibility of two contact persons chosen among the personnel working at the ward, there was also a growing tendency by the contact persons to maintain responsibility for the follow-up of their patients after discharge, instead of referring them back to the outpatient unit.

REDUCTION OF THE ADMISSION BEDS AND INTEGRATION OF OUT- AND INPATIENT SERVICES

As a further step in the reorganization of the services, a reduction of the available beds for admission was decided on, and the possibility of a full integration of the out- and inpatient services was considered. These reforms will be the subject of this chapter.

A continuous monitoring of admission and occupancy rates at the three admission wards revealed an average utilization of about 75 percent of the available beds. This result was interpreted as suggesting that the intensified outpatient units and the increased involvement in follow-ups by the personnel at the wards was succeeding in containing the demand for admission (and the need for it). Also, the admission wards could be easily closed temporarily, either in turn or two at a time during the major holidays and during summer vacation. Since there were no consistent significant differences in the kinds of patients admitted to each ward, it seemed appropriate to close the ward at the mental hospital in line with our goal of limiting utilization or abolishing the facility.

We predicted, however, that a reduction in available admission beds would probably increase the need for more comprehensive outpatient interventions. For this reason we obtained the agreement of the administrative authorities of our county that all of the personnel who would become available as a consequence of the phasing out of the mental hospital's ward should be transferred to, and divided between, the two admission wards at the general hospital, and that all personnel should participate in outpatient activities. In addition, we planned to have the two outpatient teams disband and have their personnel integrated with the staffs of either of the two wards.

These plans, which have now been implemented, have been inspired by the principles for the organization of psychiatric care outlined in the recently passed Italian Psychiatry Reform Law (Legge 180) (Perris, 1980) that one of us (CP) had had an opportunity of following at close quarters during their implementation, and by a similar approach tried for some time in a psychiatric sector in the south of Sweden (SPRI, 1982).

Structure of the New Organization and Its Practical Functioning

Wards

The two 15-bed wards are located at the opposite sides of a corridor in a modern five-story psychiatric building. They share a dining room and part of the space for day activities, both of which are located between the two units. Each ward has only twin and single rooms. Additional space for day activities and for group sessions is available in each ward. The wards are contiguous, but separating doors can be locked whenever required, and the wards can work independently of each other. Space for occupational therapy and physiotherapy and a gym hall are located on other floors of the building, which also includes research and teaching facilities, offices, and a small day hospital for the assistance of deinstitutionalized patients who live at home or in special group homes during a transitional phase of their readjustment to community life.

The outer doors of both wards can be locked, but that is done only when the condition of the patients present in each ward might require a secure setting, not on a rigid, straightforward rule (see below for details), except at night.

Each ward has the responsibility for one of the two subsectors mentioned previously, and each constitutes, with the personnel tied to it, a rather independent out- and inpatient unit.

Staff

The number and category of personnel at each unit are shown in Table 7-1. Doctors, psychologists, social workers, occupational and physiotherapists, the head nurses, and the two mental nurses of the former outpatient teams work on a Monday-to-Friday basis during office hours, whereas all the other personnel work according to the traditional shift system in use in most hos-

Table 7-1. Number and Category of all Staff Members in each Integrated Unit*

Category	Unit A	Unit B
Senior psychiatrist	1	2
Resident	2	2
Psychologist	2	1
Social worker	1	2
Head nurse	2	3
Psychiatric nurse	5	5
Mental nurse	12	12
Occupational therapist	1	1
Physiotherapist	1 for both units, at present	

* One psychiatric nurse and four mental nurses are consistently on night duty for the two units. These are not included in the table.

Table 7-2. Lowest and Highest Personnel Density in Unit B at Different Times.

Time	Head nurse	Psychiatric nurse	Mental nurse
Morning (weekday)	1 (2)*	1–4	5–8 (1)*
Afternoon	1 (2)*	2–5	7–10 (1)*
Evening	—	1–1	2–2
Morning (holidays)	—	2–2	2–5
Afternoon	—	2–3	4–5
Evening	—	1	—

*Those who work on a Monday-to-Friday basis and only during office hours.

pitals. The lowest and highest density of people available at different times of the day, besides those working on a Monday-to-Friday basis mentioned previously, is shown in Table 7-2. During the night, five people are on duty for both wards: four mental nurses and one psychiatric nurse. However, an additional mental health nurse can be temporarily assigned for night duties from a special pool whenever the condition of some patient(s) requires special supervision. An internal emergency alarm system connects all the wards in the building. The outer doors are consistently locked evenings and nights.

The staff in each ward is fairly stable. It is composed mostly of people with a long experience of working in psychiatric care settings and a high level of psychiatric education. A fair number among the psychiatric nurses and the mental health nurses has received formal psychotherapeutic training or is currently in training.

The staff in each ward is divided into three "supervision groups" with responsibility for both in- and outpatient care and for interventions in the community. Each of these subgroups is composed of representatives of different personnel categories. Although they are not all completely alike, we have tried to maintain some balance in the composition of each group. Some minor differences among the two units also occurs. Each group is in charge of a certain number of patients in the ward, according to the principle mentioned above of a two-to-one fixed tie with each patient in the care of the group. Working schedules differ slightly in the two units, but the general structure is the same in the two wards.

Each supervision group in turn is on special duty for 2 consecutive days, to assist the person among the senior staff (above) who is on call for a first screening of the patients in need of acute care. If a patient who had been seen by any member of the group as an outpatient has to be admitted, then those who have seen him/her will become the contact persons during the patient's stay in the ward and will have the responsibility for the follow-up after discharge. This system allows for a fair, random allocation of the patients to the different supervision groups and to the different contact persons.

Functioning of Each Unit in Daily Work

All of the patients and the personnel in the ward meet every morning between 8:00 and 8:30 A.M. after having participated in a joint short morning gym program. At this meeting the condition of each patient in the ward is surveyed, and practical needs of individual patients are assessed. Patients have an opportunity for expressing their wishes for unscheduled activities outside the unit, e.g., occasional visits to the town, to a bank, to the social insurance offices, or to relatives.

A second general planning meeting, in which both the personnel on duty in the ward and the other members of the unit's staff participate, is then held between 8:30 and 9:30 A.M. During this meeting, problems concerning patients requiring a consistent management policy from all of the people tied to the ward are discussed, and an appropriate approach is agreed on. Depending on the condition of the patients present each day, it is also decided at this juncture whether the outer door has to be kept locked. In discussing why it has to be so, possible alternatives regarding a particular day schedule for the most disturbed patients are investigated. Also, an assessment is then made of how many people have to be in the ward for the care of the patients present that very day. When such an assessment has been made, all the others among the unit's staff are expected to be available for outpatient work. As a rule, people belonging to the supervision group on special duty, as mentioned above, are expected to share most of the responsibility for the care of inpatients as well.

A short history of patients who have been referred for psychiatric consultation or who have requested consultation for themselves by a telephone call during the previous day are shortly reviewed by a senior staff member. A division of the tasks then occurs among the available personnel according to the needs and types of patients asking for care. These tasks may consist of an office consultation or home visit by one or more among the available staff.

Every Friday individual occupational and physiotherapy programs are agreed on for the coming week, within the frame of a more comprehensive plan for care tailored for each patient.

When time is available, as most often occurs, problems of a more general scope are discussed, or the history and psychopathological development of some particular patient are discussed in greater depth. Since trainees attend this morning session when they are available, there is an opportunity for in-service education.

Screening of Patients Applying for Care

Patients in need of psychiatric care may apply in person at the main desk, make a phone call, or be referred for consultation from any health care service in the catchment area. Patients coming acutely to the reception area are screened by a qualified member of the staff on duty, in turn, and assigned to the most appropriate level of care.

Patients who have made a phone call or have been referred by some other health care service in the community are discussed at the ward round as described above, and the most appropriate intervention is planned.

Supervision

Each of the supervision groups meets twice weekly for a 1½-hour session with the leader of the group. At this junction individual treatment plans are agreed on and then followed up at subsequent sessions. The planning applies to each patient that any one of the group members has in charge, either while in the ward or on an outpatient basis. When planning, efforts are made to cover a follow-up period and to be sure that tasks are appropriately distributed among the group members. In one of the units (see below) the supervision also encompasses the application of a cognitive therapeutic orientation in the approach to the patients.

Planning for Weekends and Holidays

We favor, whenever possible, that the patient spend their weekends at home or with some relative. However, it happens very frequently that a sizable number among them are in a state that precludes this possibility. There is an attempt to ease the difficulty that ensues because of the lack of activities that are available during weekend and holiday time for those patients who cannot leave the unit on their own. Personnel among those who will be on duty during the weekend in each ward meet together every Friday to plan some joint activity for the patients in the two wards and to share the responsibility for those who are severely disturbed. Such activities may consist of short excursions—visits to a coffee shop, to the movies, to some exhibition, or to whatever else is accessible at the moment. If outdoor activities cannot be organized, then some joint activity in the wards is planned, for example, games or small parties.

Connection with Other Units at the Mental Hospital

Of the wards at the mental hospital, those loaded with older patients have a very low turnover and are not currently used for transfer of patients. Most of the patients at those wards would more properly belong to a geriatric section, whereas some of them would probably be suitable for care in a hospital. Plans to reorganize this part of the system are now in progress. One ward, together with the night hospital, is an important part of the rehabilitation chain. When some patient from the acute units is found in need of prolonged rehabilitation and has to be transferred to one of those wards, then his contact person will socialize him with the transfer and discuss the planned rehabilitation with the personnel at the rehabilitation wards. Visits to the ward to which the patient is supposed to be transferred are a consistent part of the socialization efforts. The last ward at the mental hospital is currently reserved for chronic, severely disturbed, and destructive patients and for a few forensic patients. When an occasional transfer to this ward occurs, it involves patients discharged on trial who show a severe impairment. Before being sent back to the original ward, the are admitted temporarily to either of the admission wards for a check of their current state of functioning.

Role of Each Category of Staff Members

Since the composition of the staff in the two units, as shown in Table 1, is not completely alike, we focus on the following only for one of the units, although the general principles are applicable to both. There is neither a complete blurring of the professional roles in each ward nor a strict hierarchical structure, but everyone contributes with his/her particular training to some duties.

Doctors

One doctor is assigned to each of the supervision groups. The two senior doctors at ward B are also the leader/supervisors of their group, whereas the leader/supervisor of the third group is a psychologist. This distribution of roles has been warranted because this particular ward is trying to apply a special cognitive therapeutic orientation, and therefore it was necessary that each group had an experienced cognitive therapist as a leader (Perris, Palm, Perris, Rodhe, Palm & Abelson, 1985.

The doctors supervise all the medical aspects of care. The residents are also responsible for the medical examination of each patient in the ward and for the appropriate conduct of medical treatment of the patients in their group.

Current medical-administrative duties (certificates, prescriptions, etc.) are the responsibility of the doctor in each group. A duty of the senior doctors is the decision to retain a patient who has been committed at the end of the observation period prescribed by the law. Junior doctors from all sectors also are on call for the whole department according to a day and night schedule. Doctors also are responsible for firsthand consultation/liaison with the other departments at the General Hospital. It is also a duty of the doctors to supervise and to assist the medical students during their periods of practice in the ward and to contribute to teaching and research programs going on at the department.

Psychologist

Besides being the leader of one of the subgroups, the psychologist works directly with both in- and outpatients, especially with those judged suitable for psychotherapeutic interventions. In turn with the doctors and one of the social workers, each psychologist (also those at ward A) participate in the first screening of the patient needing acute care and in their distribution among the staff members of each group as described above. Together with one of the psychologists at ward A, ward B is also responsible for a consistent liaison with one of the primary care centers belonging to the subsector. When required, the psychologist is responsible for the administration of psychological diagnostic tests to patients who do not directly belong to her group. Further, she is responsible for the supervision of those among the personnel from the two units who are in psychotherapeutic training and participates in teaching and research programs.

Social Workers

The social workers' most specific contribution is to intervene whenever a link has to be established between the unit and the various social agencies in the community. In this respect they are at the disposal of the whole unit regardless of whether the patient in need of such advice belongs to any of their groups. One of them participates in the first screening of patients applying for care, as described above. The other is in charge of the distribution of patients in need of supportive long-term contact among the staff members of the unit and of the supervision of these contacts. Both being trained in psychotherapy, most of their work, however, is in direct one-to-one contact with outpatients. The social worker of ward A is tied with a primary care center.

Head Nurses

Ward B has three head nurses because the outpatient team that become incorporated in this ward had two head nurses with different tasks. Among them, one is in charge of the ward. It is her duty to coordinate the work in the ward and to distribute tasks among the personnel who will work in the ward each day. Although belonging to one of the supervision groups, this particular head nurse is not directly involved as a contact person with any inpatient but participates, with her psychotherapeutic training, in outpatient activities. As the head of the ward, she has to be well informed about the condition of each patient. She has the administrative responsibility of the personnel in the ward; she acts also as the coordinator of the research programs going on in the ward and participates actively in research.

Another head nurse is the coordinator of interventions in the community by other nurses or mental health nurses. He contributes by distributing tasks concerning home visits and supervises them. He is also (as one of the head nurses at ward A) in charge of a certain number of patients currently in family care. Being trained in psychotherapy, he meets with a few patients on an outpatient basis.

The third head nurse, also trained in psychotherapy, is in charge of single outpatients for long-term treatment. She conducts therapeutic groups with outpatients of various kinds and in particular a special group for Finnish-speaking people. She is also the coordinator of the neuroleptic clinic of the subsector, of which she shares the responsibility with a senior psychiatrist.

Other Psychiatric Nurses and Mental Nurses

They have the direct responsibility of being the contact persons of the patients in the ward and for participating in outpatient activites. As a rule, they also have the tasks of following up the patients after discharge under the supervision of the leader of their supervision group. They lead most of the activities in the ward and assist the patients in their compliance with the assigned activity schedules. A few among them are formally trained in psychotherapy, and see outpatients on a one-to-one basis. However, all of them have short- or long-term supportive contacts with single patients, and a few among them lead supportive groups under supervision. One mental nurse from each ward also leads social-encounter groups with chronic patients in the community.

Occupational Therapist and Physiotherapist

Their role is to contribute with their specific competence to the planning and carrying out of the activities appropriate of their specialization. Both individual patient programs and programs open to all the patients in the ward are agreed on according to the routine mentioned above. Because of their work overload they can only occasionally take care of outpatients. Among their duties is that of supervising and assisting the trainees belonging to their professional group.

Trainees

Trainees from all professional categories are almost consistently present in the wards during the school terms. In general, they assist the ordinary personnel of their own category in their duties. Their impact is particularly appreciated for their involvement in activating the patients present in the ward. They participate in turn in the planning meeting every morning but not in the supervision sessions. Such routine is obviously not the result of deliberate discrimination but the necessity of keeping the attendance at the larger meetings to a reasonable number of people.

IN-SERVICE EDUCATION

Besides the regularly scheduled twice-a-week supervision sessions, programs of in-service education covering various aspects of psychiatric theory and practice are going on at random intervals once weekly in each ward. Since the department is a part of a university teaching hospital, lectures and seminars in which the staff of the units can participate occurs weekly during the terms. Several among the staff have received or are at present receiving formal psychotherapeutic training, either with the department or at the State Institute of Psychotherapy. In ward B an educational program of cognitive therapy orientation is going on, integrated with practice supervised by the leaders of the supervision groups. This program will be extended to ward A if its application proves successful from the results of an evaluation program that is now in progress. External courses are regularly organized by the Educational Section of the Administration of Psychiatric Care, and a sum of money is put at the disposal of the department for participating in external courses each year. All members of the staff are encouraged to participate in such activities.

Research

Several research programs are going on in both wards. These consist, first of all, of a comprehensive evaluation program of the present model of care, encompassing all of the consecutive admissions to each ward during one year and a follow-up of some 300 patients for one further year. A longitudinal, prospective monitoring of patients who start long-term lithium treatment has been going on for some years. This project also continues after the organizational change. A psychiatric nurse is in charge of coordinating this program in both wards. Personnel in both wards participate in the rating of inpatients' behavior in research programs concerning the trial of new treatments or the study of particular morbid conditions.

Some Preliminary Comments

The organizational model that we have described so far has been implemented, but too short a time has elapsed to draw any far-reaching conclusions. Thus, we can present at this point only our preliminary impressions.

The model that we have adopted differs from traditional ones principally because all staff at the two units described in this article participate in both inpatient and outpatient care as well as in interventions in the community. Thus, we are able to provide continuity of care at both an ideological and a personal level through a patient's whole episode of illness, whether or not it requires hospital admission. Also, if a patient should suffer a relapse, he will meet people with whom he is well acquainted.

The link with the primary care centers, which we aim to develop further, represents another aspect of our efforts in ensuring continuity of care at all levels. Although aiming at continuity, we try to apply this principle with some degree of flexibility. Whenever appropriate and feasible, we leave some freedom to the patient in the choice of his/her contact persons, within the limits imposed by our system. In a similar way none among the staff feels compelled to become the contact person for any particular patient if he prefers not to do so.

The implementation of the organizational change described in this chapter has been preceded by a few months of preparatory work. A working group composed of representatives of all three wards involved in the change, who were also representatives of their different trade unions, have participated constructively in the planning.

There was optimism and enthusiasm in meeting the challenge but also fears and worries. Among the latter were a main worry about the feasibility of coping with the sudden reduction in the number of beds, a preoccupation about the suitability of the wards to accommodate severely disturbed psychotic patients in a larger number than previously, and a worry about the feasibility of managing effectively all of the personnel who would be linked to each ward. There was also an understandable uneasiness at the prospect of changing working conditions and, for those who had to move to a new ward, their working place.

We were also uncertain as to whether we would be able to identify meaningful tasks for all people working at each unit, or whether the linkage of all personnel with a ward would be at the cost of outpatient interventions. So far, most of the worries have melted away, and most of the negative expectations have dissipated. We are now experiencing that we are able to intervene in a more timely, more in-depth—and more appropriate?—way on an outpatient basis, thus being better able to prevent unnecessary hospital admissions.

The planning of daily activities for each single patient, and in consequence the efforts to keep them engaged with goal-oriented activities, contributes to maintaining the fairly pleasant atmosphere of the wards and allows for keeping the wards open most of the time despite the fact that almost all of the patients admitted to the wards suffer from a severe and acute psychotic disorder.

The possibility of delegating tasks traditionally proper for doctors to other professionals, and the opportunity of an intensive supervision for all members of the unit's staff have had a momentous motivation-promoting impact on all categories of personnel, who feel that their participation in the work is meaningful and rewarding. At the same time, availability of different categories of personnel with different levels of education and training permits tailoring to the most appropriate type of contact for each patient, which probably will increase effectiveness and contain costs.

There are undoubtedly some among the older staff members who still feel uncomfortable in the new role and who perhaps long for the old routines. We hope, however, that even those will grow in their new roles. We are aware that a full stabilization in this new model of care will occur only after a much longer process of adaptation, during which old schemas will have to be relinquished and new ones will have to be incorporated. It is our intention to report forthcoming results of the evaluation program that is now in progress and to be describe the further development of our approach.

Summary

A new model of psychiatric care implying a complete integration of outpatient and inpatient activities recently has been implemented in the Umea psychiatric sector in northern Sweden. The model implies that all personnel tied with the sector work at the wards, at the outpatient clinic, and in the community, independently of the professional category to which they belongs, but in relation to level of their professional education and competence. The application of such model has the following advantages: It allows for quick intervention when a patient is in need of care; it permits application of the principle of "continuity of care" in the sense that the patient is tied with the same people both as an outpatient and when in hospital; it permits the assignment of every patient to the most appropriate level of care; and it contributes to a sizable reduction in the number of admissions. The model is adaptable to other hospital settings and will have the effect of maintaining a continuum of care.

References

Andersen, K., Dimitrijevic, P., Jacobsson, L., Palm, U., Perris, C., Rapp, W., Smigan, L., & Strandman, E. (1978). Integrering av ett psykiatriskt sjukhus och en psykiatrisk universitetsklinik. *Lakartidn, 76,* 2563–2564.

Bachrach, L. L. (1981). Continuity of care for chronic mental patients: A conceptual analysis. *American Journal of Psychiatry, 138,* 1449–1456.

Becker, M. H., Drachman, R. H., & Kirscht, J. P. (1974). A field experiment to evaluate various outcomes of continuity of physician care. *American Journal of Public Health, 64,* 1062–1070.

Dahlgren, M., Gottfries, C.-G., Perris, C., & Jacobsson, L. (1975). Forsok med sektoriserad-decentraliserad oppen psykiatrisk vard i Umea sjukvardsdistrikt. *Lakartidn, 72,* 581–584.

Gottfries, C.-G., Ivanov, B., Jacobsson, L., Lindberg, M., & Perris, C. (1978). Oppen psykiatrisk vard i Lycksele—psykiatrisk mottagning med begransad psykiaterinsats. *Lakatidn, 75,* 1289–1291.

Gottfries, C.-G., Jacobsson, L., & Perris, C. (1976). A pilot trial of sectorized and decentralized psychiatric care in Northern Sweden. *Social Psychiatry, 11,* 27–32.

Granet, R. B., & Talbott, J. A. (1978). The continuity agent: Creating a new role to bridge the gaps in mental health system. *Hospital & Community Psychiatry, 29,* 132–133.

Jacobsson, L., & Perris, C. (1973). Re-organization of psychiatric services in a particular geographical area. *Proceedings of the Second International Symposium on Rehabilitation in Psychiatry*, Orebro, Sweden. Unpublished manuscript.

Legge no 180, 13 maggio 1978. *Gazzetta Ufficiale della Republica Italiana 1978, 133*, 1491–1494.

Perris, C. (1978). Sectorized psychiatry: Effects upon psychiatric care in an area of sparse population. *Nordic Council Arct Med Res Rep, 22,* 92–97.

Perris, C. (1980). Avinstitutionalisering i italiensk psykiatri. *Lakartidn, 77,* 1979–1981.

Perris, C. (1982). Changing pattern of psychiatric care in Sweden: An example from the County of Vasterbotten. In *Servizi sanitari e psichiatria,* D. Kemali et al. (Eds), (pp. 171–189). Rome: Il Pensiero Scientifico Editore.

Perris, C. (1983). Integration of a mental hospital and a university department of psychiatry at a general hospital. Five years follow-up. In *General hospital psychiatry,* J.J. Lopez-Ibor et al. (Eds.). Amsterdam: Excerpta Medica; International Congress Series, *621,* 64–71.

Perris, C., Palm, A., Perris H., Rodhe, K., Palm, U., & Abelson, M. (1985). Implementing a cognitive therapeutic orientation in a fully integrated out-patient and in-patient psychiatric unit for acutely ill at a university hospital. *Acta Psychiatrica Scandinavica,* Submitted.

Smigan, L., & Perris, C. (1983). A prospective study of long term lithium treatment. An interim report. Read at the International Symposium on Lithium and Rubidium Therapy, Venice.

Socialstyrelsen. (1978). Psykiatrisk halso- och sjukvard. Forslag till principprogram. Socialstyrelsen redovisar 5.

SPRI. (1982a). Utveckling av 80-talets allmanpsykiatri. *SPRI report* 75.

SPRI. (1982b). Psykiatri i omvandling: Psykiatriska kliniken i angelholm. *SPRI report* 107.

Chapter 8

A COGNITIVE APPROACH TO GROUP THERAPY WITH HOSPITALIZED ADOLESCENTS

Robert W. Grossman
Beverly Freet

Group psychotherapy in various forms has been part of residential treatment of adolescents for many years. Much of the early work was probably stimulated by Slavson's work with latency-age children in what he called "activity group therapy" (Slavson, 1943; Kraft, 1975). Most of these early groups were done from the psychoanalytic perspective.

By the late 1960s and early 1970s, there was a proliferation of conceptual frameworks for doing group psychotherapy as well as a growing body of research supporting its therapeutic efficacy and suggesting some of its limitations (e.g., Yalom, 1971). Carl Rogers and his associates, for example, had developed an approach to group therapy based on his client-centered approach (Rogers, 1970). By this time, their approach had been strongly influenced by the T-group method of the National Training Laboratories (Bradford, Gibb, & Benne, 1964). Some of his followers were advocating an almost completely unstructured approach to group therapy (Rogers, 1970, p.6).

Reality therapy, developed by William Glasser (1965) and his colleagues, evolved by this time as well. Like Rogers, his viewpoint was developed in opposition to the psychoanalytic viewpoint but was much more structured in its approach to group therapy. Glasser specifically focused on developing involvement, confronting irresponsible behavior, and teaching patients to be more responsible.

J. L. Moreno's work in psychodrama began possibly even earlier than Slavson's work (Moreno & Toeman, 1942) and, as well as establishing its own tradition, provided a lot of the techniques incorporated into the Gestalt groups done by Fritz Perls (1969). Eric Berne and his associates developed and popularized the transactional analysis (TA) approach to group psychotherapy (Berne, 1966). Robert and Mary Goulding (1979) even evolved a TA-Gestalt approach to groups.

The most structured and problem focused, however, were the groups of the behaviorists as well as the cognitive-behavioral therapists like Arnold Lazarus (1972, 1975) and Albert Ellis (1975; Ellis & Harper, 1973).

When the director of the state hospital in which we were working asked us to make group psychotherapy available to the adolescent inpatients, we had many different conceptual frameworks available to us. Whichever framework we chose, it had to allow us to meet the constraints imposed by the director: It had to serve patients of widely differing handicaps and emotional disorders, and it had to be an ongoing, open-ended group to which new patients could be added at almost any time.

Because of these practical constraints and the nature of our patients, a cognitive-behavioral approach proved most effective. In this approach we had the foundation for three features that were essential to our work:

1. It allowed us to conceptualize clearly our work with each patient in a "true interaction" model of mental illness.
2. It encouraged us to present therapuetic concepts in ways that could be understood quickly by even severely handicapped patients.
3. It emphasized developing structure and organization for each session, which proved vital in helping patients gain the behavioral control needed to progress to more sophisticated therapy skills.

The Conceptual Model

The first feature, developing a real interaction model, was a slight conceptual departure from standard theory for doing psychotherapy. When we started the group in 1972, it was fashionable to assume that all children's emotional problems were caused by "terrible" parents. It wasn't hard to see, however, that each child in our hospital had caused extreme difficulty in their relationships with the staff in the hospital. Some were even able to create conflicts between staff members, and most were able to get staff to feel depressed and anxious at one time or another. If the child could create difficulties for these individuals, wasn't it just possible that they contributed similarly to the origin of problems with their parents? Following this line of reasoning led us to conceptualize each of our patients in terms of six questions:

1. What handicap, personal attribute, or trait of temperament may have made this child especially difficult for his/her family to manage?
2. How might this difficulty disrupt the family and bring out its weaknesses?
3. In what ways might the child have learned to exaggerate his/her handicap, attribute, or trait into a "manipulative style" that took advantage of the family's weakness?
4. What cognitive distortions or dysfunctional self-instructions did the child have that controlled this exaggerated form of the handicap?
5. Over time, how did the child's "manipulative style" distress parents and other adults in the community enough to push them toward hospitalizing the child?
6. In what ways did the "manipulative style" and its cognitive underpinnings manifest themselves in the behavior of the child in the hospital and, more specifically, in group therapy sessions?

This model and these questions helped focus our attention on the cognitions that contributed to their emotional problems. It turned out that this viewpoint often led directly to the cognitive and behavioral changes that allowed children to get out and stay out of institutional settings.

An example of the use of this system can be seen in the case of a child with a severe attention-deficit disorder accompanied by hyperactivity. This child's parents described unmanageable temper tantrums, almost from birth. The mother poignantly described an infant who could not be comforted, screaming loudly in the crib until he was "blue in the face." Clearly, this was the "handicap" or "personal characteristic" that taxed the family's coping capacity. It seemed logical to hypothesize that such a child learned to exaggerate 36is temperamental attribute to the point that he manipulatively threw a tantrum whenever he didn't get his own way. Severe tantrums allowed this child to avoid unpleasant tasks in the short run, but in the long run his parents, peers, teachers, and neighbors found such behavior intolerable. Even in the hospital, where we carefully monitored the rewards and deprivations in a sophisticated behavioral treatment program, we were worn out by this child. He was a child who bit people, threw things, and banged his head on the floor until he bled for such insignificant frustrations as losing a pool game.

We didn't discover the cognitive processes that underlay this behavior until one day he began a tantrum in group therapy by screaming, "You hate me! Everyone hates me! The whole world's against me!" These wild cognitive distortions were the underpinnings that justified and amplified this young man's violent behavior. If the whole world was against him, his only chance to survive might indeed have been to throw a tantrum.

In fact, however, only one person had said he couldn't do something he wanted to do. This cognitive distortion led him to overreact dramatically to this situation. The manipulative effect of these tantrums on others was to get them to "walk on eggshells" around him. Essentially, he intimidated everyone because there was a threat of a tantrum behind even the smallest request he made. Over time, everyone got tired of dealing with him, except some kids who enjoyed triggering dramatic, entertaining shows any time their lives were boring. His siblings at home, fellow students in school, and other patients in the hospital seemed to delight in frustrating this youngster just to see him explode.

It was a bit harder to see how the truly psychotic child's handicap became a manipulative device until we noticed how tired we were after trying to work with such children for even short periods of time. We began to call this the "I don't think well enough to solve *any* problems" manipulation. It was true that rational thinking and reality testing were extra hard for schizophrenic adolescents; however, it was also apparent that they often exaggerated their difficulties to get out of tasks they could do but didn't feel like doing. Adults were pressured into doing their work for them. Similarly, retarded adolescents and antisocial ones found ways to use their special traits to take advantage of others.

It is important to note that there was no assumption that any of these manipulations were conscious. In fact, many of them were developed without the child or the parents being aware of these effects. What was important was that the effects were there and were maintained by the views of the world and the self implicit in the child's cognitive processes.

Presentation of Therapeutic Concepts

Second, because we had various types of patients, with problems ranging from retardation and attention deficit disorders or impulsive and aggressive behavior to psychotic hallucinations and delusions, it was important to do therapy in a framework that could be easily understood. To this end, all major therapeutic concepts were operationalized in briefly stated cognitive rules. These rules evolved into an approach to therapy very much like Meichenbaum's Self-Instruction or Stress Inoculation Therapy (1971). Rules or self-instructions were presented in group settings, practiced in homework assignments (Maultsby, 1971), tried out in group therapy interactions, and applied in other areas of their lives.

Completed *written* homework was required for attending group therapy. (There is an extensive section on the development of structural rules in the next section.) The structure of written homework and clear agendas for each of the sessions made the process of group therapy available to many patients who were otherwise too uncontrolled and unskilled to participate in traditional groups. For example, having written homework assignments done ahead of time so they were available to read during the session made social interaction possible for some kids who were too retarded or too psychotic to think of things to say on the spot. Patients would often get help on their homework from the hospital ward staff, teachers, and teacher aides. Because of this help, even the most socially inept kids often had good things to contribute. Some of them were rewarded with praise from peers for the first time in their lives, because of the structured homework assignments and the help they received from the staff. Structured homework made the group sessions better, improved the kids' relationship with the hospital and school staff, and led to an improvement in the patients' self-esteem.

STRUCTURE OF THE SESSIONS

Third, because so many of our patients were impulsive, we found it necessary to structure our group therapy for behavioral control before encouraging self-analysis and feelings exploration. Many of the rules for group structure were implemented to manage the patients' tendency to act out or misbehave. As a collection, these were referred to as "Group Therapy Rules" and "Constructive Behavior Tools." The "rules" served as the basis for teaching rudimentary social skills, and the more abstract "tools" became guidelines for evaluating larger segments of behavior.

After these rules and tools were operating, we found we could go on to "Self-Observation Skills" and "Rational Self-Analysis," which were like the traditional focus of cognitive psychotherapy.

Group Therapy Rules

We used a group as the setting for therapy because many opportunities for social interactions arose as a natural consequence of getting a group together. In addition, we thought a group setting that involved both male and female patients would motivate the students to cooperate in therapy. Group therapy was one of the few regular opportunities they had to interact with the opposite sex outside of school. The motivational value of this should not be underestimated. They had a strong desire to be there and an interest in relating to each other. In the group, then, we could work on shaping the way they related to each other.

When we first started group therapy in the Children's Unit, the kids spent most of their time criticizing or cutting each other down. There were hospital rules about violence, and so the children knew that they would be put on ward restriction for at least a week if they behaved aggressively. This meant they would miss group therapy as well as losing all opportunity to leave their ward during that time. In addition, they knew the ward staff could be called to the group therapy room to subdue any patient who was out of control, and that this would result in seclusion in a locked room for at least an hour. This hospital-wide policy was enforced consistently and so was a built-in rule of group therapy.

The students, however, were absolutely professional in their ability to hit each other verbally where they hurt the most. If one of the boys was the least bit concerned about his masculinity, he was called a "fag." If a girl was worried about her femininity, she was invariably called a "dyke." If a girl was even a little guilty about using her physical attractiveness to get attention from guys, the other kids knew instinctively that calling her a "whore" or a "slut" would hurt her terribly.

The first rule we developed was (A) *You aren't allowed to do any name calling*. The penalty for calling someone a name was then to give them a "nice one." This meant the offender had to give a solidly positive compliment about the personality of the person he just called a name. Immediately, the name calling came to a halt. These children could fire hostile comments with devilish ease, but it was worse than having a tooth pulled to compliment each other. This rule caught them at a weak point in relationship skills. They didn't have the skills to give genuine compliments to peers. To help develop these skills, we often gave the homework assignment to write a "nice one" for every person in the group. The therapists as well as the kids had to come with a written compliment for each person in the group just to get into the next group session. By modeling and repeated practice, they slowly gained this essential social skill.

The second rule was (B) *Only one person is allowed to speak at a time*. Simple as this seems, this was a difficult rule for most of our children to follow. It was absolutely essential, to allow even a minimum of group work to be done. Hyperactive children especially had so much trouble with this rule that we developed a system that gave them an opportunity to catch themselves before being sent out of group and back to the ward. The penalty was "If you get three strikes, you're out of the group for the day." This gave a child two warnings before he/she was asked to leave. Surprisingly enough, when we instituted this rule, it took two months of biweekly sessions before the first child had to be sent out of the group. The three-strikes standard was flexible enough to give hyperactive children the space necessary to gain control. Even later, we rarely had to send a child out of group. They intuitively accepted the standard as fair. It wasn't unusual, however, for a child to get two strikes before settling down. We soon found that the teachers in the school and the staff on the wards made use of this rule and standard. Occasionally, a patient would report using this rule as a "self-instruction" in conversations outside of group. It was surprising to some that people liked them better when they didn't try to talk when others were speaking.

The third rule also seemed simple, but it led to some therapeutically powerful discoveries. We noticed that many of the kids weren't paying attention when others were talking, and these same people weren't watching the person talking. The third rule we developed was (C) *Look at the person who is talking.* As we used this rule, we discovered that, invariably, when children were looking away, their minds were wandering away.

It seemed that all of our kids' handicaps were associated with attentional problems: "Psychotic" children would fade off into their fantasy world as their gaze faded off onto some distant point in the room; hyperactive ones would glance quickly away as they became distracted from the topic by an irrelevant noise; sociopathic adolescents would look away as they avoided hearing anything that might be painful or disturbing; mildly retarded individuals looked at the floor or the walls when the topic became too complex for them to follow. In each case, explorations of the effects of wandering visual attention proved important in the therapy.

What was even more exciting was that whenever we got a child to look persistently at the people who were talking, he would be able to pay more attention to what was being said: The "psychotic" child stayed more in our world; the hyperactive child was less distractable; the sociopathic child faced more painful things; the "dull" child began to ask questions when he didn't understand. It wasn't easy for any of them consistently to follow the conversation with their eyes; however, as they developed more skill and persistence with their eyes, they overcame attentional deficits at the same time.

Out of this discovery came our fourth and fifth rules. The test of whether or not someone was paying attention was if they could repeat the conversation word-for-word: (D) *If you cannot repeat exactly what was just said, then you aren't paying attention.* Parroting each word, of course, was not always correlated with understanding the meaning of the words. The test for understanding we developed was putting the message into one's own words: (E) *If you are listening carefully enough to translate the message accurately into your own words, then you are understanding what is being said.*

These were difficult tasks for our kids. If they couldn't do this well, then we had to teach them to attend better before they could make progress in learning anything else in therapy. We said seemingly simple things like "T, you just stopped talking in the middle of a sentence. You do that often, and it's one of the main things that lead people to think you're crazy."[1]

Someone else would ask, "T, what did Dr. Grossman say to you?"

T's response was "He said I stopped in the middle of a sentence and ... well ... ah ... I don't know what else he said. Would you please repeat it?" To get him to remember this simple idea, we often had to break it down into a three- or four-step process and go over it four or five times before he could remember what he was told; e.g., (a) "I stop talking in the middle of sentences";

---

[1] It is important to note that the group members used the word *crazy* to refer to that aspect of their personality that got them hospitalized. We used it because it was their word and had that connotation for them, not because we were labeling them.

(b) "I do it often"; (c) "It is one of the things that lead people to think I'm crazy."

When he was asked to put it into his own words, he often said something like "One of the reasons people think I'm crazy is that I often stop in the middle of a sentence. You know, when I pay careful attention, I don't stop in the middle of a sentence. That means that if I don't want people to think I'm crazy, I need to force myself to pay attention. Neat!" It was amazing to see what some of these "low-functioning" kids could do when we took the time to make sure they were attending to the information that was given to them.

Paying attention alone was not enough, however, to relate to people. Building effective relationships also required that the children respond to others. They needed to give their reactions to others, in words. Our next rule, therefore, was (F) *It is necessary to respond with words whenever spoken to.*

We expanded this by saying, "It is most important to respond in words whenever you are spoken to directly, but it is also important to learn to give some of your reactions when you are just listening to a conversation between others. If you don't give some verbal response when spoken to, people think you are 'strange.' They even consider you a little 'withdrawn' if you *never* add something voluntarily to a discussion. Adding things spontaneously can be overdone, of course, but some verbal reactions are necessary just to let people know you are listening."

We found that students failed to respond in the group situation only if they weren't paying attention or if they had some kind of excuse that inhibited them. The focus of the homework for this rule was on our favorite excuses to avoid talking. Over time, we developed a list of common excuses, so the patients would know what kinds of thoughts to look for. If someone didn't respond when spoken to, we could always ask them if they were saying something to themselves that stopped them from responding. If we found that they were inhibited by a thought like "What I have to say isn't important," then we could help them come up with a self-instruction to counter this dysfunctional thought. Just reminding themselves with a phrase like "Say something, so they don't think you're weird" often was enough to unblock some students.

Our next bit of structure was (G) *You should also offer some things to the conversation when you aren't directly spoken to.*

We found the safest responses were the positive ones, so in group we encouraged each other to (H) *Respond openly with your positive reactions.* This fit very well with our rule (A) about giving "nice ones" to make up for name calling. The kids themselves came up with the elaboration of this rule when one of them said, "You can always find something you like about someone, if you look hard enough. You may not *want* to find it, but you *can* if you work at it."

It was amazing to see how high a set of standards the kids set for themselves. Whenever anyone did any hostile name calling, they had to come up with a "good one" for the person they were angry toward. Children were often asked to come up with second or third "good ones" if the first ones weren't judged to reflect honest positive feelings. Sometimes a group even got to the point of demanding "creative" positive responses.

Another way to respond to a conversation that we taught was simply called a "checking out" response. Whenever a child was confused or irritated by something that was said to him, he was encouraged to (I) *Check out what was said by repeating back part of the message in the form of a question.* This rule was a natural extention of our attentional rules (D) and (E), above. Since we trained students to attend so carefully they could repeat what was said word for word, this became an easy rule to follow. In fact, some withdrawn schizophrenic and mildly retarded students became "conversationalists" simply by using these skills. They found they always had something to say in conversations just by "checking out" what was said. It was also interesting to see other patients discover how many of their fights and arguments dissolved as soon as they "checked out" what they heard. It was surprising to find out how many disagreements with people come from misinterpreting what others said to us. Just checking to make sure they understood the other person eliminated a large proportion of their conflicts.

Another rule that was helpful in handling negative reactions was (J) *Send feeling messages rather than calling names.* For example, we would rather someone said, "You've interrupted me. I'm really irritated" than to have them say, "You shouldn't do that, you slob!" We found that this method led to clearer messages and it helped us avoid a lot of unproductive arguing. Some children were surprised to discover that these messages also worked very well with their parents. Parents somehow just reacted more calmly to a child who said he was irritated than they did to being called a "slob" by that child. By getting the children to follow our guidelines for behavior in group therapy, they got a chance to evaluate the rewards they earned from doing these behaviors. Outside of group therapy, they often tried these same behaviors to see if the results achieved in their "real" world corresponded to what they found in group therapy. Of course, they absorbed and used these skills only to the extent that they worked for them in their "real" world.

Summary List of Rules

(A) You aren't allowed to do any name calling.

(B) Only one person is allowed to speak at a time.

(C) Look at the person who is talking.

(D) If you cannot repeat what was said exactly, you aren't paying attention.

(E) If you are listening enough to translate the message accurately into your own words, then you are understanding what is being said.

(F) It is necessary to respond verbally whenever spoken to.

(G) You should also offer some things to the conversation when you aren't directly spoken to.
(H) Respond openly with your positive reactions.
(I) Check out what was said by repeating back the message in the form of a question.
(J) Send feeling messages rather than calling names.

Constructive Behavior Tools

"Having adults around who are firm without being belligerent and kind without being an easy mark" was the way we described the complex set of conditions that led to character development. We abstracted this notion from reading Ellis's book titled *How to Live with a Neurotic* (1969). We provided these conditions in our rule enforcement in group therapy and by focusing attention on specific behaviors and concrete accomplishments of children rather than excuses. This focusing was done by asking people to display what we called "constructive" behavior in the group therapy sessions, rather than just talking about problems or giving excuses. We also discussed eight specific ideas to give the patients cognitive reference points for "being constructive."

1. We defined being constructive as caring enough to say what you think about someone when asked to give feedback, even though it may get them angry at you. This, of course, had to be balanced by being sure one didn't name-call for the sake of being mean or getting back at a person. For adolescents to become aware of the way they affected other people, they needed to hear from others. At first there seemed to be an unwritten rule that you didn't talk about an irritating aspect of someone's personality unless you were in a fight or argument. Then you mentioned it to hurt them. The idea that you might give each other negative information that could be used to improve oneself was a totally new concept. The key was to tie the negative information-giving to "when it was requested" and "being caring enough."

The rule of giving "nice ones" if any name calling occurred gave the group leverage to correct a member who was too zealous in their communication of negative feedback. The therapist was often said to be guilty of this charge, so usually had to follow up each criticism with a compliment. This habit of the group often made negative information easier for a child to accept and harder to ignore because it tended to break down any "all-or-nothing" interpretations of such feedback (Beck, Rush, Shaw, & Emery, 1979). When negative information came with some positive clarification, it was much more easily assimilated.

2. We worked toward showing children that being constructive meant being able to "lose face" in the short run, when one of your important long-run goals would be achieved by it. By words and actions the therapists showed they were willing to "lose face" by admitting mistakes and discussing examples

of their interpersonal problems. This was the best way to communicate that nothing horrible occurred when one admitted he/she was wrong or had problems. As one of the kids said, "It is a little painful for you in the short run, but people often respect you for it in the long run."

3. Being constructive was also defined as being "fair" with people. We worked especially hard on being "fair" in the expression of our negative feelings. Irritation and anger were to be expressed in a way that allowed others to decide whether or not they wanted to deal with our feelings. We said things like, "Name calling is dumping feelings on others by trying to hurt them. It's not a 'fair' way." Using statements that began with the word *I* and being ready to accept responsibility for exaggeration were two of the ways to be "fair."

4. Being constructive was saying "won't" instead of saying "can't." A child who said, "I can't do it" often meant, "I won't do it, and you can't make me!" The goal of this tool was to get the children to accept responsibility for their decisions. Here we pointed out that "it is better to refuse to do something when we just don't want to do it than to say we can't do it." This definition of constructive was aimed at the special manipulative tool used by many psychotic children, as described above, but all of our children used this excuse to avoid behaving responsibly at one time or another.

5. We said, "Working constructively is evaluating possible gains and losses *before* taking action." For example, a child who was caught being disruptive in group after being warned twice was out of group for one session. The choice was to think before you act and stop being disruptive or leave for the day. No excuses were accepted. As we often pointed out, "Only one person speaks at a time, and if you are whispering or gesturing enough to catch the therapist's attention while someone else is talking, you are being disruptive in group. For this you get warning number one. If you give, or try to give, an excuse, you get your second warning, and if you continue to press your case, you are out for the day."

6. Being constructive also involved building up your "emotional bank accounts" with people. The goal was to have enough in your "emotional bank account" with people to get what you want from them "off the interest" from your account. This analogy was used to teach the students how to evaluate the long-run consequences of their behavior. For example, whenever a child described a temper outburst that she used to get something from her parents, some member of the group asked, "What did that do to your 'bank account' with them?" This gave the children a cognitive tool to use, which highlighted the fact that even though she got her way in that situation, she probably irritated the adults enough that they would want to take something away from her in the long run. In fact, we pointed out that "people won't stand to have you around them if you constantly 'bankrupt' your account with them. For example, judges often agree to send kids to the hopsital if they have 'bankrupt' accounts with more than one set of important adults, like parents, teachers, and police."

7. Constructively earning your privileges, rather than manipulating for them was a way to build up your "emotional bank accounts." For example, if someone wanted money to use downtown, there were always several ways to get it. They might whine, cry, and tell their parents they are getting "depressed," so they need some money to go downtown to cheer themselves up. They might try "stamping their feet," if their mother refused to give it to them, as a careful way to remind her they could break things and throw wild tantrums if she didn't give them the money. A more constructive approach would be to tell their mom that they wanted some money to go downtown, and then ask if there were any jobs around the house for which she would be willing to pay them.

This was an example of a constructive approach, a way to *earn* one's privileges and at the same time to increase one's "emotional bank account" with one's mother. If they did this kind of thing often enough, they would build up so many positive feelings in their "account" that Mother would gladly let them have some money even if she didn't have any jobs that needed doing. They would have earned her trust and have enough in their "emotional bank account" to do what they wanted "off the interest."

8. Whenever constructive behavior occurred in group, we got the constructive child to notice his/her feelings. This was an effective way to notice the mild but long-lasting reward of self-esteem that could only be earned through responsible, constructive behavior. As we said, "We don't believe we can give you self-esteem. We can suggest ways in which you may want to try to earn it, but you alone can put the suggestions into action. After you try it out, you will know if it helped you earn self-esteem."

Summary List of Tools

Being constructive is

1. Caring enough to say what you think about someone when asked to give feedback, even though it may make them angry at you.
2. Being able to "lose face" in the short run, when one of your important long-run goals would be achieved by it.
3. Being fair with people.
4. Saying "I won't" instead of saying "I can't."
5. Evaluating possible gains and losses *before* taking action.
6. Building up your "emotional bank accounts" with people.
7. Earning your privileges rather than manipulating for them.
8. Noticing your feelings after you've behaved constructively.

Self-Observation Skills

We found that most children were completely unaware of the mental processing that went into the planning of their behavior. From their viewpoint, they just seemed to sense situations and react automatically, with little or no awareness of how their minds worked. Helping them become aware of the mental processes that occurred between sensing and reacting allowed them to select and have better control of their responses to the environment. Under this heading, we worked on two subgoals: first, helping kids make more useful distinctions among their various mental experiences; second, helping them become aware of a wider range of potential reactions to any given situation.

It is important to note that all this mental- and emotional-awareness development was done within the context of the rules for building social skills and developing character. Helping children become more fully aware of deep anger without having the rules and tools to manage that anger could have been physically dangerous for the therapist as well as therapeutically destructive for the children. Only after we clearly established rules for behavior and the cognitive tools for evaluating behavior did we begin to emphasize self-observation skills.

In this context, emotional exploration gave the children many more places to catch themselves before acting in an unconstructive manner. For example, we developed a handout, based on Ellis's four basic processes (Ellis & Harper, 1973, p. 17) that taught the children to differentiate among their (a) senses, (b) thoughts, (c) feelings, and (d) actions.

Once children could notice the difference between (a) hearing or *sensing* a thing that irritated them, (b) *thinking* about the meaning of that stimulus, (c) *feeling* the irritation, and (d) *acting out* their retaliation, they had four places in which to catch themselves before hurting someone. For example, if they used rule (1) about "checking out" what they heard, they might short-circuit a fight by realizing they were misinterpreting what they heard; if they paused after feeling irritated to consider the possible consequences of retaliating, they might catch a violent impulse before it got expressed in action.

One experience in particular highlighted this point. The therapist was mentioning to a severely socially impaired child that she wasn't the only person in group who had difficulty paying attention to what was going on. "S is like you in that he has difficulty paying attention, too. But——"

Across the room and to the right came a thundering interruption. "You pig! You no-good mother-fucking bastard! I'd like to smash you!" S was pointing his finger directly at the therapist, and every muscle in his body was tight. In fact, he could just barely hold himself in his chair as he strained up and down on the seat.

"Man, I know you're angry with me, but I don't know why," the therapist said (looking directly at S). "If you want to tell me, that's fine, but get upstairs into a quiet room if you aren't going to talk about it." On several occasions in the past, S had chosen to go upstairs to his ward when he didn't want to discuss his anger. There were three or four attendants there who could physically restrain him if necessary and place him in a seclusion room during a violent outburst. The rules were clear to S and the rest of the group members, even if he was "fighting mad."

He was just barely able to restrain himself from tearing the therapist apart, as someone else in the group asked him, "What did Dr. Grossman say that got you so angry? S, what did you hear him say?" (Pause. . . .)

Another group member broke the silence. "I don't think he likes you comparing him to M. No way that he's that out of it. He has never been as bad as she is."

The therapist then asked, "Is that it, S? Is that what you heard me saying? That you are as out of it as M?" His head nodded in the affirmative. "There's no way I meant *that*, man. Even at your worse, we could have a good time talking and playing pool, remember?"

"Yeah, I remember." Relief occurred for everybody as S began to smile.

"Now, what did you hear me saying, and how did you exaggerate it?"

S comfortably relaxed in his chair again and said, "You said I have some of the same problems paying attention as M, and I do, but I heard you putting me down, man, saying I was as low as her, man, and I didn't like that. She don't say nothing to nobody. She's really out of it, and I have never been that bad. It really hurt bad when I thought you were saying I'm as bad as her."

Later we were able to work with him on how he exaggerated a "put-down" enough to get so angry he wanted to kill, but the key to this whole feeling exploration was based on our rules about handling things "costructively." Left to try to control his hatred of the therapist at that moment, without the clear-cut rules, we could have had one bloodied therapist and one messed-up child to work with. There was no doubt in the therapist's mind that S had an urge to kill him at one point in that session. By the time it was over and he was giving the therapist his "good ones" for the names he had called him, S said, "Doc, you know, you're the only person in this whole damn hospital that understands me."

Still, he couldn't have contained his urge to smash the therapist if the norms and rules for constructive behavior had not been established at the outset. Most of these kids were just not ready for exploration and arousal of feelings before a group structure for managing behavior had been established. When used in conjunction with our structure, however, self-observation skills had a tremendous impact on a child's progress. Our ability to work through hatred feelings was a signficant step. The staff never again had to restrain S forcibly. He had clearly learned to distinguish between feeling angry and smashing somebody. After the episode was over, the co-therapist said, "You know, S and Bob, you owe M some 'good ones,' too."

S smiled and said, "You're right. Give me a second to think of some."

When children were taught to pay attention to the differences between what they heard, thought, and felt, it was just a short step to teach them that all people mis-hear things now and then, which often leads to getting unnecessarily angry. Then it was easy to point out that "because we all mis-hear things sometimes, it is important to remember to *check out* what we perceive to see if it is accurate before we take action. This is especially true when anger and fighting are involved, because they can lock you up for fighting and hurting people. It's silly to get yourself locked up just because you didn't take the time to check out what you thought you heard."

Essential to our program for increasing the self-analytic skills of each child was that we also carefully pointed out the differences between *what* someone said and the *way* they said it (verbal and nonverbal communication). We said, "The way something is said often has more effect on us than what is said, because feelings are often carried in the nonverbal aspect of the message. People are often in the midst of a conflict with others because they react to the way someone said something rather than what the person said." As the children became aware of this, they were often able to reduce the number of conflicts they had by checking out both the verbal and nonverbal aspects of the messages they received.

For example, the therapists were often perceived as being "angry" toward a child when they were really just "very concerned" about the child's welfare. The kids often misperceived the affection and concern embedded in the therapists' "forceful" reaction to them. When students checked out how the therapists felt (by asking them how they felt, rather than interpreting their nonverbal communication as anger), they were often surprised by the genuine concern and affection the therapists expressed to them. Most important, they often found a similar miscommunication was also operating in their relationship with their parents.

Using self-observation skills, we also tried to help children get labels for their internal experience that more accurately corresponded to their nonverbal behavior. For instance, we found that one child's label for being "not upset" was associated with behavior that would be defined as "very upset" or "extremely angry" by most people. One day in group, J couldn't stop moving, talking, or interrupting others. The therapist said to him, "J, you seem to me to be excited or upset about something."

J said, "No, if I were upset, you would be all bloody now. You'll know when I get upset." On further questioning, we found out he had just missed his afternoon cigarette. He stayed after school to help a teacher move some boxes and missed the scheduled smoking time on the ward. He was angry at the attendant who wouldn't listen to his legitimate excuse for being late. After we talked this over, and the therapist agreed to check with the attendant the next day, J was able to calm down and work effectively in group therapy for the rest of the hour. If he changed his definition for the word "upset," J would have been more effective with people. He would more accurately tell them what to expect. If he warned the group that he was upset or angry, they would know that they should gently discuss the matter with him, rather than just ask him to stop being rude to others. When he said he wasn't upset, that confused them and they didn't know what to expect. When the internal state was more accurately labeled, the child became more effective with people.

To expand further the range of feeling awareness, we also tried to get the children to increase their differentiation among their feelings. We might help a child sort out and label some of the "hurt" feelings involved in feelings of "anger" or "dislike." They often got amazingly different reactions from their parents when they said something like, "Boy, that hurt when you called me a liar," instead of reacting with an angry "Screw you! You never loved me! All you do is criticize me!" More appropriate differentiation was part of developing a set of skills for self-observation.

RATIONAL SELF-ANALYSIS SKILLS

We found that these children were especially difficult to work with because they subtly distorted and avoided reality. In order to get them to develop more emotional resources and solid character structures, we found that we had to teach them to discover how they distorted things that were said to them. This involved what we called rational self-analysis skills and was similar to cognitive psychotherapy for less severely disturbed individuals.

A theme that evolved in our work was that these distortions often operated to get someone else to do one's work for him or her. In other words, most distortions seemed to provide the child with an excuse to live totally for the "now" and let the "future be damned." Thus, cognitive distortions served the function of allowing the child to develop "a very poor character." Even if these distortions came partly from some organic disorder, they usually had the net result of excusing the child from some disagreeable task or responsibility. This was the manipulative aspect of mental or emotional illnesses. As stated in the introduction, it seemed useful to think of this developing around a child's natural handicap in order to take advantage of their family's weaknesses.

When we were trying to help a child figure out his distortions, we usually asked, "What must you be thinking to give yourself an excuse to get others to do your work or to avoid thinking about the long-run consequences of your behavior?" The idea that all or most distortions of reality occurred in the form of "distorted internalized sentences" was especially useful in this context (Ellis & Harper, 1973). We suggested that we often got other people to do our work for us by telling ourselves something distorted about what we saw and heard. Consequently, whenever a child behaved irresponsibly, irrationally, or unconstructively, we asked, "What did you tell yourself to get yourself to do that?"

We found that the hyperactive child described in the introduction would often tell himself something like, "Dad *never* gives me my way. He's *always* letting my brother go out at night, never me." If Dad *never* gave in to this child, then he might need a full tantrum to get "fair" treatment, but, when asked, most children would admit that there was at least a tiny bit of exaggeration involved when they used words like *never* and *always*. Dad, indeed, might have treated the brother better, but it was a rare father who *never* gave in and so could only be managed by full-blown, violent temper tantrums. In fact, as we discussed, the only time such violence is "constructive" is when one's life is in danger and there is no way to run. There was a better way to handle Dad, and that was usually by building one's "emotional bank account" with him so he could trust one to be out after dark.

We also looked for cognitive distortions behind any avoidance of information. For example, one day J said, "M, I think you have really said a lot of good things in group today." M just looked at the floor.

Another child said, "Boy, M, you really ignored J. How did you feel when he said that to you?" M looked up, then down at the floor again.

The therapist said, "That would have made me feel pretty good to have J say that to me." M smiled and nodded her head. "Why don't you tell him how it made you feel?"

M then looked quickly at J, smiled, and said, "Thanks, J, that made me feel good."

J then added, "Boy, I'm glad you said that. I thought I had hurt your feelings, somehow."

In this example, M avoided reaction to J by just being quiet. Getting her to respond was the first step in helping her learn to recognize one of her cognitive distortions. We later found out that she had what Beck calls an "automatic thought" (1979). She thought to herself, "Boys *never* say nice things to you except when they're after your body, so don't pay any attention to what J's saying." We also noted that these distortions got others to do her work for her. Other group members jumped in and helped M do some of her thinking and risk taking. Once she noticed this, she began to feel that she had a choice about whether or not to use these behaviors. Her interpretations and behaviors were no longer out of her control.

We found that all the children in our group were better able to deal constructively with reality after we helped them verbalize or "put accurate sentences to" the reactions they had in situations where their behavior was unconstructive. Once they began putting their reactions into words, the members of the group were able to help them find the "exaggerated sentences" that they used to magnify and distort their view of the situation. As these were pointed out, one could usually see how the inappropriate behavior followed from the distortions.

This process was modified and individualized for each child. However, we found some consistency among groups of children. For example, with children whose major problems were due to hyperactivity and attention-deficit disorders, the practice time was much greater. Some of them seemed to have a central nervous system disorder that made them extremely susceptible to overarousal, so they had to work extra hard to catch themselves in the process of exaggerating. Once they started the process of exaggeration, they seemed to have only a fraction of a second to catch themselves. They also seemed to backslide more readily than other children, even after they understood the whole process. This meant, of course, that it took an extraordinary amount of time, effort, and persistent repetition on our part to help these children control their tendency to exaggerate.

With children whose problems were complicated by below-average intelligence, the basic learning process was slow. It required not only that we teach the children to put their feelings into words, but we also had to teach them some alternative sentences to use. These sentences had to be broken down into very small steps, and each step was gone over time and time again, because most of these children had verbal learning problems. The process was slowed down and drawn out because of their handicap. Once they caught on to their distortion processes, however, they were less likely than the hyperactive child to backslide.

With the children who had distortions of reality mainly due to psychotic processes, learning new sentences wasn't enough. Not only did they exaggerate the crisis nature of their environment, but they had not learned some of the very basic coping skills that many of us took for granted. The therapist, therefore, not only had to help them identify the exaggerations and discover the advantages gained by their distortions, but he also had to help them develop more effective ways for achieving their goals. In a step-by-step fashion, we had to foster the development of new ways that had less negative consequences for the child. Because there was a lot of socialization involved, this often took extra time. Another time-consuming problem was that their attention often wandered off to their fantasy world. With one patient who constantly saw angels, this meant that each phrase had to be repeated several times before she got the message. Sometimes her span of concentration was so short that only one or two words could be kept together at one time. This handicap was the most difficult to work with, but we saw significant progress made using this framework. Slowly but surely, this patient chose to pay more and more attention to the members of the group and less and less to her hallucinations.

With the children whose problems were mainly the result of character disorders, the distortions were due less to unconscious processes than in the other children. Their distorted responses were more consciously aimed at achieving some short-run objective. With these children, we had the task not only of pointing out the exaggerations implicit in their distortions, but we also had to be sure to discuss the consequences of their behavior with them. First, they needed to know that we were aware of how they gave themselves excuses to get upset, so that they would win in the short run. We often did this by asked simple questions, like "What did you gain by it?" or "What are the advantages of doing it?" Next, they had to see how this same behavior destroyed the long-run relationships they had with people. This often had to be clarified for them in sentences that had enough emotional impact to be remembered, like "That's why your family can't stand to have you live with them. You're always ripping them off! Instead of carrying your responsible share of the load, you just clean them!" The goal was then to get these children to think about and emphasize the long-run consequences of their behavior. This gave them a reason for the development of the skills necessary to reduce their exaggerations. The analogy of the "emotional bank accounts" with people worked especially well in this regard.

Thus, rational self-awareness, like careful self-observation, was always coupled with other aspects of treatment. Rarely were we able simply to offer insight into distortions and have a positive therapeutic gain. These insights always had to be coupled with other goals of treatment, such as character building and social skill development, before any noticeable therapeutic gains were achieved. We always considered self-understanding to be incomplete unless there was a corresponding improvement in the child's behavior in group therapy and ultimately a constructive change in how the child was getting along in the rest of his or her world. Rational self-analysis, then, in many ways was the last step in treatment, rather than one of our major preoccupations. Once we got children to the point of being able to use such skills, they were usually ready for outpatient treatment.

REFERENCES

Beck, A. T., Rush, J. A., Shaw, B. F., & Emery, G. (1979). *Cognitive theory of depression*. New York: Guilford Press.
Berne, E. (1964). *Principles of group treatment*. New York: Oxford University Press.
Bradford, L. P., Gibb, J. A., & Benne, F. D (1964). *T-group theory and labatory method*. New York: John Wiley & Sons.
Ellis, A. (1969). *How to live with a neurotic*. New York: Award Books.
Ellis, A. (1975). Rational emotive group therapy. In *Basic approaches to group psychotherapy and group counseling* (2nd ed.), G. M. Gazda (Ed.) (pp. 287–316). Springfield, IL: Charles C. Thomas.
Ellis, A., & Harper, R. A. (1973). *A guide to rational living*. Hollywood, CA: Wilshire Books.
Glasser, W. (1965). *Reality therapy*. New York: Harper & Row.
Goulding, R., & Goulding, M. (1979). *Changing lives through redecision therapy*. New York: Brunner/Mazel.
Kraft, I. A. (1975). Group therapy with children. In *Comprehensive textbook of psychiatry* (2nd ed.), A. M. Freedman, H. I. Kaplan, & B. J. Sadock (Eds.), (pp. 2229–2239). Baltimore: Williams & Wilkins.
Lazarus, A. A. (1975). Multimodal behavior therapy in groups. In *Basic approaches to group psychotherapy and group counseling* (2nd ed.), G. M. Gazda (Ed.), (pp. 150–174). Springfield, IL: Charles C. Thomas.
Maultsby, M. C. (1971). Systematic written homework in psychotherapy. *Psychotherapy Theory, Research, and Practice, 8*, 195–198.
Meichenbaum, D. B. (1971). *Cognitive factors in behavior modification: Modifying what clients say to themselves*. Waterloo, IA: University of Waterloo.
Moreno, J. L., & Toeman, Z. (1942). The group approach in psychodrama. *Sociometry, 5*, 191–194.

Perls, F. S. (1969). *Gestalt therapy verbatim*. Lafayette, CA: Real People Press.
Rogers, C. R. (1970). *Carl Rogers on encounter groups*. New York: Harper & Row.
Slavson, S. R. (1943). *An introduction to group therapy*. New York: The Commonwealth Fund and Harvard University Press.
Yalom, I. (1971). *The theory and practice of group psychotherapy*. New York: Basic Books.

Part II

APPLICATIONS IN MEDICAL SETTINGS

Chapter 9

COGNITIVE THERAPY WITH CANCER PATIENTS

J. William Worden

Cancer continues to be one of the major medical challenges of our lifetime. It is estimated that one out of every four persons will receive the diagnosis of cancer at some point in his lifetime. Historically, the cancer patient has most often been approached as a terminal patient, and psychosocial interventions have been geared to helping that individual cope with the impending finality of his life. The literature is replete with information on how to help the terminal cancer patient toward an appropriate death (Weisman, 1972). There is very little in the literature for helping the living cancer patient cope with the exigencies of the disease. The reality is that cancer is not always a fatal prognosis. With today's treatments increasing numbers of cancer patients are either cured or are given a much longer disease-free time period. Living with cancer imposes significant stresses on the patient and requires well-developed adaptive coping skills. To live with cancer is much more than adapting to the treatments and their various side effects. There is a whole host of psychosocial issues with which to cope, many of which require much more from that patient than coping with the threat to mortality. To understand cancer as merely a biological event is to overlook the innumerable biopsychosocial factors that demand strategic coping from the patient and his family. Fortunately, there has been a growing recognition of these factors in the past 15 years, and an attempt is being made to deal with these. For many patients health, family, work, finance, self-image, friendships, and psychological and bodily concerns are as important as existential concerns.

To understand better the wide range of concerns to be dealt with by the cancer patient, we undertook a longitudinal study of newly diagnosed cancer patients. Patients with five different tumor sites, chosen for a wide range of disabilities and treatments, were followed at monthly intervals from time of diagnosis to 6 months and then at 3-month intervals to 1 year. Patients were consecutive admissions to the medical and surgical services of the Massachusetts General Hospital with the first diagnosis of cancer (Weisman & Worden, 1977). From this longitudinal study we identified a group of poorly coping cancer patients. These were patients with high levels of emotional distress and poor resolutions to the problems with which they were coping. To evaluate coping we used a problem-solving paradigm that looks at what a person does with a problem to bring about both resolution of that problem and relief from emotional distress. Coping behaviors of patients were assessed over a whole host of problems and over time. We discovered that poorly coping patients had basically two main deficits in their coping repertoire. First, they tended to overuse coping strategies that are less effective in bringing about resolution of problems, though some may bring about a temporary sense of relief—such as getting drunk. Second, and perhaps more important, these patients were not able to generate a number of alternative coping strategies. They would try one or perhaps two approaches to problems, and if these did not work, they would stop trying. Good copers, on the other hand, were able to try a number of approaches to problem solving and to keep going until something was effective and brought about some degree of resolution. Also, good copers were able to evaluate and to rank-order their approaches to problem solving without giving each strategy an equal weighting.

Equipped with this information, Dr. Harry Sobel and I set about to design a problem-solving intervention for cancer patients who were identified as poor copers. We were able to design and test the Cancer Problem-Solving Instrument (CPSI) described in this chapter.[1] Once the instrument was developed, we embedded it in a 4- to 6-week training program for these patients to test out its effectiveness in improving coping skills in a group of patients identified as poor copers (Sobel & Worden, 1980).

We believed that a problem-solving cognitive-behavioral approach would be useful from several standpoints. First, it would address the coping deficits of the patients for whom we were creating it. Second, as a short-term, focused on the "here and now," educational intervention it would enable the clinician and the patient to collaborate in the promotion of patient self-control and patient responsibility for health. These goals are consonant with what we saw to be the expectations of medical patients. The "average" medical patient does not expect to receive nor does he want psychotherapy following a cancer diagnosis. In fact, many traditional psychiatric consultations with cancer patients can fail because the clinician may be too focused on pathology. In our experience cancer patients and their families do not want help with their feelings, worries, and fears, but rather they want help in getting well physically

---

[1] Available from Guilford Press, 200 Park Avenue South, New York, NY 10003.

as well as help in solving immediate problems and planning for future tasks. A cognitive, problem-solving intervention is consonant with these expectations. Also, such an intervention, based as it is on an educational model, avoids the stigma of traditional psychotherapy, especially of medical patients who are not seeking it out.

There is still a third advantage to a program such as ours, and that is cost effectiveness. Increasing health care costs make it difficult to provide long-term psychosocial support to the cancer patient, many of whom will return for multiple treatments and perhaps have several recurrences. A brief problem-solving intervention that is effective can multiply its effect over time. It is our experience that patients as students will continue to practice their newly learned skills on their own long after the initial four-session contract. Our program offers them an opportunity to learn a method for coping with problems while continuing to live with cancer.

The overall aim of our program is to correct deficits in coping, lower levels of distress, reclaim personal control, teach problem-solving methods, and improve morale. More specifically, we want to influence a patient's coping through an educational means. Michenbaum (1977) divided behavioral change into three components: self-observation, recognition of incompatible thoughts and behaviors, and cognitions concerning feasible change. That is, one does not just spontaneously alter ways of thinking or behaving. Much thought and practice go into the process.

We conceptualize coping as first confronting and clarifying a problem then considering alternative ways to attack a problem. Distressed cancer patients are encouraged to examine their situation, then to articulate their understanding of what might interfere with good coping and to explore options that are within reach in order to find a feasible satisfactory solution. Good copers are able to face a perceived problem with hope and then imagine a range of consequences that might come about by using different strategies.

Our program is a short-term, structured, problem-solving approach for helping distressed cancer patients. Patients are taught how to recognize, confront, and solve commonly encountered cancer problems. This approach focuses on the process of problem solving and how to do it (Janis & Mann, 1977; Spivack, Platt, & Schure, 1976).

Many current psychosocial interventions with cancer patients are aimed at helping the patient cope with a particular personal problem. Most of them do not provide patients with the general methodology for solving future problems as they arise. We, on the other hand, offer the patient an opportunity to learn a specific step-by-step approach to problem solving, then to practice the process with the therapist, and to apply the procedures to personal problems related to the illness. We attempt to teach and to reinforce active coping skills.

In this intervention patients are presented with a variety of common problems that cancer patients encounter in the course of their illness, and then they are taught a precise decision-making process. Problems are simulated through a series of drawings (CPSI) designed to initiate problem solving. A description of these cards with their themes and objectives can be found in Table 9-1. The patient is shown a series of paired cards depicting a cancer-related problem and a second card showing the same problem solved. The intervention centers around the intermediate steps necessary to get from the problem to some type of resolution. Patients are taught how to generate and how to evaluate various strategies that could lead to solution. Patients also are taught to develop an awareness of the interpersonal context of many vexing problems and to see how these can contribute to generating or blocking intermediate steps to an adequate resolution. It is important that patients not only be able to conceive of alternative solutions but to recognize the intrapsychic and interpersonal consequences of each approach considered. Problems are defined and redefined. Approaches are evaluated and ranked, consequences are cognitively considered in order to dissolve self-imposed blocks to behavioral action. The objectives are to strengthen internal controls and to reinforce flexibility about coping strategies, choice in goals, and personal resourcefulness.

The intervention follows the general principles of any short-term psychotherapy. The major requirement in short-term therapy is to establish a focus and to stick with it. This therapy is designed to do that. In the first session the patient is introduced to the program, its procedures, and rationale. A four-session contract is established, and the patient is told that we will look at common problems faced by many cancer patients and the best way to solve them in the most practical way. Ideas for problem solving will be taught, and

Table 9-1

Card	Theme	Purpose
1	Loneliness & isolation	To reinforce social assertion & responsibility
2	Morale & self-management	To reinforce limit-setting & the seeking of support
3	Sexuality & contact	To facilitate self-initiation, with spouse or lover
4	Body self-esteem & general mood	To help adjust to surgery and disfigurement
5	Communication	To facilitate information seeking and direct confrontation with medical personnel
6	Body self-image & social adjustment	To encourage the return to prior activities without fear of people's thoughts
7	Exisistential plight & time limitation	To support a discussion on future planning & the realities of a life-threatening illness
8	Social alienation & self-identity	To encourage interpersonal communication, self-control and adaptation to living with cancer
9	Emotionality & personal growth	To help patients understand emotional release, sharing of concerns and feelings, and important relationship between thoughts and feeling
10	Dysphoria & depression	To facilitate an effective style for coping with depression, anger, fears of treatment, and dying.

patients are encouraged to practice these skills on their own problems. No CPSI cards are shown at the first session. Rather the patient is introduced to the idea of relaxation training and relaxation procedures are demonstrated. Relaxation is presented as a time-out procedure for managing stress and for coming up with practical and successful means of problem solving (Benson, 1975). After explaining the rationale for "homework" as a way of reaching the goal of self-management, the patient is given an assignment for the week, which involves daily relaxation training. In addition to the instruction offered in the office, the patient is given to take home either a written handout of instructions on relaxation or a tape cassette made in the session of the procedure.

At the second session the instructor checks on progress with relaxation training. Any problems are noted, and the patient's own daily assessment of relaxation depth is examined by means of a series of analogue scales that the patient has been keeping. In this session patients are given additional practice in relaxation and are taught to be aware of and to use covert language such as spelling the word *relax* as they pay attention to their breathing.

In this session the first of the CPSI cards is now introduced. The first cards are selected on the basis of their low distress value and are not necessarily the problems currently facing the patient. The patient is shown the card posing the problem and also a similar card with the problem solved. The therapist works with the patient to generate possible strategies for solving that particular problem and ways to establish priorities among the various possible approaches. The therapist will suggest additional approaches to supplement those of the patient. Remember, this intervention was developed for a subpopulation of patients known to be poor copers, who are unable to generate many alternative approaches to problem solving and who overuse ineffective strategies.

The therapist again reiterates the purpose of the program as well as the training cards. Among these are (a) learning ways of solving a concern should something arise in the patient's life; (b) discovering that other people have problems similar to the patient's and what they do to solve them; (c) understand more about how thinking, feeling, and behaving are all interrelated; and (d) learning to approach problems in a step-by-step manner so as to prevent feeling overwhelmed.

Homework for the period between the second and third sessions involves more training in relaxation. This is tailored to the needs of individual patients on the basis of their skills and/or deficits in using the procedure.

The third session places a heavy focus on problem solving. The process of problem solving is reviewed (see Table 9-2), and a number of new training cards are introduced and worked with. At this point the therapist explores current personal problems with the patient and the approach is applied to these. For homework, the patient is encouraged to practice the approach on problems that are current or arise during the week. Patients also are instructed in how to evaluate the effectiveness of various approaches that they might apply to a given problem. Here the attempt is to encourage the awareness of

Table 9-2. Steps in Problem Solving

1. Clearly define the uppermost problem.
2. Recognize how you feel about the problem.
3. Relax and try not to think about a solution for a while.
4. Consider all possible solutions, even some "BAD" ones.
5. Try to imagine how other people might solve the problem.
6. Evaluate the pros and cons of each solution.
7. Arrange the various solutions into a listing, starting with the least desirable or least practical one.
8. Make a choice.
9. Briefly consider some favorable or positive aspects of the original problem. Can you think about it differently?

From: Sobel & Worden, 1980, with permission.

success as a graded outcome rather than the binary focus on success or failure. At the end of the third session patients are reminded of the four-session contract and asked to consider if this will be enough time or if they might need more. In our experience most people feel that four is sufficient. For those who request more, additional sessions are added—usually two.

During the fourth session the patient and therapist together evaluate the effectiveness of the approach in dealing with problems during the preceding week. Patients still using relaxation tapes are encouraged to practice without tapes. New sets of training cards are presented, and/or the approach is applied to the patient's current concerns. With many patients role playing is used in this session. The patient plays the therapist (and the therapist, the patient) and instructs the therapist-patient how to handle a specific simulated problem. This is useful not only for skill building, but it enables the therapist to spot any gaps in the patient's understanding of the process. The problem-solving steps are reviewed, and the patient is given a handout about these steps. The need for further sessions is evaluated, and if none is needed, the therapist terminates the formal sessions. If patients should run into future problems, they are always welcome to recontact the therapist.

The effectiveness of this approach to improve coping and to reduce emotional distress was evaluated in a 3-year study funded by the National Cancer Institute (CA Four hundred newly diagnosis patients with cancer from 5 primary tumor sites (breast, colon, lung, Hodgkin's disease, malignant melanoma, and gynecologic cancer) were screened at the time of diagnosis with an instrument developed to identify poorly coping patients (Worden, 1984). Patients identified as poor copers were randomly assigned to this short-term intervention. When compared with nonintervened controls, those receiving this cognitive intervention had lower distress levels and better coping resolutions than the group not receiving the treatment when both groups were assessed over time. The number of problems faced was no different for each group.

The intervention was not designed to reduce the number of problems but rather to improve problem resolution and with that to reduce emotional distress (Weisman & Worden, 1984).

Many cancer patients who are distressed believe that change is impossible, despair will persist, effort is futile, and a better outcome is beyond hope. Their morale is low because personal control is enfeebled. Self-esteem is often compromised because preexisting problems have been joined by feelings and thoughts of weakness, helplessness, and discouragement. The philosophy behind this cognitive intervention is that change is possible, that patients can be helped to take steps on their own, and that problems can be revised into manageable proportions. Therefore, we encourage the cancer counselor/therapist to function in the role of the guide and instructor and lead patients toward this end.

Acknowledgments

The author is grateful to Dr. Harry Sobel and other members of the Omega Project staff at the Massachusetts General Hospital for the development of this intervention. This research was funded by grants from the National Cancer Institute.

References

Benson, H. (1975). *The relaxation response.* New York: Morrow.
Janis, E., & Mann, L. (1977). *Decision-making.* New York: Free Press.
Michenbaum, D. (1977). *Cognitive behavior modification.* New York: Plenum Press.
Sobel, H. J., & Worden, J. W. (1979). The MMPI as a predictor of psychosocial adaptation to cancer. *Journal of Consulting and Clinical Psychology, 47,* 716–724.
Sobel, H. J., & Worden, J. W. (1980). *Helping cancer patients cope: A problem solving intervention program for health care professionals.* New York: Guilford Press.
Spivack, G., Platt, J., & Schure, M. (1976). *The problem-solving approach to adjustment.* San Francisco: Jossey-Bass.
Weisman, A. D. (1972). *On dying and denying.* New York: Behavioral Publications.
Weisman, A. D., & Worden, J. W. (1977). *Coping and vulnerability in cancer patients: A research report.* Boston: Massachusetts General Hospital.
Worden, J. W. (1984). Screening newly diagnosed cancer patients. *Journal of Psychosocial Oncology, 1,* 1–10.
Worden, J. W., & Weissmen, A. D. (1984). Preventive psychosocial intervention with newly diagnosed cancer patients. *General Hospital Psychiatry, 6,* 243–249.

Chapter 10

COGNITIVE APPROACHES TO MANAGEMENT OF THE TYPE A BEHAVIOR PATTERN

Julaine Kinchla

Studies of coronary heart disease (CHD) have repeatedly shown that men and women who exhibit the type A behavior pattern are at increased risk for premature disease (Blumenthal, Williams, Kong, Schanberg, & Thompson, 1978; Haynes, Feinleib, & Kannel, 1980; Rosenman, Brand, Jenkins, Friedman, Straus, & Wurm, 1975). The type A behavior pattern has been found to be associated with coronary atherosclerosis in at least four studies to date (Krantz, Sanmario, Selvester, & Matthews, 1979; Frank, Heller, Kornfeld, Sporn, & Weiss, 1978; Blumenthal et al., 1978; Zyzanski, Jenkins, Ryan, Flessas, & Everist, 1976). This chapter will discuss a cognitive approach to the clinical management of the type A pattern as an attempt to develop a framework for preventive and therapeutic interventions (Review Panel, 1981).

In her book *Type A Behavior Pattern*, Virginia Price (1982) presents an excellent review of the type A behavior pattern and a therapeutic approach based on cognitive social learning theory (Bandura, 1977). The present chapter expands on the cognitive approaches to the treatment of the type A pattern, drawing on the wealth of clinical methods developed by cognitive behavior therapists, most notably Aaron T. Beck and David D. Burns. Cognitive interventions for many of the components that will be discussed evolved in the context of developing effective treatment for depression and other emotional disorders. They also appear to be quite promising approaches for altering core dysfunctional beliefs associated with this type A pattern.

> From a clinical point of view, efforts to reduce the Type A behavior pattern have generally not been very effective. At best, these efforts seem to result in only temporary change. Persons' beliefs about themselves and their

actions appear to get in the way of sustained behavior change. It seems apparent that the behavior pattern is an outgrowth of the way Type As *view* themselves and the world, and that these views need to be examined and, if possible, changed if permanent reduction in Type A behavior is to be effected. (Price, 1982, p. 65)

The approach described here should be compatible with most cognitive/ affective/behavioral therapies, both group and individual. The rest of this paper consists of two main parts: First, ways in which normal cognitive strategies are misused in the type A pattern; and second, ways in which cognitive therapy can be applied to basic features of type A behavior.

MISUSED COGNITIVE STRATEGIES IN THE TYPE A PATTERN

It is beyond the scope of this discussion to provide a review of cognitive therapy, theory, and practice. [For more detailed discussion the reader is referred to the text by Beck, Rush, Shaw, & Emery (1979) and to *Feeling Good* (Burns, 1980a)]. There are however, some cognitive strategies that appear to to be misused in the type A pattern so frequently that they deserve special attention.

All-or-Nothing Thinking

This refers to the tendency to evaluate things in absolutistic or dichotomous categories (Burns, 1980a; Beck et al., 1979) as either black or white, win or lose, success or fail, aggressor or victim. This type of thinking is simplistic and may have appeal because it appears efficient, but it overlooks the dimensional aspects of most events—shades of gray do not exist.

Participants in the Recurrent Coronary Prevention Project "often fear that if they reduce their fast-paced approach to life, they will become slothful. They are afraid that if they learn how to concentrate their attention on just one thing at a time, they will no longer be able to 'polyphase' (i.e. think about or do more than one thing at a time). They express concern that if they say 'no' to an opportunity because of too many commitments, they will never get another opportunity" (Price, 1982, p. 178).

Overly Selective Attention

This refers to a tendency to overfocus and overcontrol one's attention, directing it toward select aspects of environmental information. Type A's appear to appraise and encode information concerning their liabilities and failures, selectively, whereas type B's appear to choose information revealing their positive qualities (Lifshitz & Zeichner, 1983). The process of selectively abstracting negative information may be related to the strategy of identifying areas that need improvement and may facilitate the subsequent performance of type A behaviors.

Another way that selective attention helps maintain type A behaviors is in what may be considered a constriction of attention—that is, focusing on a narrow band of information, selectively excluding other aspects. This is similar to "denial" and often may be at critical levels in type A patients (Hackett & Cassem, 1976). Matthews and Brunson (1979) found that type A's suppress all stimuli that are peripheral to the main task they are trying to accomplish. It has been speculated that this leads them to be unaware of the early symptoms and warning signs of CHD. Another consequence of restricting attention to a narrow-band width of information is that individuals appear concrete. Type A's need to have their attention focused on other, broader meanings; they do not provide these meanings spontaneously. Such concreteness is not necessarily a function of ability or capacity but may be due to attentional processes.

Personalization

This is a tendency consistently to exaggerate one's own importance, beyond normal egocentricity. This is often accompanied by making judgments from an egocentric frame of reference, such as attributing one's own views to others and not questioning whether they have their own frames of reference, or seeing oneself as the central figure around which all others revolve. This type of extreme egocentricity is described in a chapter by Beck on "Cognitive Approaches to Stress" (Beck, 1984). "He views all events as though he were the central character in a drama; the behavior of all other characters has meaning only insofar as he relates it to his own 'vital interests'. He personalizes events that are essentially impersonal and perceives confrontations and challenges when others are conducting their own lives—oblivious of him" (Beck, 1984, p. 352).

Attributions of Causality

Beliefs concerning why things happen are referred to as causal attributions and have been found to have a profound effect on well-being (Kelley, 1967). It has been postulated that type A's make different attributions about their accomplishments than Type B's. Type A's appear inclined to attribute their success to effort, to trying hard. Thus, when they fail, they are likely to make the attribution that they didn't try hard enough and will fault themselves for not trying harder (Margolis, McLeroy, Runyan, & Kaplan, 1983). Type B's, on the other hand, appear disposed to attribute at least some of their skills to ability and to use outcomes to help develop a somewhat realistic assessment of this ability. They demonstrate an acceptance of the notion of limited capacity and appear more likely to alter standards according to outcomes (Burman, Pennebaker, & Glass, 1975; Glass 1977; Snow, 1978).

Features of Type A Behavior and Cognitive Therapy

Seven components or features of the type A pattern that appear to have the most overlap with issues commonly dealt with in cognitive therapy are the following:

1. Time urgency
2. Perfectionism
3. Achievement striving
4. Low self-esteem
5. Excessive job involvement
6. Hostility
7. Depression

(For a more complete description of components of the type A behavior pattern see Price, 1982, chapter 5). Cognitive/affective/behavioral interventions will be discussed for each of these components.

Time Urgency

Time urgency is the drive to do far too many things in far too little time. Burman et al. (1975) found that type A's fail to alter response rate and work just as hard whether or not a deadline is externally imposed, whereas type B's regulate the work rate depending on the prevailing situation. Consequently, type A individuals often have a number of time-related attitudes that they may be unaware of but that are useful to explore; e.g., time is their enemy or, at least an adversary; time is precious and steps must be taken to conserve it and protect it as much as possible, etc. While they are working on a task, there is a tendency to monitor the time dimension continually, switching attention to it countless times. However, as much of an enemy as time can become to such individuals, it appears to be a love-hate relationship—although they feel besieged by time pressure, they impose deadlines on themselves. This self-defeating time urgency offers a promising place to begin intervention.

A first step is to encourage clients to keep records of what they do throughout the day, using the Daily Activity Schedule (Beck et al., 1979). Clients not only can log their activity but rate them on two different dimensions, mastery and pleasure. One benefit of this is to help bring into awareness that they are trying to do too much in too little time. After analyzing the raw data and the patterns from the Daily Activity Schedule the client can be encouraged to restructure the activities in a more realistic way. This requires helping individuals prioritize. If an individual can recognize that choices must be made, the mastery-pleasure ratings may help guide those choices. Some activities that are low in both mastery and pleasure may be candidates for the bottom of the list; other activities high in pleasure or mastery may be considered to have a higher priority. Sometimes this exercise unveils the finding that an individual is not deriving much satisfaction from any of the many things he is struggling to get done each day. When an individual has too many activities that are unrewarding, developing pleasureful activities and pleasuring skills may become a focus of the therapy for a period. Some activities may have a high priority because of an appropriate sense of duty or commitment, and some things that are frustrating and unrewarding for a time may bear fruit later on. It also may be important to do things for others that may not necessarily be all that rewarding at the time. Friedman (Friedman, Rhoresen, & Gill, 1981) also recommends individuals ask themselves which of their activities will have lasting value, such that they would still be important in 6 months. Clients should be encouraged to prioritize their daily activities with the long- and short-term goals and values in mind. There should be a balance of work and relaxation, productivity and play, giving and getting. Although type A's tend to pride themselves on their organizational abilities, the problem is usually that they have never stopped to reflect on what it is they're organizing. Training them to be more reflective can help them to develop a more meaningful value system.

Some occupations are more likely than others to present time deadline demands that are beyond the individual's control. Examples would include meeting advertising or journalism deadlines, clerical work for a demanding boss, law, media work, and blue-collar occupations with inflexible time schedules. Where this is a feature of an individual's situation, teaching him/her methods to help cope with demands and pressures more effectively and with less stress can be helpful.

Training them to relax is one way to help clients deal with time urgency. Type A's often don't give themselves permission to relax until they are exhausted. Relaxation training can be taught in the first few sessions (e.g., Benson, 1975; Beck, 1984). A modified progressive relaxation procedure that incorporates imagery techniques can be expanded to include positive coping imagery for time urgency. For example, after one or two tension-release cycles with the various muscle groups, the client can be instructed to think about a particular relaxing scene. One is then asked to imagine a stressful situation in which he/she experiences time pressure. One is then guided to restructure this scene, seeing oneself proceeding calmly and masterfully, identifying the maladaptive strategy being employed, constructing problem-solving alternatives, and correcting erroneous cognitions. Another tension-release cycle may follow the positive coping imagery to induce deeper relaxation. Combining both cognitive and behavioral activities in the relaxation intervention appears to enhance its effectiveness (P. LaRiccia, November 1983, *personal communication*).

Working on communication skills is appropriate, especially where interpersonal conflict, such as an overly demanding boss, is an issue (See, for example, Lange & Jakubowski, 1976). Teaching clients to understand that there are important differences between assertiveness and aggression and that they have the right to express their needs but not the right to get what they want can be helpful educational steps. Providing opportunities to role-play appropriate assertive behavior helps develop their skills. Negative expectations that occur during the role play can be explored and discussed. The perception that being assertive is a viable problem-solving alternative can help them feel less angry or helpless when confronted by job demands.

The "tic-toc" technique (Burns, 1980a, p. 100–103) is useful for helping identify "task-interfering cognitions" and developing more productive "task-orienting cognitions." The time-urgent pattern often involves many distracting throughts about time that clients may be aware of. This technique helps them identify how they're keeping themselves under pressure. They can learn to concentrate better on the task at hand, not on time.

As we shall see in a later section, it's not the job characteristics alone that determine whether a position is stressful; one's attitudes can also be important. For example, if being late is interpreted as a sign of failure, than you will feel miserable and unhappy if you're held up in traffic getting to an appointment. However, if you have the expectation that try as you will events beyond your control will sometimes conspire to make you late, then when you're held up in traffic you can tell yourself this is just one of those times. One might feel mildly unhappy but not distressed, aggravated, and pressured. Helping individuals identify and modify potentially dysfunctional attitudes also can be a part of the treatment.

Perfectionism

Typically, the type A individual expects a high performance level, not only of himself, but also of those around him. This may produce an obsessive attention to details, whether they are important or not. Price (1982) notes that getting these individuals to set lower performance standards is often quite difficult because such standards are not perceived of as worth working for. An example from a recent type A client helps illustrate the meaning he assigns to a lower standard. This person saw his performance as falling into two categories—either all A's or failure—and was aware of having used this rule since seventh grade. To him, therefore, working to a lower standard simply meant failure; he was convinced he had to achieve top marks and viewed any other outcome as equivalent to flunking out.

In an article on *Reflections on Perfection,* Asher Pacht (1984) puts into perspective the problem of developing an attainable therapeutic "goal is not 180 degrees of change. For the vast majority of patients, 20 to 30 degrees of change is far more than enough. The message must be clear—we seek acceptance of 'imperfection' as a goal rather than the achievement of perfection" (p. 389). It is well to remind clients of this moderation. While "some imperfection is good, more imperfection is not necessarily better" (Pacht, 1984, p. 386). With their all-or-nothing thinking tendencies they will automatically equate any mistake or imperfection with total failure. This distinction is also made by Burns.

> I want to make clear what I mean by perfectionism. I do *not* mean the healthy pursuit of excellence by men and women who take genuine pleasure in striving to meet high standards. Without concern for quality, life would seem shallow and true accomplishments would be rare. The perfectionists I am talking about are those whose standards are high beyond reach or reason, people who strain compulsively and unremittingly toward impossible goals and who measure their own worth entirely in terms of productivity and accomplishtment. (Burns, 1980b, p. 34).

In a chapter in *Feeling Good*, "Dare to Be Average!—Ways to Overcome Perfectionism," Burns (1980a) describes several clinical techniques which can be helpful in modifying perfectionism. Assigning such reading is a good first step in educating a client about perfectionism. In a cost/benefit analysis of this problem, the individual is encouraged to identify the belief of "rules" he/she is using and then list the advantages and disadvantages of employing each rule. He/she can be reminded that almost every rule has disadvantages as well as advantages. Our task as intelligent decision makers is not to follow rules that lead only to good things and no bad things but to consider gains relative to costs, that is, determine a cost-benefit ratio for any rule or belief. This useful exercise helps focus on the consequences of an attitude.

Questioning clients about perfectionistic rituals and their consequences helps them become aware of thought patterns that are more or less automatic. Such recognition sets the stage for attitude change. However, it is important to encourage the client to experiment with new behaviors to make the reconstructive effort complete. Any of the techniques recommended in the *Dare to be Average* chapter are helpful in engaging the client in "collaborative empiricism" (Beck, 1979) to test the assumptions that are part of the old thinking style. Some minor facet of everyday work experience is often a good place to start. For example, a woman who ran a highly successful arts program for a public school system had the habit of making 10 Xerox copies of everything. She was convinced she wouldn't be adequately prepared for requests with fewer than 10 copies, but she was annoyed at how much time it took her to perform this task every time she went to file something. We designed an experiment in which she would only make two Xerox copies, and we would then test the assumption that she wouldn't be prepared to meet the demands for those copies. The experiment was designed to run for 1 week only, but she was so pleased with how the new system worked that she voluntarily decided to keep it. A few sessions later she had the revelation that not only did she not need 10 copies, she didn't even need 2—one copy would suffice quite nicely! Although it was a minor change, this success greatly increased her confidence in making other changes.

Achievement Striving

Achievement striving refers to an incessant struggle to obtain accomplishments, power, status, material goods, or success, often against opposing forces. It is the *struggle* to achieve which often seems the most characteristic aspect of the type A's daily routine. Tasks are pursued and additional projects taken on in a nonreflective way, often toward poorly defined goals. This syndrome seems to involve the assumption that it is important to stay busy at all costs, even if it means ignoring physical symptoms.

Price (1982) discusses the role selective attention may play in suppressing awareness of personal limitations. "A person who is excessively reliant for a sense of well-being on accomplishing a lot and on other persons' recognition of his accomplishments cannot afford to notice anything that might disrupt his ability to continue to perform at full capacity" (p. 182–183). If a person were to note the cost in terms of physical exhaustion, mental fatigue, deterioration in personal relationships, and lack of personal satisfaction he/she might not be able to persist long enough in the effort to succeed in achieving his/her excessively high goals. Another way of understanding this is as denial in the service of maintaining the struggle. Weissman and Hackett (1961) define denial as "the conscious or unconscious repudiation of part or all of the available meaning of an event to allay fear, anxiety, or other unpleasant affects." Hackett and Cassem (1976) reported 68 percent of postinfarction patients used major or moderate levels of denial.

There are many useful techniques for helping individuals recognize information that is outside their awareness, i.e., which they are denying. Table 10-1, adapted from Price's book (1982), is one such tool. It is useful for focusing on the consequences of behavior, which type A's have learned so well to deny. It helps provide the client with information as well as a useful cognitive task, that of looking for consequences. When future consequences again appear to be minimized and denied, this can be pointed out and discussed using a similar model.

Another relevant activity is the use of pleasure-predicting techniques. One form this might take is provided in Table 10-2 and is discussed in more detail in *Feeling Good* (Burns, 1981, p. 96). Its value is twofold: first, it is a self-help exercise that gives individuals a structured way to work on this problem on their own; and second, it focuses attention on an attribute of their activity that they often ignore: how much they enjoy what they're doing. Paying attention to what it feels like to be involved in what they are doing is often missing information to a type A; this has been described as having a product-versus-process orientatin (Price, 1982). This technique can help shift attention from the product to focus more on the process of the activity.

Changing the type A pattern is also accomplished by the basic cognitive therapy techniques of helping the individual explore the meaning system he/she is using, uncovering silent assumptions, and identifying attitudes concerning achievement and self-esteem. Therapists' questions concerning history

Table 10-1. Summary of the Probable Consequences of the Type A Behavior Pattern

Factor		Consequences
Environmental Social/interpersonal	Positive	Recognition, social approval
	Negative	Interpersonal conflict and tension
		Tendency not to have close relationships with spouse, children, colleagues, or others
Material	Positive	Money
		Material goods
	Negative	
Personal	Positive	Self-pride
Cognitive	Negative	Inability to concentrate
		Worry
		Excess reliance on other's approval
		Chronic lack of satisfaction
		Hypervigilance
Physiological	Positive	Surge of norepinephrine gives sense of abundant energy
	Negative	Overactivation of sympathetic nervous system, including increased heart rate and increased blood pressure
		Possible addition to excess norepinephrine
		Increased cholesterol and triglyceride levels
		Reduced blood coagulation time
		Increased sludging
		Muscular tension

Adapted from Price, 1982, p. 124.

can be helpful here, often assisting individuals in identifying their learning history with regard to achievement and self worth. Exploration of the deep structure of belief systems probably will occur in the later phases of therapy.

A twenty-eight-year-old woman was compulsively filling her days with myriad tasks and obligations, always feeling "pressured." She was frequently irritable and angry, falling into bed at night exhausted, suffering from tension headaches and depression. She had all the signs of the type A pattern. Early months of therapy focused on depression, recognizing anger, assertiveness training, and time urgency. It was not until the ninth or tenth month that she was able to pinpoint the assumption she was using: because she dropped out of college she was a failure and she would not be a worthwhile person until she obtained her college degree. Recognition of this attitude concerning achievement and of how unrealistic it was in light of her present situation and values was a major turning point for her.

Low Self-Esteem

Type A's appear to believe that people who achieve a lot are somehow better than others. They seem to have bought the equation "worth equals achievement" and have come to base their self-esteem on proving their worth.

Table 10-2. Pleasure Predicting Sheet

Activity Schedule Activities with a Potential for Pleasure or Personal Growth	Companion (If alone, specify self)	Predicted (0–100) (record this before each activity)	Satisfaction Actual (0–100) (record this after each activity)

In a chapter entitled "Your Work Is Not Your Worth," Burns identifies the type A view. "You...believe it is basically *true* that people who are superachievers are more worthwhile—the big shots seem 'special' in some way. You may be convinced that true happiness, as well as the respect of others, comes primarily from achievement" (1980a, p. 291).

One implication of this belief is that one's worth fluctuates with one's accomplishments. That is to say, self-worth goes up and down with one's achievements and with approval from others. It is instructive to examine what some possible motivational functions of this fluctuation are. Often individuals caught up in this pursuit readily point out the rewarding functions of hard work and achievement (Price, 1982). What may be overlooked, however, is that these individuals are also working for negative reinforcement. In reinforcement theory terms (Skinner, 1953) negative reinforcement is associated with a response that avoids or terminates an aversive stimulus. When approval is not forthcoming, it leads to a precipitous drop in self-worth; when circumstances conspire to prevent one from accomplishing what was planned, it is interpreted as a sign of failure, and self-worth plummets. Such low levels of self-esteem may function as aversive states that individuals work to avoid. Thus, much of their effort may be understood as avoidance behavior, and it is not surprising to observe that their behavior often takes the rigid, stereotyped form that characterizes animals working to avoid shock. However, like the animal that persists on pressing the lever long after the shock has been turned off, these individuals may maintain their high rate long after the disastrous consequences of nonachievement have stopped.

Whereas we hypothesize that type A's often experience low self-esteem, other research appears, on the surface, to contradict this view. Recent studies report a high degree of self-involvement in type A individuals, where self-involvement refers to interest and focus on the self in terms of physical, personal, material, and interpersonal properties (Scherwitz, McKelvain, Laman, Patterson, Dutton, Lysim, Lester, Kraft, Rochelle, & Leachman, 1983). In the MRFIT study the number of self-references (i.e., statements in which they used *I*, *me*, *my*, or *mine*) correlated positively with the number of previous myocardial infarctions, the extent of CHD, and with type A. In this study, a high sense of self-efficacy and a tendency toward self-aggrandizement was a consistent psychological correlate of the manifestations of CHD (Scherwitz et al., 1983).

The psychological pattern associated with heart disease thus appears to pose a paradox between the issues of low self-esteem and high self-involvement (Price, 1982; Dunbar, 1943). More research and clarification are needed to explore this hypothesis that the chronic self preoccupation type A's present with does not stem from a good sense of self-adequacy; the self-involvement observed is a function of poor self-esteem. Or as one forty-year-old type A man states this thesis: "Because I'm inadequate, the problems I encounter are of my making. As I feel more adequate, I don't blame myself for my problems."

A cost/benefit analysis is one useful method for helping an individual explore the value of using the rule that they have to prove their worth to others by working for it. This idea might have particular appeal to organizational type A's because it is an approach they pride themselves on using in their company or business. It may require a few sessions to work out all the advantages and disadvantages of proving your worth by your work. Often, in the process of doing this, new ideas are introduced that the person will want to examine before completing the list. This activity is valuable in helping to identify more clearly all of the consequences of the belief.

Sometimes an individual may not complete the cost/benefit analysis before deciding the strategy of proving his worth to shore up low self-esteem is not one that he wants to continue. It is an important step of recognition for a person to say "It's my low self-worth that's the problem. I wouldn't have to do all this if I felt better about myself." Many individuals are not able to make this step early in treatment. Thus, the goal of bringing the low self-esteem into awareness may be considered an advanced stage of learning and best achieved by gradual steps. However, whether it takes a short time or a long time, helping guide the individual to become aware of a poor self-image brings them to the point where he/she can then begin to process this.

For instance, they can then begin to question why being rejected or criticized is such a feared outcome and can begin to assess realistically the consequences of such an event. Very often individuals recognize that disapproval from others does not constitute the feared event they had fantasized, and further that others' disapproval has little relation to their self-esteem. A quite simple but useful cognitive model is the idea that self-esteem can be thought of as a pie, in which the various prospective sources of self-esteem are thought of as slices. Most people seem to make up their self-esteem from several sources: work, relationships with others, and an unconditional sense of self-worth, for instance. Sometimes people devote almost the whole pie to achievement and may have only a tiny slice derived from an unconditional sense of self-worth. One goal of therapy might be to help them redress this disproportion so that there is a better balance from all the sources of self-esteem. In this way it is possible to make explicit that developing a sense of adequacy, security and worth that is unearned is a valid task, one that is at the very core of the type A pattern.

Excessive Work Involvement

The relation between occupational stress and heart disease has been the focus of considerable research. The early occupational health literature suggested there was an association between work environment variables and CHD and focused on occupational factors that were thought to carry CHD risk (Cooper & Marshall, 1978). Air traffic controllers were found to have a greater incidence of hypertension than other occupational groups (Rose, Jenkins, & Hunt, 1978). However, similar findings were not made in a study by Reynolds

(1974) with employees who were responsible for the first moon rocket launch. Inconsistencies such as this led investigators to question the assumption that job-related variables were correlated with the development of CHD in a simple way, and they began to examine the manner in which personal characteristics interacted with work environment. Cooper and Marshall (1978) developed a person-environment fit concept with proposed coping behaviors, maladaptive behaviors, and CHD were influenced by the interaction between environmental stressors and worker characteristics.

In their initial conceptualization of the type A pattern, Friedman and Rosenman (1974) proposed that the pattern emerged when an individual encounters an environmental challenge. Subsequent research has confirmed that differences between type A's and type B's are more consistently observed in response to challenging, rather than nonchallenging tasks (Dembroski, Macdougall, Herd, & Shields, 1979; Egerem, Sniderman & Roggelin, 1982; Jennings & Choi, 1981; Rhodewalt, Hays, Chemens, Wysocki, 1984; Schlegel, Wellwood, Copps, Gruchow, & Sharratt, 1980). Thus, the current view is that susceptible individuals encounter job situations that elicit type A behavior, and consequently, higher coronary risk. Karasek and his colleagues (1981) have proposed a model in which two types of job characteristics, job demands, and job decision latitude interact to produce increased CHD risk. Their study of a large random sample of working Swedish men showed situations that combined a hectic and psychologically demanding job with low personal freedom were associated with highest CHD symptoms and signs. This research would seem to suggest the hypothesis that type A's who are predisposed to perceive environmental events as challenges to their self-esteem may be particularly reactive in job situations where high performance demands are coupled with low decision latitude and low personal freedom.

In terms of interventions, this appears to be one context in which it is helpful to work on personalization, to help correct the tendency for individuals to attribute too much of the outcome to factors they can control. A more accurate attribution might be to focus attention on the things within their ability to control and assign external factors the responsibility for the rest. Another goal is to get type A's to recognize and to shift the unusually low challenge-detection threshold they appear to have. Occasionally, job demands are so severe and a sense of time urgency is so overdeveloped that restructuring may not bring about a better adjustment. It may be worthwhile to consider other job alternatives. Working on job involvement may be extremely difficult early in treatment since identity can be such a major part of an individual's self-esteem. Having had an opportunity to establish a somewhat successful track record on other tasks may be essential to prepare for the hard work of questioning the attachment to work.

It may help to consider how much an individual is invested in the system. Frequently there is overinvestment in it, what Beck refers to as "personalizing the system" (Woolfolk & Lehrer, 1984, p. 301) When an individual overidentifies with his/her system, the means often become more important than the end. Cognitive techniques such as identifying automatic thoughts, recognizing and correcting the inappropriate use of cognitive strategies and identifying underlying assumptions are useful ways to alter these job-related problems.

Hostility

Anger, hostility, and competitive, aggressive behaviors are prime characteristics of the type A pattern (Friedman & Rosenman, 1974; Williams, Haney, Lee, Kong, Blumenthal, & Whalen, 1980). Indeed, Friedman (1981) and Williams et al. (1980) believe this may form its core characteristic. Williams and colleagues (1980) found that the hostility scale of the MMPI was associated with clinically significant CHD. Patients in all groups scoring higher than 10 on the Hostility Scale showed a 70 percent rate of significant disease, whereas only 48 percent of those scoring below 10 had a significant occlusion. Shekelle, Gale, and Ostfeld (1983) obtained results that support these findings. Williams (1980) hypothesizes that the most toxic component of the type A pattern may be hostility. As evidence appears to be accumulating that anger plays a central part in this pattern, it raises the possibility that none of the above features contributes to CHD without the anger component.

Hostility may present differently in different individuals. In many the emotional anger may be missing. Instead what can be said to be present is hostility in the form of physiological activity. This arousal may include sympathetic activation with discharge of norepineprhine, vascular changes, and increased heart rate. (For a more detailed discussion of this, see Price, 1982, chapter 9). While type A's appear to be hyperreactive (Krantz & Durel, 1982) to specific situational stimuli, they may not label this physiological reactivity as anger. When questioned, they may deny anger but are often able to categorize the feelings as "aggression." Other emotional labels they may identify are irritation, impatience, frustration, resentment, and vengeance.

The type of stimulus-response contingency most frequently associated with this arousal involves the person making a *quick* response to a *small* and *unexpected* situation (Powell, 1983). This description helps clarify three important characteristics of this maladaptive arousal:

1. Type A's may handle big problems well; it's the small things at which they may be dysfunctional. Since each of us encounters a large number of small obstacles each day, it is the chronicity of these events that are the problem.
2. Type A's have been characterized as striving for control (Glass, 1977); unexpected events may be challenges to that control and therefore particularly arousing. Although they may be good at dealing with planned events, type A's may have a difficult time dealing with uncertainty.

3. Finally, the quickness of their response appears to be a dysfunctional part of this hyperactivity. Their gestures and speech may be noticeably accelerated and they appear to believe that they are expected to act quickly.

The belief system of a type A plays an important role in maintaining the hostile, competitive behavioral style. One set of beliefs centers around expectations that others, and not they, should change (Powell, 1983). Type A's are usually very good at working to change their environment and may automatically externalize; i.e., their wife shouldn't take so long, the waiter should be more attentive, or their secretary should be more precise. It is very hard to get them to see it is their own attitudes that are important. Another set of attitudes are concerns that others will be nasty, that the world is not a nice place, that one cannot depend on people to be nice (Williams et al., 1980). Given the potentially critical role chronic anger arousal may play in the establishment of coronary artery disease, it seems particularly important to modify aggression in the type A individual.

One obvious strategy is to teach clients to become aware of their physiological arousal—to keep records of when it happens, to describe what their sensations are, to try to scale it so they acquire some notion of intensity, and to notice how long it lasts. These are valid ways of helping focus attention on the internal information they otherwise ignore. One advantage of a group setting is that gestures one is unaware of (or is systematically denying) can be pointed out by others who are also struggling with this problem; however, a therapist can also give such feedback. They can be encouraged to focus on their annoyance or resentment and give themselves permission to experience these feelings. However arrived at, the process of becoming aware, of paying attention to one's internal arousal, is a novel strategy for the type A.

Another method is educating the patient regarding anger and its uses. Since type A's are often all-or-none thinkers, it is important they not make the simplistic assumption that all anger is bad. It may be helpful to discuss some principles of assertiveness to help them conceptualize a middle-of-the-road alternative to aggression versus being a wimp. It is useful to present the idea from sports psychology that there is an ideal level of arousal for most tasks. Too much arousal can be as deleterious to performance as too little (Kiester, 1984a). It would be nice if they could train themselves to control their arousal so it is typically at the point where ability is maximal. Olympic athletes, pro football wide receivers, and tennis champions can function as convincing role models for demonstrating the value of cognitive rehearsal and positive coping imagery in controlling emotional overarousal (see, for example, Kiester, 1984b).

Another helpful approach is to learn to identify the cognitions that occur when one finds oneself aroused. These often are negtive thoughts such as "This is unfair," "You can't depend on people to do things right," "He's a nasty person," Ellis and Harper (1975) identify irrational ideas frequently associated with anger, as well as steps for challenging and answering the faulty thinking involved. Teaching constructive ways to answer irrational statements is a good problem-solving alternative. This approach can be combined with progressive relaxation to help reduce the physiological arousal. Cognitive rehearsal guiding them to visualize themselves handling the situation in a calm, controlled way can be incorporated in the relaxation training. Working on all these strategies usually takes several sessions, and may take many.

As knowledge increases of the variety of situations and of the types of cognitions associated with arousal, it becomes possible to identify and modify some of the underlying expectations. For example, the attitudes that others should do things my way, or I should get what I want can be replaced with the attitude that this is an unfair world, a more functional alternative. The underlying expectation that others should change is also important to question. The ultimate goal is to get them to recognize that it is their own attitudes that are important and that one cannot demand that the world adjust to one's needs.

Depression

Depression refers to feeling sad, blue, down in the dumps, or low, with loss of interest or pleasure in usual activities. The idea that type A pattern involves depression is an interesting and somewhat new hypothesis (Price, 1982). Although evidence that depression is a component of the type A pattern is lacking, there are some interesting connections. Several of the cognitions and beliefs that have been identified are typical of the thinking patterns observed in depressives—for example, the notion that one is not viewed as being worth very much (Beck et al., 1979). A common finding during recovery following a heart attack is that 2 to 3 days after admission many cardiac patients become depressed (Wishnie, Hackett, & Cassem, 1971). Some of the signs are vegetative, such as sleep disturbance and fatigue; however, other aspects of depression are also present, such as sadness, feelings of extreme gratefulness, and tearfulness. Price has speculated that in certain type A individuals depression may be more common than in others, i.e., perhaps women are more likely to present with depression than men. In some individuals feelings of low self-esteem and of not being appreciated may be more likely to lead to depression; in others anger arousal may occur. It would be important to identify the beliefs that differentiate between individuals who tend to get depressed versus those in whom any angry state is more likely.

One of the striking clinical features of these individuals is the consistency with which they report having shaped beliefs about achievement and self-esteem in childhood and adolescence. Although data to document this impression are somewhat scarce, recently Shekelle et al. (1983) found the hostility scale (HO) of the MMPI to be positively associated with 20-year mortality from CHD. This is strongly suggestive that onset of this pattern, at least as it relates to anger, is detectable at least 20 years earlier. Exactly which aspects of earlier stages of development are important here remain to be searched out. One likely candidate would seem to be parental interactions and the way in which beliefs may have been developed and maintained in the parent-child relationships. Anecdotally, it seems that a large number of type A individuals report a driving parent, either mother or father, who attached recognition to accomplishment in some way. It is not hard to envision the result of belieivng that one has to work for one's worth and the conditioned association that may have evolved between such depressive cognitions and achievement striving.

Obstacles to accomplishment, such as illness, exhaustion, confinement, and the like are especially likely to be a problem for type A's since they are not able to maintain their hard-driving efforts to prove themselves worthy of high esteem. It seems likely depression is much more ego-dystonic to the type A than is the superachieving or aggressive state. Nevertheless, when it occurs, it can be a therapeutically useful opportunity because in this state it is possible to access cognitions that are unavailable other times, particularly statements that reveal the degree to which negative self-appraisal and feelings of worthlessness are at the core of the self-system. To type A individuals depression represents the failure of the strategies they have evolved to cope with the feeling that they are unloved and unlovable. Working on the depression provides an opportunity to evolve more positive, adaptive, and less health-threatening strategies for maintaining self-esteem than those they have used in the past.

One advantage of accurately identifying the depressive components of this pattern is that very effective tehcniques have been developed for the treatment of depression (see, for example, Beck et al., 1979; Burns, 1980a). Success at developing self-control over depression can encourage a type A to tackle regulation of some of the other areas of the pattern that are also dysfunctional.

It is sometimes difficult to get cardiac patients to recognize their type A risk factor and take steps to alter this. However, it would apper to be the case that even type A's will consider therapy when depressed and appear willing to come for help to get relief from this problem. Thus, therapists should pay close attention to their depressed patients and be alert for the possibility that the type A behavior pattern also should be diagnosed. History is quite relevant in making this determination, especially if there are signs or symptoms of coronary artery disease, myocardial infarction, or coronary artery bypass surgery. The Jenkins Activity Survey (JAS) is a questionnaire that has been found to be predictive of initial and recurrent CHD events (Jenkins, Zyzanski, & Rosenman, 1976) and is a useful tool for assessing the pattern. Usually when presented with the appropriate information and educated concerning this type A pattern, clients will accept a treatment plan that includes modifying this risk factor.

The following case history indicates how such a treatment plan evolved in the case of a depressed thirty-nine-year-old man. He was a self-employed, successful career consultant, divorced 1 year earlier, with two teenage children. About 6 months after his divorce he lost his drive to keep working as hard as he had before and shortly thereafter began to feel depressed. His Beck Depression Inventory at the first session was 23, but there were indications he was in significantly more distress than the score indicated.

Initially, treatment emphasized cognitive therapy techniques for depression. His depression began to improve, but the thought records he had kept provided evidence of many type A cognitions. His history indicated he'd established himself as an early success in his field and had often worked long hours, e.g., 70 hours a week over a 10-year period. In addition, he'd been diagnosed as having signs of coronary artery disease at age thirty-five. The Jenkins Activity Survey was administered to assess the pattern in a standardized way.

When his scores were found to be quite high, he was educated concerning the type A pattern and the rationale for a cognitive/behavioral approach to the problem. Steps in treatment included progressive relaxation training and keeping daily stress records, as well as identifying cognitions associated with his reactions. He became aware for the first time how often he was annoyed, irritated, frustrated, or angry and how consistently this was associated with somatic arousal. Cognitive coping was rehearsed along with relaxation techniques and these were helpful in developing some control over the arousal. As the patterns of underlying beliefs and expectations were explored, he began to search for where this pattern had come from. It seemed clearly related to a family system that featured a strong, domineering, workaholic mother and a passive, compliant father who was usually swept along in his wife's ambitions. As the oldest son, the client was put in charge of caring for his younger siblings; he clearly remembered growing up with the conviction that he was not loved and his only value to his parents lay in helping them care for the other children. Family communications seemed to center around work and what it got you, and shouldering obligations in a responsible way. As these underlying attitudes were brought into awareness he was able to explore them in the context of his present needs and situation. He gradually began to exchange the competitive model for one based on cooperation; he learned to interact with his children, girlfriend, and colleagues assertively rather than aggressively and benefited from the more satisfying and productive relationships this led to. He was able to counter the excessive pressures he put on himself to be a success and scale down his work involvement to a more manageable level.

A final comment concerning the diversity of the type A population seems in order. Every individual is different and, thus, not all features and interventions mentioned will be relevant in each case. One individual may have great trouble with time pressure but not have overinvolvement in work. Strong achievement beliefs in one person may be accompanied by a tendency toward self-aggrandizement and anger; the same beliefs in another may be paired with ready knowledge of low self-esteem and depression. Since different features predominate in different individuals, it is important to explore the data base with the client to develop a meaningful treatment plan.

Acknowledgment

The author wishes to express her gratitude to Theodore Weiss, M.D., who provided guidance, support, and encouragement, and who gave her the opportunity to get to know the heart patient.

References

Bandura, A. (1977). *Social learning theory.* Englewood Cliffs, NJ: Prentice Hall.
Beck, A. T. (1984). Cognitive approaches to stress. In *Principles and practice of stress management,* R. L. Woolfolk & P. M. Lehrer (Eds.), (pp. 255–305). New York: Guilford Press.
Beck, A. T., Rush, A. J., Shaw, B. F., & Emery, G. (1979). *Cognitive therapy of depression.* New York: Guilford Press.
Benson, H. (1975). *The relaxation response.* New York: William Morrow.
Blumenthal, J. A., Williams, R. B., Jr., Kong, Y. H., Schanberg, S. M., & Thompson, L. W. (1978). Type A behavior patterns and coronary atherosclerosis. *Circulation, 58,* 634–639.
Burman, M. A., Pennebaker, J. W., & Glass, D. C. (1975). Time consciousness, achievement striving and the type A coronary prone behavior pattern. *Journal of Abnormal Psychology, 84,* 76–79.
Burns, D. D. (1980a). *Feeling good: The new mood therapy.* New York: William Morrow.
Burns, D. D. (November, 1980b). The perfectionist's script for self-defeat. *Psychology Today,* 34–52.
Cassem, N. H., & Hackett, T. P. (1971). Psychiatric consultation in a coronary care unit. *Annuals of Internal Medicine, 75,* 9–14.
Cooper, C. L., & Marshall, J. (1978). Sources of managerial and white-collar stress. In *Stress at work,* C. L. Cooper & R. Payne, (Eds.). London: John Wiley & Sons.
Davidson, D. M., Winchester, M. A., Barr, C. T., Alderman, E. A., & Ingels, N. B. (1979). Effects of relaxation therapy on cardiac performance and sympathetic activity in patients with organic heart disease. *Psychosomatic Medicine, 41,* 303–309.
Dembrowski, T. M., MacDougall, J. M., Herd, J. A., & Shields, J. L. (1979). Effects of level of challenge on pressor and heart rate response in type A and type B subjects. *Journal of Applied Social Psychology, 9,* 208–228.
Dunbar, H. F. (1943). *Psychosomatic diagnosis.* New York: Paul B. Hoeber.
Egerem, L. F., Sniderman, L. D., & Roggelin, M. S. (1982). Compettitve two-person interactions of type-A and type-B individuals. *Journal of Behavioral Medicine, 5,* 55–67.
Ellis, R. A., & Harper, R. A. (1975). *New guide to rational living.* N. Hollywood, CA: Wilshire Brook Co.

Frank, K. A., Heller, S. S., Kornfeld, D. S., Sporn, A. A., & Weiss, M. D. (1978). Type A behavior pattern and coronary atherosclerosis. *Journal American Medical Association, 240,* 761-763.

Friedman, M., Rhoresen, C. E., & Gill, J. J. (1981). Type A behavior: Its possible role, detection, and alteration in patients with ischemic heart disease. In *Heart—update V,* Harst et al. (Eds.). New York: McGraw-Hill.

Friedman, M., & Rosenman, R. H. (1974). *Type A behavior and your heart.* New York: A. A. Knopf.

Glass, D. C. (1977). *Behavior patterns, stress, and coronary disease.* Hillsdale, NJ: Edbaum Associates.

Grimm, L. G., & Yarnold, P. R. (1984). Performance standards and the type A behavior pattern. *Cognitive Therapy and Research, 8,* 59–66.

Hackett, T. P., & Cassem, N. H. (1976). White collar and blue collar responses to heart attack. *Journal of Psychosomatic Research, 20,* 85–95.

Haynes, S. G., Feinleib, M., & Kannel, W. B. (1980). The relationship of psychosocial factors to coronary heart disease in the Framingham Study; III. Eight year incidence of coronary heart disease. *American Journal of Epidemiology, 111,* 37–58.

Jenkins, C. D., Zyzanski, S. J., & Rosenman, R. H. (1976). Risk of new myocardial infarction in middle-aged men with manifest coronary heart disease. *Circulation, 55,* 342–347.

Jennings, R. J., & Choi, S. (1981). Type A components and psychophysiological responses to an attention-demanding performance task. *Psychosomatic Medicine, 43,* 475–487.

Karasek, R., Baker, D., Marxer, F., Ahlbom, A., & Theorell, T. (1981). Job decision latitude, job demands, and cardiovascular study of Swedish men. *American Journal of Public Health, 71,* 694–705.

Kelley, H. H. (1967). Attribution theory in social psychology. In D. Levine (Ed.), *Nebraska Symposium on Motivation, 15,* 192–238.

Kiester, E. (July, 1984a). The uses of anger. *Psychology Today, 18,* 26.

Kiester, E. (July, 1984b). The playing fields of the mind. *Psychology Today, 18,* 18–24.

Krantz, D. S., & Durel, L. A. (1982). Psychobiological substrates of the type A behavior pattern. Presented at the American Psychological Association Annual Meeting.

Krantz, D. S., Sanmario, M. I., Selvester, R. H., & Matthews, K. N. (1979). Psychological correlates of progression of atherosclerosis in men. *Psychosomatic Medicine, 41,* 467–475.

Lange, A. J., & Jakubowski, P. (1976). *Responsible assertive behavior.* Champaign, IL: Research Press.

Levenkron, J. C., Cohen, J. D., Muller, H. S., & Fisher, E. B. (1983). Modifying the type A coronary-prone behavior pattern. *Journal of Consulting and Clinical Psychology, 51,* 192–204.

Lifshitz, J. L., & Zeichner, A. (1985). Selective attention processes in the type A (coronary prone) behavior pattern, in press.

Margolis, L. H., McLeroy, K. R., Runyan, C. W., & Kaplan, B. H. (1983). Type A behavior: An ecological approach. *Journal of Behavioral Medicine, 6,* 245–258.

Matthews, K. A., & Brunson, B. I. (1979). Allocation of attention and the type A coronary-prone behavior pattern. *Journal of Personality and Social Psychology, 37,* 2081–2090.

Pacht, A. R. (1984). Reflections on perfection. *American Psychologist, 39,* 386–390.
Powell, L. (1983). Workshop on the type A behavior pattern. Presented at Society for Behavioral Medicine Convention.
Price, V. A. (1982). *Type A behavior pattern.* New York: Academic Press.
Review Panel on Coronary-Prone Behavior and Coronary Heart Disease. (1981). Coronary-prone behavior and coronary heart disease: A critical review. *Circulation, 63,* 1199–1215.
Reynolds, R. C. (1974). Community and occupational influences in stress at Cape Kennedy: Relationship to heart disease. In *Stress and the heart,* R. Eliot (Ed.) Mount Kisco, New York: Futura Publishing.
Rhodewalt, F., Hays, R. B., Chemers, M. M., & Wysocki, J. (1984). Type A behavior, perceived stress, and illness: A person-situation analysis. *Personality and Social Psychology Bulletin, 90,* 149–159.
Rose, R. M., Jenkins, C. D., & Hunt, M. W. (1978). *Air traffic controller health change study.* Galveston, TX: Authors.
Rosenman, R. H., Brand, R. J., Jenkins, C. D., Friedman, M., Straus, R., & Wurm, M. (1975). Coronary heart disease in the Western Collaborative Group study: Final follow-up experience of 8½ years. *Journal of the American Medical Association, 233,* 872–877.
Scherwitz, L., McKelvain, R., Laman, C., Patterson, I., Dutton, L., Lysim, S., Lester, J., Kraft, I., Rochelle, D., & Leachman, R. (1983). Type A behavior, self-involvement, and coronary atherosclerosis. *Psychsomatic Medicine, 45,* 47–57.
Schlegel, R. P., Wellwood, J. K., Copps, B. E., Gruchow, W. H., & Scharratt, M. T. (1980). *Journal of Behavioral Medicine, 3,* 191–205.
Shekelle, R. B., Gale, M., & Ostfeld, A. M. (1983). Hostility, risk of coronary heart disease and mortality. *Psychosomatic Medicine, 45,* 109–114.
Skinner, B. F. (1953). *The science of human behavior.* New York: Macmillan.
Snow, B. (1978). Level of aspiration in coronary prone and noncoronary prone adults. *Personality and Social Psychology Bulletin, 4,* 416–419.
Weissman, A. D., & Hackett, T. P. (1961). Predilection to death: Death and dying as a psychiatric problem. *Psychosomatic Medicine, 23,* 232–257.
Williams, R. B., Haney, T. L., Lee, K. L., Kong, Y-H., Blumenthal, J. A., & Whalen, R. E. (1980). Type A behavior, hostility coronary atherosclerosis. *Psychosomatic Medicine, 42,* 539–549.
Wishnie, H. A., Hackett, T. P., & Cassem, N. H. (1971). Psychological hazards of convalescence following myocardial infarction. *Journal of the American Medical Associaton, 215,* 1292–1296.
Zyzanski, S. J., Jenkins, C. D., Ryan, T. J., Flessas, A., & Everist, M. (1976). Psychological correlates of angiographic findings. *Archives Internal Medicine, 136,* 1234–1237.

Chapter 11

ISSUES IN THE DIAGNOSIS AND COGNITIVE THERAPY OF DEPRESSION IN BRAIN-DAMAGED INDIVIDUALS

Mary Ruckdeschel Hibbard
Wayne A. Gordon
Susan Egelko
Karen Langer

Stroke is the most common cause of brain damage onset in older Americans and is ranked as the primary cause of chronic functional impairments in adults (Brust, 1983). Advances in medical care have made it possible for 70 percent of those experiencing strokes to survive and to live an average of 7 additional years (Executive Summary, 1979). In fact, according to the National Center for Health Statistics (1977), there are more than 1 million stroke survivors in this country. Current literature suggests that 30 to 60 percent of these stroke survivors are depressed (Finklestein, Benowitz, Baldessarini, Arana, Levine, Woo, Bear, Moya, & Stroll, 1982; Folstein, Maiberger, & McHugh, 1977; Kerns, 1980; Robins, 1976; Robinson & Benson, 1981; Robinson & Price, 1982; Hibbard, Gordon, & Diller, 1985). This chapter will examine issues pertinent to both the diagnosis and the treatment of depression, a common sequela of brain damage, in these adults. These issues will be discussed within the context of understanding some of the common cognitive, behavioral, and physical changes that occur following brain damage.

Cognitive and Behavioral Changes Following Brain Damage

One must be aware of the diverse cognitive and behavioral changes that are observed in the brain-damaged people when attempting either to diagnose or to treat their depression. These changes often cloud or even mask the reliability of the patient's self-report of his/her affective state. Within the cognitive therapy model, depression is viewed as consequence of a triad of dysfunctional thoughts that revolve around oneself, one's environment, and one's future. In this model, cognitive distortions are assumed to occur primarily in ideational material that typically has a depressive content (Beck, 1967). Thoughts in other domains are not presumed to be distorted. In brain-damaged individuals, it is possible for distortions to exist in most cognitive domains, i.e., in both affect-laden and neutral areas. Depending on severity and location of the brain damage, a stroke patient can experience any or all of the following cognitive changes: impairments in general alertness/attention, faulty perception, decreased memory, poor concentration, altered ability to understand or communicate verbal and affective information, and a loss of voluntary control of emotional expression. Thus, descriptors of depressogenic thinking in non-brain-damaged people—e.g., rigidity, minimization, overgeneralization, and concrete thinking—are common features of the cognitive processes of brain-damaged individuals independent of whether or not the person is depressed.

Each of the cognitive changes alluded to in the above paragraph will be briefly described below:

1. Alteration in general alertness. Patients with even mild brain damage often will experience fluctuating levels of arousal and alertness. These symptoms are often subjectively interpreted by the patient as "fatigue," and they may be present for many months following the onset of the stroke. A patient with more extreme alertness difficulties (i.e., hypoarousal) may have difficulty maintaining sustained attention and often reports frequent episodes of falling asleep for brief periods of time throughout the day. These symptoms are often falsely interpreted as indicators of a lack of interest or motivation or as a sign of depression.

2. Impaired perceptual functioning. Brain-damaged patients, especially those with right-brain damage (i.e., a left-sided paralysis), may experience a decreased ability to receive and integrate correctly sensory, visual, or auditory information from their environment. Rather than integrating all of the information available in a situation prior to responding, these individuals tend to act impulsively and base their responses on a small detail of the stimulus field. This incorrect view is then generalized to the remaining parts of the situation. Thus, there are many sources of distortions that are consequences of the perceptual disturbance that are secondary to brain damage. These deficits include loss of spatial and time perspective, inability to maintain eye contact, and abrupt discontinuation of normal pleasurable leisure activities, e.g.

reading, due to faulty visual information processing. These perceptual difficulties can be mistakenly interpreted as signs of depression.

3. Memory impairments. Patients may experience transient or permanent, short-term and/or long-term memory losses following brain damage. Recall of affective material may be lost or inaccurately remembered. These deficits may interfere with both the diagnosis of depression and attempts at its treatment.

4. Concentration deficits. Concentration deficits that are often independent of depressive symptoms are common complaints in brain-damaged individuals. These difficulties usually become apparent when the patient attempts to process verbally or visually complex information. Increased levels of fatigue tend to make the problem worse. Careful exploration of the nature of the patient's complaint is required, as the source of the problem might reside in a coexisting memory or perceptual disorder. Questions asked of the patient may need to be simplified, using short, simple sentences, and evaluation of whether the patient has actually comprehended the issue being discussed is often necessary.

5. Impaired verbal communication skills. Following left-brain damage (i.e., a right-sided paralysis), patients may experience difficulty with both comprehension and expression of language. These deficits can vary from being quite subtle to being quite obvious. In the extreme case, patients who have lost *both* language *comprehension* and *expression* abilities would be unable to engage in a normal verbal interchange because they could neither understand nor communicate spoken language. These patients may have little awareness of their language deficits. Patients with less severe *comprehension* difficulties may be able to understand individual words but lose the meaning of a series of words when they are combined together to form a sentence. In contrast, patients with *expressive* difficulties have adequate language comprehension but compromised language skills. Words may be mispronounced or substituted with incorrect statements. The type and severity of these basic communication impairments will necessarily dictate the specific modifications that are needed in therapeutic interaction with the individual.

6. Impaired affective communication skills. Following right-brain damage (i.e., left-sided paralysis), patients have intact verbal skills, but they may experience difficulty expressing or comprehending emotional nuances in either spoken language or nonverbal (i.e., facial or body gesturing) communication (Ross & Mesulam, 1979; Ross & Rush, 1981). For example, patients with *expressive* affect communication difficulties may be unable to inflect their speech or use facial gestures with the intended affective intonation (e.g., raising voice pitch to sound angry, looking sad when feeling sad). As a result, people's external appearance and/or dialogue may be incongruent with their internal mood state. For example, while the patient may sound flat and monotone, he/she may be feeling extremely upset and anxious. Thus, the self-presentation does not correspond to the person's mood. Conversely, patients with affect

comprehension difficulties may be unable to interpret correctly the affect conveyed with spoken words or the facial expressions of those surrounding them. For example, the patient may confuse an angry statement for one that is sad. As a result, the patient, acting on false information, may respond in an emotionally inappropriate manner. These often subtle affect communication deficits create additional interpersonal stress for patients. The clinician needs to focus on the *verbal* description of patients' emotional state rather than rely on the *expected congruence* between verbal and affective expression in patients with these affect communication deficits.

7. Altered control of emotional expression. Brain-damaged patients may experience changes in their ability to control emotional expression that may be easily misinterpreted as a reflection of their actual mood. When faced with a task that he can not competently complete, the brain-damaged patient may suddenly begin to swear, act aggressively, become hyperemotional, or use compensatory boasting. This sudden shift in behavior in the face of failure has been called a "catastrophic reaction" (Gainotti, 1972). Another aspect of altered emotional control is uncontrolled lability. This lability is most often manifested as sudden crying or even as laughter and can be triggered by discussion of even covertly affect-laden material. Both catastrophic reactions and lability are secondary to specific brain pathology and are typically not within the voluntary control of the patient. The emotional behaviors expressed during the outbursts are usually unrelated to the brain-damaged patient's internal affect state. Distraction and a change of topic often will serve to dissipate this upsetting type of behavior.

In summary, the clinician working with a depressed brain-damaged individual needs to be cognizant of the potential interaction between the cognitive sequelae of the brain damage and the affect state of the patient. It is suggested that the clinician explore which of these sequelae are present in a patient through direct inquiry with the patient during the initial clinical sessions or from a neuropsychological evaluation and/or medical report, as any of these sequelae can influence the way in which the professional interprets both the patient's behavior and his mood.

PHYSICAL SEQUELAE OF BRAIN DAMAGE

In addition to the cognitive and behavioral changes discussed above, the brain-damaged individual is faced with permanent physical impairments that further impact on diagnosis and treatment of depression. Reality-based concerns—such as mourning the loss of some body function, life role changes, altered body image, and stigma—need to be considered when evaluating and treating an individual. Symptoms of depression can stem both from actual physical limitations and from cognitively distorted thought processes. For example, if the patient is socially isolated, dependent, and passive, are these symptoms the result of a mobility impairment, fatigue, or the patient's distroyed view of how others view him/her? Feelings of dissatisfaction and general lack of pleasure also can stem from either physical or cognitively distorted sources. For example, activities that were pleasurable before the brain damage (e.g., taking a shower, going to a restaurant) may now be perceived as totally nonpleasurable because of competing negative sensations such as pain or spasm or the stigma of being seen in public as a disabled person. This same dissatisfaction, however, also may arise from the patient's rigidity, which does not allow for any appreciation of shadings or small amounts of pleasure. Events may be interpreted as either "all bad" or "all good."

In summary, the physical, as well as cognitive, sequelae of brain damage needs to be considered when working with the depressed brain-damaged individual. The potential interaction of these concomitant sequelae often make it clinically difficult to separate the consequences of brain damage from a manifestation of depression per se.

THE NATURE OF DEPRESSION IN BRAIN-DAMAGED INDIVIDUALS

Approximately 30 to 60 percent of adult brain-damaged patients who have had strokes are depressed (Finklestein, et al., 1982; Folstein, et al., 1977; Kerns, 1980; Robins, 1976; Robinson & Benson, 1981; Robinson & Price, 1982; Hibbard, et al., 1985). Given the prevalence of depression in stroke patients, a pertinent diagnostic issue is whether such depression is a *transitory* (i.e., grief) reaction or a *stable* affective response.

A review of the available literature suggests that depression following stroke is chronic in nature (Ahlsio, Britton, Murray, & Tores, 1984; Feibel, Beck, & Joynt, 1979; Gordon & Diller, 1983; Robinson & Price, 1982; Robinson, Starr, Lipsey, Rao, & Price, 1984). Gordon and Diller (1983) have reported that the depression scores of right-brain-damaged patients at 4 months and at 1 year post-discharge from inpatient rehabilitation are both elevated and stable. In addition, relative to age-matched community volunteers, these patients were found to be inactive and isolated, as indicated by a measure of daily time usuage. For example, the stroke patients engaged in fewer different types of activities, spent 10 percent more time sleeping, spent 8 percent less time participating in household tasks, and spent five times less time out of the house compared to the nondisabled group. Fiebel, Beck, and Joynt (1979) found that 37 percent of a sample of 85 stroke patients who were 4 months post-rehabilitation discharge were moderately to severely depressed and 56 percent were socially isolated. Similarly, Robinson and his colleagues (1984) report that during the first 6 months following the onset of stroke, the incidence of depression increased from 44 to 60 percent; 95 percent of those who were initially depressed remained depressed; and 29 percent of those who initially were not depressed became depressed during this time period. Furthermore, Robinson and Price (1982) noted that this depression may remain for periods of up to 2 years post–stroke onset.

The chronicity of the depressive symptoms observed in brain-damaged patients suggests that the type of depression being reported does not fit the *DSM III* classificaton of a grief response or bereavement. It also would be inappropriate to classify this type of depression as endogenous, since the somatic or more vegetative complaints of these patients are common in other medically ill populations as well (Buckberg, Penman, & Holland, 1984). Thus, the nosology provided by the *DSM III* fails to provide for an accurate classification of depression in this population. Given the prevalence and chronicity of this depression in brain-damaged individuals, accurate diagnosis and effective treatment is critical, since prolonged periods of depression compromise the brain-damaged person's quality of life, impede recovery, and increase the person's perceived functional impairment.

Despite the magnitude of the clinical problem, the treatment of the depression afflicting stroke patients has received little symstematic attention. For example, a review of the literature reveals only a handful of cases describing the effective treatment of depression in these patients (Folstein, et al., 1977; Ross & Rush, 1981) and only one adequately designed experiment of a specific approach to depression treatment (Lipsey, Robinson, Pearlson, Rao, & Price, 1984). Thus, it is not surprising to find that only a small proportion of depressed stroke patients receive any form of intervention, whether antidepressant medication, cognitive therapy, or any other systematic approach to the problem. Indeed, Fiebel, Beck, and Joynt (1979) report that despite the prevalence of depression and social isolation noted in the stroke patients living in the community, few of these individuals have been referred and/or treated by the existing community mental health professionals.

Why are these patients' needs so poorly addressed by the mental health professional community? Two factors may explain the puacity of treatment: the inadequacy of both conventional diagnostic tools and diagnostic criteria, and the lack of modification of traditional models of psychotherapy for use with medically and cognitively impaired individuals who are post-stroke. To address these clinical needs, the remainder of the chapter will focus on modifications in diagnosis and cognitive therapy required for effective psychological management of the brain-damaged individual.

Diagnostic Issues in the Assessment of Brain-Damaged Patients

Most psychiatric and psychological tools used to assess depression have been developed and standardized on young psychiatric populations. Many of the traditional markers of depression in this population are not useful discriminators of depression in an older population. For this reason, it has been suggested that the tools used to assess depression in older populations require modifications (Yesavage, Brink, Rose, Lum, Huang, Adey, & Leirer, 1983). This issue assumes greater significance when the clinician is confronted with assessing older, medically ill brain-damaged individuals. In these individuals, physical, somatic, and cognitive functioning have been altered as a result of a stroke. Functional losses are often extensive and permanent. Thus, it is often clinically difficult to separate the consequences of the stroke from manifestations of depression. For example, weight loss of 15 pounds in an obese patient who had been placed on a medically prescribed reduction diet is hardly a manifestation of depression. Likewise, a patient rendered paralyzed as a result of the brain damage will clearly experience increased fatigue when attempting to walk. Consequently, the clinician needs to explore the etiology of any reported somatic complaints with the patient to determine the extent to which symptoms are secondary to physical sequelae of brain damage or are a sign of depression.

Given this context, the following suggestions are provided which have been found to be useful in evaluating depression following brain damage:

1. In stroke and other seriously ill medical populations (Bukberg et al., 1984; Schwab, Bialow, Clemmons, & Holzer, 1967), somatic complaints are not particularly useful discriminators of either the presence or severity of depression. For example, Gordon and his colleagues (1984) undertook an exploratory item analysis of both somatic and nonsomatic items on the BDI and HRSD in 32 stroke patients. In comparing the frequency of specific item endorsement of severely and mildly depressed patients, none of the somatic items differentiated between these two subgroups of patients. For this reason, it is suggested that somatic symptoms of depression should not be heavily weighted in diagnosing depression in this population. The clinician must carefully assess the more intrapsychic, i.e., nonsomatic, symptoms in order to determine the presence and severity of depression in this population.

2. Medically ill older people may find the items included in standard depression inventories, such as the BDI, jarring or difficult to interpret. For example, questions about suicidal intent (i.e., whether life is worth living) and concerns about the future have obviously different meanings to individuals who are simultaneously reaching the later stages of their lifespan and who are suddenly rendered partially paralyzed. Questions about sexuality often make the elderly defensive (Yesavage et al., 1983) and may be inappropriate if the patient is institutionalized. Consequently, the items selected for inclusion in the assessment of depression in this population need to be given careful clinical consideration.

Given the permanent nature and severity of the physical and cognitive disability secondary to stroke, items not traditionally explored in standard approaches to assessing depression need to be added when evaluating the stroke patient's affect state. Bukberg, Penman, and Holland (1984) suggest that feelings of hopelessness, helplessness, and worthlessness are valuable indicators of the severity of depression in cancer patients. These same intrapsychic symptoms are appropriate additions to the assessment of depression in the older brain-damaged individuals as well.

3. Older individuals are more often resistant to psychological evaluation than younger patients (Jarvik, 1976; Salzman & Shader, 1978). This resistance

may in part be due to the fact that the source of referral for intervention is often not the individual but his/her physician, family, or the rehabilitation team. Additionally, resistance often will surface when the patient is confronted with a depression inventory that focuses solely on increasing extremes of dysphoric self report. For example, Hibbard (1984) found that reading aloud to the patient all response choices for each Beck Depression Inventory (BDI) (Beck, Ward, Mendelson, Mock, & Erbaugh, 1961) item increased the patient's resistance to the task. However, embedding the BDI items within a structured interview helped to enhance a patient's cooperation and ability to complete the task. Two additional approaches have been found to be useful in reducing a patient's resistance to psychological evaluation. First, the clinician should determine the extent and severity of somatic complaints prior to probing more intrapsychic symptoms. Second, the clinician should intersperse the evaluation of recent positive affective experiences (e.g., What things have really made you feel good lately?) within the clinical interview.

4. Existing assessment tools need to be modified so that they are cognitively less demanding and more easily understood by the brain-damaged patient. For example, the BDI requires the respondent to choose one of four possible responses to each item. The patient is asked to read all responses and then choose the one that best reflects his affective state. This format is often too difficult for a brain-damaged patient to complete. A patient's difficulty with this task may stem from several sources: (a) the patient's ability to comprehend language may be compromised so that he is unable to make the subtle distinctions among the choices; (b) the patient may have perceptual impairments that render him unable to read the choices accurately; (c) the patient may concretely/idiosyncratically interpret each response and therefore be able to generalize his feelings to a response that accurately reflects his/her general affective state; or (d) the patient may have a memory deficit that renders him unable to remember the four choices before deciding on the appropriate response. To accommodate these difficulties, it is suggested that self-report items to read to the patient by the clinician. To further minimize the cognitive demands of the task, the responses to each BDI item should be divided into a no/yes problem format. If a patient admits no difficulty in a given domain, only the (O) response of the BDI item is read to the patient. If difficulties are discussed, however, the patient is read each of the remaining three BDI responses individually and asked to choose the most appropriate response. Item content should be simplified as needed to ensure adequate comprehension.

5. A final issue to be considered in the diagnosis of depression in brain-damaged individuals is a tendency to minimize the presence/severity of their cognitive, physical, or emotional deficits (Kerns, 1980; Gainotti, 1972; Hibbard, 1984). Minimization can be evaluated by the direct comparison of a patient's actual behavior/abilities with his/her self-report of abilities. For example, a patient who exhibits severe minimization may report that his left arm is "just tired." Yet clinical observation reveals that the patient's left arm is totally paralyzed. This discrepancy between self- and observer report is a classic example

of how the patient, although aware of some difficulty with his left arm, minimizes the extent of the difficulty. This minimization is more typically observed after right-brain damage (i.e., a left-sided stroke) and represents an actual "lack of awareness" of the extent and severity of an individual's deficits as opposed to "denial" in the classic psychoanalytic sense.

This lack of awareness also can extend to the affective domain. A patient who admits to being mildly depressed may appear more severely depressed to the observer. Thus, the diagnosis of depression needs to incorporate an assessment of the presence and severity of minimization by the patient. To evaluate this issue, simultaneous ratings of depressive symptoms by both the clinician and the patient (via self-report) are suggested.

Issues in Cognitive Therapy with Brain-Damaged Individuals

Beck and his colleagues (Beck, 1970; Beck, Rush, Shaw, & Emery, 1979; Beck et al., 1961; Kovacs, 1980; Kovacs & Beck, 1978) describe depressed persons as making broad global judgments regarding events that impinge on their lives. The meanings that flood their consciousness are typically extreme, negative, categorical, absolute, and judgmental. Their emotional responses thus tend to be negative and extreme. This description, combined with dysphoric thoughts surrounding self, environment, and future, seem to describe aptly the typical cognitive processes of depressed brain-damaged patients.

If psychotherapy is to impact on the dysphoric mood of these individuals, the therapist must first address the pervasive cognitive distortions of these individuals. Given this framework, the choice of a cognitively based psychotherapy approach to depression treatment is a logical one. The focus of cognitive therapy—i.e. to correct the rigid and concrete distortions of the individual—is seen as a primary goal of therapy with the depressed brain-damaged person. Cognitive therapy offers several advantages for clinical use with this population. The type of therapy is (a) behaviorally oriented; (b) time-limited; (c) highly active and directive; and (d) focused on the current problems in an individual's life. Additionally, cognitive therapy provides a patient with a set of specific behavioral/cognitive skills with which to deal with ongoing cognitions and situations that serve to maintain both depression and social isolation. These skills are appropriate strategies for dealing more effectively with both neutral and affective cognitive processes.

In dealing with the cognitively compromised depressed patient, some suggestions for the modification of traditional cognitive therapy are provided. These suggestions are aimed at increasing a patient's ability to competently complete tasks assigned and maximizing his ability to profit from the cognitive interventions:

1. Given the pervasive nature of inactivity and social isolation in this population, behavioral techniques, such as activity planning and mastery/pleasure ratings, should assume a greater role in therapy. The aim of these techniques

is to expand the diversity of social activities engaged in by the patient and enhance feelings of mastery over the patient's physically and cognitively altered environment.

2. Because of the many realistic physical limitations of the patient, expansion of activities to include positive social interactions should be stressed. These types of activities require less physical mobility and therefore are more easily achieved by the patient. The stress is, therefore, on residual abilities and assets, not deficits.

3. All tasks assignments should be modeled by the patient and the therapist within a session. A task may need frequent repetition until the patient has mastered its component parts. Once the skill is *overlearned*, it can then be attempted outside the therapy session.

4. Task assignments need to be cognitively simplified to meet the abilities of the brain-damaged patient. Duration of assignments needs to be initially brief and slowly expanded. While most cognitive assignments are in the written domain (e.g., recording of dysfunctional thoughts is a written task), auditory documentation via a tape recorder may be indicated to enhance recall for the patients with motoric difficulties, concentration, or memory deficits.

5. Establishing a therapeutic liaison with a spouse or interested relative to help the patient with assignments outside of a session is often a helpful strategy.

6. The crux of cognitive therapy is aimed at identifying and reality-testing cognitive distortions that serve to maintain a person's depression. For many brain-damaged individuals, this type of activity is cognitively too demanding to be independently accomplished outside the therapy session. For most patients, challenge and correction of cognitive distortions will evolve from materials that surface within the clinical session.

CLINICAL CASE EXAMPLE

A clinical case utilizing the structured clinical interview is presented to illustrate how the clinician can integrate information obtained from neuropsychological testing, medical records, and psychological assessment to accurately assess a brain-damaged patient's affect state. This case illustrates how expressive affective communication problems combined with severe perceptual difficulties masked the actual severity of the individual's depression.

Patient name: E. K.
Age: 64 years
Occupation: Retired bookkeeper
Marital status: Widow

Pertinent Medical History

Mrs. E. K. has a past history of two completed left-sided strokes. Her initial stroke was relatively mild, resulting in minimal residual weakness of her left arm and leg. Two months later the patient experienced a second and more severe left-sided stroke. Residual deficits from this stroke included marked paralysis of her left face, arm, and leg and a visual field impairment. A CT scan revealed multiple right cerebral hemisphere infarctions. She also has a past history of hypertension and obesity.

Pertinent Neuropsychological Data

Neurological assessment at the time of interview revealed marked paralysis of the patient's left face, arm, and leg and a partial visual field impairment. On further evaluation, Mrs. E. K. was found to have *severe perceptual neglect*, as indicated by extremely poor performance on a simple cancellation task and the Raven's Coloured Progressive Matrices (Raven, 1965). She had a mild affective comprehension deficit and a *severe impairment in affect expression* (i.e., she was agestural and spoke in a flat monotone voice).

Clinician Impression of Patient's Emotional Behaviors

Mrs. E. K. was seen for a structured clinical interview, as part of an ongoing research study, 4 weeks after her second stroke, while she was undergoing an active rehabilitation program.

During the clinical interview, Mrs. E. K. completed the Beck Depression Inventory (BDI) (Beck et al., 1961) and was concurrently rated by the clinician on the Hamilton Rating Scale for Depression, Modified (HRSD) (Hamilton, 1969). Mrs. E. K. appeared depressed throughout the clinical interview. Although extremely verbal and articulate regarding her present affect state, she spoke in a monotone voice devoid of any affect intonation. She was also agestural throughout the interview. Her physical appearance was unkempt and her eye contact was poor.

Mrs. E. K. was realistically aware of both her medical condition and the extent of her disability, although discussion of these issues resulted in the patient expressing a need to escape from focusing on them. For example, some of her responses are presented below:

Clinical Question: What physically happened to you that brought you to the hospital?
Patient Response: Fell down...had a stroke in February. Eight weeks later I had a second stroke. A brain scan confirmed this. Now I have no movement in my arm or leg.
Clinical Question: What are your biggest problems now?
Patient Response: Getting my son-in-law and daughter back together again. [The patient begins to cry over the recent divorce of her daughter] [Note: The patient ignores her own physical difficulties.]
Clinical Question: What are your biggest problems with yourself?
Patient Response: I don't care about myself...I use lots of escapes right now.

194   COGNITIVE THERAPY

Clinical Question: Are your worried about your medical condition?
Patient Response: Extremely...I had two strokes...I don't want another. [Cries.] I want to be free of all this...run away from everything.

Clinical Impressions

The profile of Mrs. E. K.'s self-report and clinical ratings of depression are presented in Table 11-1. Total scores on both measures are in the severely depressed range. Mrs. E. K.'s pattern of somatic complaints are typical of a physically impaired older individual; however the quality of her responses to these items suggest that both depressogenic cognitions and physical limitations are core to these symptoms. For example, while many patients admit great difficulty sleeping, Mrs. E. K. volunteers that her "mind is racing a mile a minute at night." Likewise, her feelings of *total* exhaustion and inability to

Table 11-1. Depression Profile for Mrs. E. K.

Beck Depression Inventory (BDI)*	Rating	Hamilton Rating Scale for Depression (HRSD)**	Rating
Somatic Items		*Somatic Items*	
Insomnia	2	Insomnia, initial	1
Fatigability	3	Insomnia, middle	2
Work retardation	3	Somatic complaints (i.e., fatigue, etc.)	2
Weight loss	3	Motor retardation/agitation	2
		Weight loss	2
		Hypochrondiasis	0
Subtotal	11	Subtotal	9
Nonsomatic Items		*Nonsomatic Items*	
Irritability	1	Anxiety, psychic	1
Indecisiveness	1	Agitation	2
Sadness	1	Anxiety, somatic	2
Crying	1	Work/interest changes	1
Pessimism	3	Depressed mood	2
Suicidal ideas	1	Hopelessness	2
Self-accusation	3	Helplessness	2
Self-dislike	3	Suicide	1
Sense of failure	2	Worthlessness	2
Guilt	2	Guilt	2
Expectation of punishment	3		—
Subtotal	21	Subtotal	17
Total	32	Total	26
	(Severe depression)		(Severe depression)

* BDI scoring is on a 4-point scale in which 0 = no difficulty, and 3 = maximum severity of a symptom. Maximum score, 63.
** HRSD scoring has been modified to a 3-point scale in which 0 = no evidence of a symptom and 2 = severe symptomalogy. Maximum score, 38.

initiate *any* tasks are in excess of what is normally observed in the stroke individual. Her extreme weight loss, more than 50 pounds, was attributed to a reduction diet and was thus seen as a positive change in the patient.

Her pattern of self-reported nonsomatic symptoms are key to the severity of her depression and the nature of her cognitive distortions. As noted in Table 11-1, she admits to maximum scoring on items related to a negative view of oneself (i.e., scores of 3 on Self-Accusation, Self-Dislike, and Sense of Failure) and one's future (a score of 3 on Pessimism and a score of 1 on Suicidal Ideas). Furthermore, she was quite verbal regarding her feelings of guilt and her wish to be punished for her past failures in life. She viewed the stroke as a just punishment. These feelings are further compounded by extreme feelings of helplessness and hopelessness.

Although admitting to increased crying episodes, the patient's description of these emotional episodes is indicative of lability secondary to her brain damage. The patient was aware that these crying episodes were often out of her control and that her outward emotional display did not always match her internal feelings. "I cry at the drop of a hat—I feel ridiculous but I cry...I cry even when I'm reading...I can't seem to stop it from happening." Despite the severity of her negative feelings toward herself and her future, Mrs. E. K. admits to only feeling "sad" and mildly irritated during the interview. The clinical observer rates her as considerably more agitated and depressed than the patient admits, hence some element of minimization of affect state by the patient was evidenced.

Summary

On both self-report and clinical ratings, Mrs. E. K. is severely depressed. Her main sources of depression revolve around her pessimistic view of herself, her past, and her future. While minimizing the full extent of her present depression, she was aware that she might become more depressed in the future if no physical improvements were noted. Despite the dysphoric verbal content of the interview, the patient speaks in a flat monotone voice devoid of affect and is unable to maintain eye contact or make appropriate facial gestures. Thus, her external affective demeanor lacks congruence with her interval affect state.

Clearly Mrs. E. K. is an appropriate candidate for cognitive therapy. Therapy would focus on both the identification and reality testing of her core depressogenic cognitions about herself, her future, and her wish for punishment.

Clinical Note

On completion of this assessment, Mrs. E.K.'s physician was contacted regarding the apparent severity of her depression. The physician was unaware of the depth of the patient's affective distress. A review of the patient's medical chart revealed no mention of depressed affect by the other members of the rehabilitation team, i.e., nursing staff, occupational therapists, physical therapists, and so on. In a prior psychological evaluation, the patient was described as "friendly, alert, and cooperative. She has chronically felt inadequate, was a worrier and felt frustrated at not achieving her potential." Although this report represented a partial picture of the patient's affective style, it clearly minimized the severity of her depression. The presence of perceptual and affect expression deficits had masked the severity of her depression to others and had resulted in the perception by other professionals that the patient was considerably less distressed than she actually felt.

In this chapter it is hoped that the context of the brain-damaged patient has provided the reader with an understanding of the complexity of diagnosing and treating depression in this population. In addition, suggestions have been offered that will aid the clinician in making an accurate diagnosis and in approaching treatment.

Acknowledgments

Work on this chapter was supported in part by a Rehabilitation Research and Training Center Grant (G008300039) on Head Trauma and Stroke from the National Institute of Handicapped Research (NIHR), U.S. Department of Education.

References

Ahlsio, B., Britton, M., Murray, V., & Tores, T. (1984). Disablement and quality of life after stroke. *Stroke, 15,* 866–890.
Beck, A. T. (1967). *Depression: Clinical, experimental and theoretical aspects.* New York: Harper and Row.
Beck, A. T. (1970). *Depression: Cause and treatment.* Philadelphia: University of Pennsylvania Press.
Beck, A. T., Rush, A. J., Shaw, B., & Emery, G. (1979). *Cognitive therapy for depression.* New York: Guilford Press.
Beck, A.T., Ward, C., Mendelson, M., Mock, J., & Erbaugh, J. (1961). An inventory for measuring depression. *Archives of General Psychiatry, 4,* 561–571.
Brust, J. C. (1983). Stroke: Diagnostic, anatomical and physiological considerations. In *Principles of neuroscience,* E. Kandell & J. Schwartz (Eds.), (pp. 677–669). New York: Elsevier/North-Holland.
Bukberg, J., Pehman, D., & Holland, J. C. (1984). Depression in hospitalized cancer patients. *Psychosomatic Medicine, 46,* 199–212.
Executive Summary of the National Research Strategy for Neurological and Communication Disorders (DHEW Publication No. 791911). (1979). Washington, DC: National Institutes of Health.

Feibel, J. H., Beck, S., & Joynt, R. M. (1979). The unmet needs of stroke survivors. *Neurology, 29*, 592.

Finklestein, S., Benowitz, L., Baldessarini, R., Arana, G., Levine, D., Woo, E., Bear, D., Moya, K., & Stroll, A. (1982). Mood, vegetative disturbance and dexamethasone supression test after stroke. *Annals of Neurology, 12*, 463–468.

Folstein, M., Maiberger, R., & McHugh, P. (1977). Mood disorders as a specific complication of stroke. *Journal of Neurosurgery and Psychiatry, 40*, 1018–1020.

Gainotti, G. (1972). Emotional behavior and hemispheric side of the lesion. *Cortex, 8*, 41–55.

Gordon, W. A., & Diller, L. (1983). Stroke: Coping with a cognitive deficit. In *Coping with chronic disease: Research and applications*, T. E. Burish & L. A. Bradley (Eds.), (pp. 113–135). New York: Academic Press.

Gordon, W. A., Hibbard, M. R., Egelko, S., Diller, L., Simmens, S., Langer, K., Sano, M., Orazem, J., & Weinberg, J. (1984). *Evaluation of the deficits associated with right brain damage: Normative data on the Institute of Rehabilitation Medicine Test Battery.* Unpublished manuscript, New York University Medical Center.

Hamilton, M. (1967). Development of a rating scale for primary depressive illness. *British Journal of Social Clinical Psychology, 6*, 278–296.

Hamilton, M. (1969). Standardized assessment and recording of depressive symptoms. *Psychiatria, Neurologia, Neurochirurgia, 72*, 201–205.

Hibbard, M. R. (1984). *Affect communication impairments in brain damaged individuals.* Unpublished doctoral dissertation, New York University.

Hibbard, M. R, Gordon, W. A., & Diller, L. Affective disturbances associated with brain damage. (1985). In *Handbook of clinical neuropsychology* (Vol. 2), S. Filskov & T. Boll (Eds.). New York: John Wiley, in press.

Jarvik, L. F. (1976). Aging and depression: Some unanswered questions. *Journal of Gerontology, 31*, 324,–326.

Kerns, R. (1980). *Depression following stroke: Self-evaluation, neuropsychological evaluation and laterality of lesion as predictor variables.* Unpublished doctoral dissertation, Southern Illinois University.

Kovacs, M. (1980). Cognitive therapy in depression. *Journal of the American Academy of Psychoanalysis, 8*, 127–144.

Kovacs, M., & Beck, A. T. (1978). Maladaptive cognitive structures in depression. *American Journal of Psychiatry, 135*, 525–533.

Lipsey, J. R., Robinson, R. G., Pearlson, G. D., Rao, L., & Price, T. R. (1984). Nortriptyline treatment of post-stroke depression: A double-blind study. *Lancet*, 297–300.

National Center for Health Statistics Profile of Chronic Illness in Nursing Homes, United States, August 1973-April 1974. (December 1977). *Vital Health Statistics: Series 13, No. 29.* Hyattsville, MD: USDHEW.

Raven, J. C. (1965). *Guide to using the Coloured Progressive Matrices.* London: H. K. Lewis.

Robins, A. J. (1976). Are stroke patients more depressed than other disabled subjects? *Journal of Chronic Disease, 29*, 479–482.

Robinson, R. G., & Benson, D. F. (1981). Depression in aphasia patients: Frequency, severity and clinical pathology correlations. *Brain and Language, 14*, 282–291.

Robinson, R. G., & Price, T. R. (1982). Post-stroke depressive disorders: A follow-up study of 103 patients. *Stroke, 13*, 635–641.

Robinson, R. G., Starr, L. B., Lipsey, J. R., Rao, K., & Price, T. R. (1984). A two year longitudinal study of post-stroke mood disorders: Dynamic changes in associated variables over the first six months of follow-up. *Stroke, 15,* 510–517.

Robinson, R. G., Starr, L. B., & Price, T. R. (1984). A two year longitudinal study of mood disorders following stroke: Prevalence and duration at six months follow-up. *British Journal of Psychiatry, 144,* 256–262.

Ross, E. D., & Mesulam, M. M. (1979). Dominant language functions of the right hemisphere? Prosody and emotional gesturing. *Archives of Neurology, 36,* 144–148.

Ross, E. D., & Rush, J. (1981). Diagnosis and neuroanatomical correlates of depression in brain-damaged patients. *Archives of General Psychiatry, 38,* 1344–1354.

Salzman. C., & Shader, R. (1978). Depression in the elderly: Relationship between depression, psychologic defense mechanisms and physical illness. *Journal of the American Geriatric Society, 26,* 253–259.

Schwab, J., Bialow, M., Clemmons, R., & Holzer, C. (1967). Hamilton Rating Scale for Depression with medical inpatients. *British Journal of Psychiatry, 113,* 83–88.

Yesavage, J. A., Brink, T. L., Rose, T. L., Lum, O., Huang, V., Adey, M., & Leirer, V. O. (1983). Development and validation of a geriatric depression screening scale. A preliminary report. *Journal of Psychiatric Research, 17,* 37–49.

Chapter 12

PROBLEM-SOLVING TRAINING AND INSTITUTIONALIZED ELDERLY PATIENTS

Richard A. Hussian

Psychologically debilitated elderly patients are making up an increasingly large proportion of the institutionalized population. Between 30 and 40 percent of the censuses of mental institutions in this country are made up of persons sixty-five years of age and older, and long-term care facilities are finding the rate of mental disorders close to that of physical illness. It should be obvious that this proportion and these problems will continue increasing.

The psychological problems manifested by this group of institutionalized elderly stem from a variety of causative and correlative factors. Predominate among these factors are those presented in Table 12-1. A combination of these factors or extremely poor response to even one factor may lead to inappropriate psychological response. It should be noted, however, that a great deal of individual variability exists among the elderly with regard to their ability to compensate for or adapt to these changes. Other factors surely interact, such as an individual's history of coping behavior, the quality of personal and environmental resources, and the level of cognitive functioning.

Inappropriate responses that may result, in part, from the factors in Table 12-1 include temporary confusional states, withdrawal from social interactions, depression, suspiciousness, agitation, deficient skills, disregard for personal hygiene or safety, and hypochondriasis. These disorders or deficits may affect as many as 50 percent of the elderly at one time or another and may complicate preexisting conditions such as central global organic dysfunction.

These problem behaviors in institutionalized geriatric populations have been subjected to a variety of well-validated behavioral treatments including those aimed at increasing communication skills, interpersonal skills, and social interactions (Blackman, Howe, & Pinkston, 1976; Hoyer, Kafer, Simpson, &

Table 12-1. Changes Associated with Aging That May Lead to Inappropriate Responses

Increased incidence of physical illnesses
Increased consumption of medication and multiple medications
Increased likelihood of personal losses
Increased probability of recent relocation(s)
Increased likelihood of dependent relationships with others
Decreased physical mobility
Decreased geographical mobility
Decreased societal interest
Decreased functioning across multiple systems
Mild to moderate memory dysfunction
Mild to moderate generalized slowing

Hoyer, 1974; Lopez, Hoyer, Goldstein, Gershaw, Sprafkin, 1980; Nigl & Jackson, 1981; Quattrochi-Tubin & Jason, 1980), social interest and affect (MacDonald & Settin, 1978), exercise (Libb & Clements, 1969), independent ambulation (MacDonald & Butler, 1974), self-bathing (Rinke, Williams, Lloyd, & Smith-Scott, 1978), eating and self-feeding (Baltes & Zerbe, 1976), participation in recreational activities (McClannahan & Risley, 1975; Quilitch, 1974), increasing personal mail (Goldstein & Baer, 1976), and the reduction of drug side effects (Jackson & Schonfeld, 1982).

Cognitive-behavioral therapies also have been shown to be effective with elderly individuals in the reduction of depression (Hussian, 1985), conversation-starting (Lopez et al., 1980), and the increase in interpersonal skills (Berger & Rose, 1977).

Problem-solving training, as described by D'Zurilla and Goldfried (1971) or components of problem-solving training also can be used in the modification of inappropriate responses to age-related problems. The rationale for the use of problem-solving training with institutionalized elderly persons follows. Descriptions of the research that does exist, protocols for the implementation of problem-solving training, and special considerations are then discussed.

RATIONALE FOR USE OF PROBLEM-SOLVING TRAINING WITH THE INSTITUTIONALIZED ELDERLY

Though cognitive-behavioral approaches to the problems of the aged have not been commonly published, problem-solving training is quite suited for geriatric psychotherapy. Client requirements are minimal and include only the presence of some verbal facility; reasonable short-term and long-term memories; the ability to manipulate problems, actions, and consequences covertly; a reasonable physical ability to effect some change on the environment; the ability to perceive sources of secondary reinforcement; the ability to inhibit immediate responding; the ability to make concrete, specific statements; the ability to ignore irrelevant information; and the ability to use mediational cues (D'Zurilla & Goldfried, 1971).

Given the presence of these abilities or their remediation, problem-solving should be a valuable supplement to geriatrics. The reasons are as follows: First, some researchers have reported that the present elderly cohort seems to exhibit less effective problem-solving behavior than younger generations (Pfeiffer, 1977). The reasons for this relative deficit may involve the *loss* of previous problem-solving ability or the total absence of a history of problem-solving ability. Table 12-2 presents some of the causes relevant to both sources of deficiency.

These deficiencies, which can be partially reduced by special accommodations in the experimental procedures, appear as poor solutions to perceptual problems, increased time required to generate correct responses (Lee & Pollack, 1980), and increased cautiousness in problem-solving situations (Botwinick, 1973). The fact that an institutionalized elderly patient, at least one hospitalized in a mental institution, has been admitted, in and of itself probably signifies some deficient adaptive behavior.

Second, the elderly appear to be faced with more situations in which efficient problem-solving skill is tested. These problems include those given in Table 12-1, which are more or less intrinsic to the age group, as well as environmentally imposed restrictions. These situations include a lack of exposure to a wide range of variable stimuli, lack of feedback subsequent to actions or verbalizations, and the decreased ability to alter events directly and immediately.

Third, many of the problems faced by the elderly, unlike those confronting younger age groups are often unmodifiable or unavoidable. Therefore, modification efforts must entail strategy training geared toward dealing with this inability directly to shape a favorable outcome rather than with the manipulation of natural contingencies.

Table 12-2. Reasons for Non-Exhibition of Problem-Solving Skills

No history of problem-solving ability
  Dependency on others throughout life
  Below normal intelligence
  Isolation
  The absence of problem situations
  More expedient methods to solve problems (e.g., money, family intervention)

Loss of previously exhibited problem-solving ability
  Extinction following problem-solving attempts
  Increased cautiousness
  Presence of anxiety or depression
  Memory dysfunction
  Lack of flexibility in the environment
  Increase in the number of new problem situations
  Cognitive dysfunction due to disease process (e.g., Alzheimer's, multi-infarct dementia)

For example, the limited mobility that may result after a stroke may be present forever at some level of involvement. This newly imposed restriction sets limits as to the amount of adaptation that can occur. Therefore, problems associated with this restriction can be resolved only by modifying one's cognitive approach (i.e., perceptions, self-verbalizations, self-statements, attitudes) to the difficulty. The depression and grief associated with the loss of a spouse also must be dealt with, at least initially, by modifying the damaging, depressive self-statements and unsuccessful coping strategies. And as Folkman and Lazarus (1980) state, it is the patient's perception of the problem situation, not the absolute magnitude of the problem, that determines the exercise of coping. With grief, other behavioral and nonbehavioral methods may be used in addition to problem-solving training. These methods might include medication and attempts to increase participation in distracting activities or to shape social and assertive skills. One's success in these areas is, in part, dependent on an initial cognitive reorganization or reappraisal. Cognitive modification techniques, such as problem-solving training, are the most direct ways to intervene at this level.

A fourth, and more speculative, reason that argues for the use of problem-solving training concerns the attitudes of the target population. This generation of elderly individuals, particularly those residing in dependency-encouraging facilities, seems to prefer response modification techniques that involve less control by the therapist. Long histories of self-reliance, particularly free from contacts with mental health professionals, tend to make interventions that involve educational rather than continued external control most appealing. Less external involvement also precludes most problems that frequently affect other treatments such as noncompliance (with medication), nonattendance (at structured activities), and nonadherence to attempts to restructure environmental events directly (as in relocation). It is quite clear that the elderly cohort does not utilize voluntary mental health services to the degree that their numbers would suggest (Kramer, Taube, & Redick, 1973), and they seldom turn to any formal organization for assistance when troubles arise (Gurian & Cantor, 1978).

The use of problem-solving training with institutionalized elderly patients, though limited, will be discussed and the procedure described. Special considerations for use in this population will then be addressed.

EVALUATION OF PROBLEM-SOLVING TRAINING

Hussian and Lawrence (1981) compared the effectiveness of problem-solving training with social reinforcement of activity in an elderly nursing home population. Hospital adjustment and depression served as dependent variables.

Thirty-six subjects (mean age, 73.6 years) with the highest scores on the Beck Depression Inventory (BDI) (mean score, 35.64) who were not deaf, blind, or receiving antidepressant medication were randomly divided into three conditions, social reinforcement (SR), problem-solving training (PS), and waiting-list control (WLC).

Subjects in the SR group were prompted to participate in daily activity classes. Attendance, participation, social interaction, and on-task behavior were social reinforced on an FR-2 minute schedule by activity staff. Reliability was calculated using a spot check by the experimenter with the number of agreements divided by the total number of commonly observed 2-minute intervals. Reliability averaged 93.5 percent.

Subjects in the PS condition received individual problem-solving training as described by Goldfried and Davison (1976). Trained activity staff and the experimenter conducted the therapy as follows:

1. A *general orientation* to problem-solving was provided. This phase included ideas on coping, mastery, the importance of exerting control, the effects of expectations on subsequent outcome, one's right to be assertive, and how deficient problem-solving skills may lead to depression, withdrawal, and "learned helplessness."

2. Problems generated in a pilot phase by other nursing home residents were then submitted to problem-solving training: *problem definition and formulation;* the *generation of alternative solutions, strategies, and tactics; decision making;* and *verification.*

3. During the final session of five, the subjects' own problem situations were subjected to the same procedure.

Waiting list control subjects received the same assessment devices (i.e., the BDI, a self-report measure of depression (SRS), and the Hospital Adjustment Scale (HAS). Measures of problem-solving ability and activity level were conducted on subjects in the two treatment groups only as a measure of the clinical validity of the procedures.

At the end of the second week, these groups were again divided so that six subjects in the SR group continued to receive social reinforcement for activity participation (SR-SR) while six began receiving problem-solving training (SR-PS). Six of the original PS group began receiving social reinforcement for activity participation (PS-SR), while six continued in problem-solving training (PS-PS). Six subjects in the WLC condition continued on the waiting list (WLC-WLC) while six were moved into an Information Control condition (WLC-IC). This latter condition involved discussions with the experimenter concerning biological, cognitive, sensory, and other changes that may occur with advanced aging.

The results are presented in Table 12-3. In addition, the outcome of the activity level measure showed an increase over the first week of treatment only for those individuals in the SR condition. There were no differences prior to the intervention.

Problem-solving ability, as expected, was significantly improved only by

Table 12-3. Results of the Hussian and Lawrence (1981) Study

I. Baseline to first treatment week
   1. PS and SR groups showed decreases on the BDI and SRS over the WLC.
II. Baseline to second treatment week
   1. PS-PS showed BDI reductions over WLC-IC.
   2. PS-SR showed BDI reductions over WLC-WLC and WLC-IC.
   3. SR-PS showed BDI reductions over WLC-IC.
   4. PS-PS and SR-PS showed a trend to reductions on the SRS.
III. First to second treatment weeks
   1. SR-PS showed SRS reductions over the SR-SR and PS-SR conditions.
   2. PS-PS showed HAS improvements over WLC-WLC and SR-SR.
IV. Baseline to the 2-week follow up
   1. PS-SR and PS-PS showed BDI reductions over WLC-WLC.
   2. PS-PS showed SRS reductions over WLC-WLC and SR-SR.
V. Baseline to 3-month follow up
   1. Significant MANOVA, nonsignificant ANOVA's.

the subjects exposed to the problem-solving training. There were no significant differences in problem-solving ability prior to the intervention.

In order to check the clinical validity of the treatment on an individual level, the levels of depression as given by the BDI were analyzed. Two subjects in each of the PS-PS, PS-SR, and SR-SR conditions showed BDI reductions from moderate or severe depression to mild or no depression. There were no individual changes in the other conditions.

It appears in this study that the conditions, which included at least 1 week of problem-solving training, led to significant reductions in depression as measured by the BDI. The follow-up data also tend to suggest that the PS component aided the maintenance of this reduction.

Berger and Rose (1977) also used a problem-solving approach in the first phase of their work with nursing home residents (mean age, 78.5). In order to generate training stimuli to increase adequate responses to various situations, the patients described problems (mostly involving peer interactions). These problems were then rated by a subset of the original problem generators as to the likelihood that they would occur in their lives and the degree of discomfort such a situation would generate. Thus, problem definition and selection was based on frequency and relevancy. These situations were then used in Interpersonal Skill Training (IRT) which comprised situation presentation, coaching, modeling, discussion, re-presentation, rehearsal, and feedback. Subjects in this IRT group outperformed subjects in a discussion control group on a behavioral measure of effective interpersonal skills. This differential held even at a 2-month follow-up. It should be noted, however, that this interpersonal skill training did not generalize to novel situations.

Toseland and Rose (1978) used a complete problem-solving training format in their study of treatment outcomes with deficient social skills. Fifty-three subjects, fifty-five years of age and older, received either role-playing (Interpersonal Skills Training), problem-solving training, or a social work group approach. The role-playing and problem-solving groups showed significant gains compared to the social work group.

On a related note, Lopez and Silber (1980) also have shown that problem-solving training can be helpful in the training of professionals who work with the elderly. These authors found that training, which included gathering information, stating problems clearly, choosing the highest priority problems, understanding the development of the problem, generation of solutions, and implementation of solutions, aided problem solving. Target problems included confusion, paranoia, anxiety, dealing with losses, grief, and annoying/disruptive behaviors.

TREATMENT SPECIFICS

When beginning problem-solving therapy with institutionalized populations of elderly, the therapist will find some minor difficulties while following the traditional procedures. Therapist involvement will tend to be greater than with many other populations. Though Kanfer and Busemeyer (1982) have correctly emphasized the need for the clinician to shape problem-solving skills in the patient rather than serving as the problem-solver, the clinician will find that the novelty of such a systematic approach will require more prompting, more concrete examples, and more emphasis on the non-critical generation of alternative solutions than with younger clients. With this modification in mind, the following procedures should prove as aids in training.

General Orientation

Emphasis should be placed on the educational aspects of the training. The importance of continual self-monitoring to determine when the new techniques should be instigated should be stressed so that the elderly client may begin appropriate problem attack skills early (Kanfer & Busemeyer, 1982). Effective problem-solving is enhanced when the client anticipates the likelihood of needing good coping ability prior to actual problem confrontation. Upcoming relocations, hospitalizations, new medication regimens, release to the home or family, and family illnesses, are situations which are likely to require the use of problem-solving strategies. A desirable outcome is more likely if the client is not overcome by anxiety, depression, or grief. Prophylactic use of the newly acquired skill should be stressed so that alternative solutions will be available prior to the need to implement them.

Clients who are institutionalized will often counter this rationale for training by arguing that the system cannot be changed, so further activity is a waste of time. The clinician may meet these objections with two arguments.

First, the elderly client may find that they will be placed in a less restrictive setting which allows for more direct impact. Therefore, these newly acquired skills may be useful when the system becomes more modifiable or a new system is encountered.

Second, the clinician should repeatedly emphasize the benefit of changing one's attitudes even when a problem situation cannot be modified directly. Acquiring the skill and using it on smaller problems often in and of itself appears to reduce anxiety and depression even though the major limitation continues.

Problem Definition and Formulation

This stage of problem-solving is most optimally presented through the use of a hypothetical problem based upon problems generated by patients in similar situations. This helps to establish rapport and lets the client know that the clinician is aware of certain high frequency problems. Before allowing the client or clients to produce a problem situation of their own, presentation of a hypothetical problem eases acceptance and prevents one client from domineering the proceedings. The most helpful topic areas include: dealing with combative residents, loss of freedom or flexibility, infrequent or disruptive visits by family members, getting attention of the staff for medical or other concerns, fear of being institutionalized for the remainder of their lives, ability of their spouse to function alone, and negative staff attitudes.

For example, the clinician may start out this phase of the training by giving the following hypothetical case:

> A sixty-six year old man is sent to a hospital like this one because he can't take care of himself anymore. Mr. Brown walks around the ward most of the day asking for his family to come get him. His head is usually down, he dresses poorly, is dirty, and does not talk to anyone. He states that he doesn't want to be here, "it's a bad place." No one cares "about me being here."

This case sets the stage for the client(s) to offer possible causes and descriptions of the problem. Most of these descriptions will correspond to their own situations but will be worded vaguely. More specific problem definitions which would lead more easily into the other phases of problem-solving therapy would be, "What Mr. Brown means is that he wants his family to visit more," or "He can't remember to fix himself up anymore and he needs encouragement."

Thoughout this phase, it is important for the clinician to stress the need for concrete, familiar terms, to encourage the use of illustrations or examples, and to reinforce information seeking. D'Zurilla and Goldfried (1971) have also suggested that the therapist stress stating problems in terms of the specific barriers or conflicts which prevent the acquisition of a particular goal which will more easily lead to the solution of the problem.

Generation of Alternatives

The concept of brainstorming should be introduced during this phase of training. Elderly institutionalized patients tend to have extreme difficulty in listing possible solutions even when the problem has been properly defined. The patient should be instructed to come up with any solutions he can, independent of any judgments regarding risk, likelihood of success, or the systemwide ramifications of the solution. These solutions can be written on a blackboard to ease the presentation. Even humorous alternatives should be listed even when these suggestions may entail totally impractical or potentially damaging consequences for the client or others.

Solutions which might be generated by uncritical analysis of the problem described above are: asking to be placed in skills training classes, contacting the social worker to help ask family members to increase visitation, watching the exit doors until one can escape, remaining in bed all day, harming other patients or disrupting ongoing activities until the proper attention is provided by the staff, etc.

Decision Making

Once the list of solutions has been generated, the clients should be told to think of the consequences of their actions. Points should be attached on a scale of -2 to $+2$ along several dimensions. These dimensions include the benefits for the client, benefits for others, short-term gains, and long-term consequences. Therefore, four sets of scores would accompany each alternative. From the example given above, Table 12-4 shows the values that might be attached to the solutions.

Table 12-4. Values Attached to Hypothetical Solutions

Solution	Self	Others	Short-term	Long-term
Request skills training	+2	+1	+1	+2
Ask for increased visitation	+2	−1	+1	+1
Try to escape	+2	−1	+1	−2
Become disruptive	0	−2	−1	−2
Place in token economy or milieu therapy	+1	0	+1	+2
Withdraw from all contacts	0	0	0	−2

The points are then tallied and the most attractive alternative(s) is/are chosen.

Once the solution(s) is/are chosen, specific strategies must then be generated and weighted which provide the course of action necessary to achieve these solution(s). These strategies are generated in the same way that the solutions were. Then, the methods for the implementation of such strategies must be generated and weighted. These methods or tactics are specific behaviors, usually in a step-by-step fashion, which must be instigated in order to complete the chosen strategies. D'Zurilla and Goldfried (1971) help to clarify this distinction.

> The only difference between the two procedures (strategy versus tactic choice) is in the objective against which the utility is to be estimated. In the case of the selection of the best strategy to pursue in a problematic situation, the value of the strategy is judged against its likelihood of effectively resolving the major issues or conflicts. In the case of the evaluation of specific means of implementing the strategy selected, the effectiveness with which the strategy is implemented is used in estimating its value. (p. 119)

Verification

Once the appropriate solution(s), strategy (strategies), and tactic(s) have been chosen, the client must be given the opportunity to act. This may be facilitated either through role-playing or by guiding the client while he or she attempts to put his or her skills to work on the problem. With geriatric patients, particularly those in institutional environments, the role-playing tactic is usually necessary. Lack of assertiveness or communication skills may prevent the client from attempting to immediately solve the problem. Premature attempts may meet with frustration and the fulfillment of negative self-prophesies. When one takes into account the difficulty inherent in trying to change these systems and the negative stereotypes of some of the staff, it becomes clear that gradual introduction to the original conflicts might be preferable.

When the therapist feels that the client(s) is/are proficient with the skill, client-generated problems are then used. The client should also be taught recording techniques which serve to document the outcome of the problem-solving attempts.

Special Considerations

Only a few modifications in the traditional problem-solving procedures are required when working with fairly intact institutionalized elderly patients.

Most of the difficulties which may be confronted with this group of clients will be due, not to age-related differences, but to variables associated with the residential setting. The following considerations are offered in order to increase the likelihood of successful implementation of the therapy.

Procedural Considerations

1. Memory limitations which are correlated with aging and intensified by cortical dysfunction make the training of new skills difficult. In cases of acute organic dysfunction, delirium, this lack of even minimal concentration may force the postponement of the intervention.

The therapist may compensate, in part, for memory deficits by using very concrete instructions and, of course, solutions and strategies; using more frequent but shorter sessions; using booster sessions; stressing concentration on internal and external cues to signal the need to implement the newly learned skill (Kanfer & Busemeyer, 1982); and by encouraging the use of memory aids. Minimally, the client should be told to write down the procedures as well as the solutions, strategies, and tactics of choice.

2. The long history of responding with less than proficient problem-solving skill may require that the clinician procede slowly with the training. Initial hesitancy to participate requires a slow introduction to problem-solving training and less structured conversations for the first few sessions are indicated.

3. The emphasis on the uncritical generation of alternatives must be repeated continually. The clinician should also repeat the fact that no negative actions will be taken for errors or less than perfect performance. Few alternatives will be generated in the absence of such instructions.

4. Special attention should be given to the availability of reinforcement provided during training and during the verification stage in particular. The therapist should not rely on naturally occurring reinforcement to maintain attendance in the training sessions, progress through the sessions, or the ultimate exercise of the newly learned skill.

Social reinforcement needs to be fairly continual in the first sessions contingent upon production, not the quality of the performance. The clinician should be certain that the strategies and solutions chosen have a fair chance of being followed by positive events. Shaping a "confrontation" behavior with goals which are not likely to be changed within the hospital should be undertaken only when accompanied by provisions for alternative action.

5. Perseveration on one topic area, usually delusional in nature, occurs quite frequently with elderly patients in mental institutions. When the patient states that he or she was placed in the facility against their will by relatives or other forces, this patient is a difficult candidate for therapy. Efforts should be made to redirect the patient's attention by interruption, extinction, and prompts and reinforcement for appropriate speech.

Problems with Generalization

Many outcome studies in behavioral geriatrics show impressive treatment gains but little or no maintenance or generalization. Clinicians may wish to incorporate the following points in their therapy in order to enhance the continuation of gains beyond the therapy session.

1. The use of extrainstitutional problems during the problem-definition stage helps to increase the likelihood of continued application after discharge. This not only increases the probability that the skill will be used outside of the facility but is ethically mandated. Teaching skills which may only be applied within the institution is, in most cases, a perpetuation of the traditional custodial-care philosophy.

These skills are less likely to be abandoned if the therapist includes as hypothetical problems some of the following: renewing old associations, self-directed medication consumption, the structuring of daily activities, how to deal with increased prices and limited resources, and how to conquer transportation problems.

2. A wide variety of problems should be used, both those intrinsic to institutional life and those which are more likely to be encountered in less restrictive settings. Experience with a large variety of problem situations should promote generalization. Though problem-solving training is purported to be a generalized strategy-training therapy, training geared to specific problems does seem to be facilitative. Possibly the deficiency in abstracting behavior often reported among the elderly helps to explain the relative success of multiple-problem training.

3. Family members are valuable to include in training. If this is not possible, family members should be told prior to the discharge of their relative about the training. These individuals may then be used to promote maintenance of therapeutic gains as "multiple therapists," act as agents of continuity, and as signals for the need for the ex-client to activate the problem-solving procedure.

4. Participation in problem-solving may be encouraged through the use of contingency contracting. Tokens or privilege level changes may be made contingent upon the use of problem-solving skill.

It is hoped that the preceding discussion and presentation will encourage the use of problem-solving training in institutionalized geriatric patients. The clinician who attempts to implement this type of therapy with this group should find a relatively high rate of success. Perhaps the most difficult barrier to overcome will be the widely held view that cognitive-behavioral techniques are somehow obviated by concomitants of aging.

Acknowledgments

The author wishes to acknowledge the valuable input of the members of the weekly professional staff meeting, Geriatric and Extended Units, Terrell State Hospital, Terrell, Texas.

References

Baltes, M. M., & Zerbe, M. (1976). Independence training in nursing-home residents. *Gerontologist, 16,* 428–432.

Berger, R. M., & Rose, S. D. (1977). Interpersonal skill training with institutionalized elderly patients. *Journal of Gerontology, 32,* 346–353.

Blackman, D. K., Howe, M., & Pinkston, E. M. (1976). Increasing participation in social interaction of the institutionalized elderly. *Gerontologist, 16,* 69–76.

Botwinick, J. (1973) *Aging and behavior.* New York: Springer.

D'Zurilla, T. J., & Goldfried, M. R. (1971). Problem solving and behavior modification. *Journal of Abnormal Psychology, 78,* 107–126.

Folkman, S., & Lazarus, R. S. (1980). An analysis of coping in a middle-aged community sample. *Journal of Health and Social Behavior, 21,* 219–239.

Goldfried, M. R., & Davison, G. C. (1976). *Clinical behavior therapy.* New York: Holt, Rinehart & Winston.

Goldstein, R. S., & Baer, D. M. (1976). A procedure to increase the personal mail and number of correspondents for nursing home residents. *Behavior Therapy, 7,* 348–354.

Gurian, B. S., & Cantor, M. A. (1978) Mental health and community support systems for the elderly. In *Aging: The process and the people,* G. Usdin & C. K. Hofling (Eds.), (pp. 184–205). New York: Brunner/Mazel.

Hoyer, W. J., Kafer, R. A., Simpson, S. C., & Hoyer, F. W. (1974). Reinstatement of verbal behavior in elderly mental patients using operant procedures. *Gerontologist, 14,* 149–152.

Hussian, R. A. (1985). The combination of operant and cognitive therapy with geriatric patients. *International Journal of Behavioral Geriatrics,* in press.

Hussian, R. A., & Lawrence, P. S. (1981). Social reinforcement and problem-solving training in the treatment of depressed institutionalized elderly patients. *Cognitive Therapy and Research, 5,* 57–69.

Jackson, G. M., & Schonfeld, L. I. (1982). Comparisons of visual feedback, instructional prompts and discreet, discrete prompting in the treatment of orofacial tardive dyskinesia. *International Journal of Behavioral Geriatrics, 1,* 35–46.

Kanfer, F. H., & Busemeyer, J. R. (1982) The use of problem solving and decision making in behavior therapy. *Clinical Psychology Review, 2,* 239–266.

Kramer, M., Taube, C. A., & Redick, R. W. (1973). Patterns of use of psychiatric facilities by the aged: Past, present, and future. In *The psychology of adult development and aging*, C. Eisdorfer & M. P. Lawton (Eds.), (pp. 428–528). Washington: American Psychological Association,

Lee, J. A., & Pollack, R. H. (1980). The effects of age on perceptual problem-solving strategies. *Bulletin of the Psychonomic Society, 15*, 239–241.

Libb, J. W., & Clements, C. B. (1969). Token reinforcement in an exercise program for hospitalized geriatric patients. *Perceptual and Motor Skills, 28*, 957–958.

Lopez, M. A., Hoyer, W. J., Goldstein, A. P., Gershaw, N. J., & Sprafkin, R. P. (1980). Effects of overlearning and incentive on the acquisition and transfer of interpersonal skills with institutionalized elderly. *Journal of Gerontology, 35*, 403–408.

Lopez, M. A., & Silber, S. (1980). Counseling the elderly: A training program for professionals. Paper presented at the meeting of the Southeastern Psychological Association, Atlanta.

MacDonald, M. L., & Butler, A. K. (1974). Reversal of helplessness: Producing walking behavior in nursing home wheelchair residents using behavior modification procedures. *Journal of Gerontology, 29*, 97–101.

MacDonald, M. L., & Settin, J. M. (1978). Reality orientation versus sheltered workshops as treatment for the institutionalized aging. *Journal of Gerontology, 33*, 416–421.

McClannahan, L. E., & Risley, T. R. (1975). Design of living environments for nursing home residents: Increasing participation in recreation activities. *Journal of Applied Behavior Analysis, 8*, 261–268.

Nigl, A. J., & Jackson, B. (1981). A behavior management program to increase social responses in psychogeriatric patients. *Journal of the American Geriatrics Society, 29*, 92–95.

Pfeiffer, E. (1977). Psychopathology and social pathology. In *Handbook of the psychology of aging*, J. E. Birren & K. W. Schaie (Eds.). New York: Van Nostrand Reinhold.

Quattrochi-Tubin, S., & Jason, L. A. (1980). Enhancing social interactions and activity among the elderly through stimulus control. *Journal of Applied Behavior Analysis, 13*, 159–163.

Quilitch, H. R. (1974). Purposeful activity increased on a geriatric ward through programmed recreation. *Journal of the American Geriatrics Society, 22*, 226–229.

Rinke, C. L., Williams, J. J., Lloyd, K. E., & Smith-Scott, W. (1978). The effects of prompting and reinforcement on self-bathing by elderly residents of a nursing home. *Behavior Therapy, 9*, 873–881.

Toseland, R., & Rose, S. D. (1978). A social skills training program for older adults: Evaluation of three group approaches. *Social Work Research Abstracts*, 873–874.

Chapter 13

GROUP COGNITIVE BEHAVIOR THERAPY FOR SEXUAL REHABILITATION OF SPINAL CORD–INJURED CLIENTS

Janie S. Weinberg

Spinal cord injuries occur most frequently in young active men, aged fifteen to thirty (AASECT, 1979; AJN, 1977; Miller, et al., 1981; Singh & Magner, 1975). All victims of spinal cord injury face a long and difficult rehabilitation process that must include learning to redefine themselves completely. No longer can they view themselves as able-bodied. The vast majority of spinal cord–damaged individuals become injured as a result of some sudden and unexpected physical trauma. They probably have not taken the time to examine their feelings toward disability or the disabled population until they become unwilling members of this group.

Much of the early rehabilitation of spinal cord–injured people focuses on aiding them to gain as much independence in their lives as possible. Sexual concerns often take on a significantly decreased importance in the rehabilitation process. Given the age group of most of the victims, this seems somewhat unusual, but sexuality and sexual functioning is often discussed very briefly or not at all.

In general, our society tends to deny the sexuality of disabled people. This is especially true for people who become paralyzed. It is often assumed that since the individual is unable to experience genital sensation they are therefore asexual. This is both damaging and untrue. In fact, paralyzed people can and do experience satisfying sexual relationships.

Sexual expression is the right of all people, regardless of their disabilities. The fact that disabled people can receive as well as give pleasure is an essential fact that is often not taught to the clients in either a hospital or rehabilitation setting. Although it is true that the nature of the sexual excitation and sexual activity may change for spinal cord–injured people, sexuality and sexual expression does persist and is still enjoyable (Weinberg, 1982).

In addition to valuing sexual expression for the dignity and pleasure it physically affords people, studies have demonstrated that sexual adjustment is related to psychological, social, and physical factors which are relevant for successful rehabilitation (Berkman, 1978); that is, individuals who are sexually rehabilitated tend to be more successful in all areas of adjustment following spinal cord injury.

Berkman (1978) found that sexual adjustment tended to follow the same pattern as overall adjustment, in which the individual learns to change his values as a result of the injury. In the initial stages of the rehabilitation process, newly injured people tend to focus primarily on the losses that have been sustained. As the rehabilitation continues, individuals learn to focus more on their remaining assets, including seeing themselves as desirable partners, finding satisfaction with sexual relationships, and engaging in sexual behaviors that do not depend solely on genital functioning.

Despite findings that sexual adjustment is correlated with overall adjustment, many clients still receive little or no sexual counseling or education during their rehabilitation process. Often the focus in rehabilitation is strongly directed toward reintegrating the injured individual back into society in terms of work and activities of daily living (dressing, feeding oneself, etc.). The focus is on restoration to work and society (Weinberg, 1982). Sexual functioning is not viewed as falling within the area of restoration or activities of daily living.

Since most clients are included in the planning for their rehabilitation, one might wonder why they don't bring the topic to the attention of their health care workers. Certainly, some do. Others feel that sex is or should be relatively unimportant in the larger scope of rehabilitation. They may be embarrassed to be concerned with such "frivolous" behaviors. The average developmental stage of the typical adolescent client does not generally allow easy discussions of sexual activity. Finally, for many, sex is a taboo topic, not to be discussed with strangers.

Health care workers may also avoid discussion of sexual information with clients. They may feel that they do not have the knowledge to discuss sexual functioning with spinal cord–injured clients. They too may be embarrassed or anxious talking about sex, particularly with the typical adolescent client. Finally, they may not even think of discussing sex, since they may hold the incorrect belief that paralyzed people cannot enjoy a rewarding and pleasurable sex life.

The view of physically disabled people as asexual is only one of many negative cognitions held by health care professionals, clients, and families of clients. A second area of negative cognition occurs when clients experience disturbances in body image as a result of the injury. They have learned of the "badness" of physical disability during their able-bodied youth. They too were told by parents to not stare or to look away instead of asking questions of people in wheelchairs. All spinal cord–injured people at some time or another view their body as the enemy. They often lack control over simple body functions such as emptying their bladder and bowel. In addition to the loss of control over function, many spinal cord–injured people evidence muscle atrophy. The "wasted" appearance of nonfunctional muscles leads to further body image disturbance and the feelings of being unattractive.

Gender role, or an individual's sense of their expression of maleness or femaleness is also subject to great disturbance following spinal cord injury. For many men, the independent, sexually aggressive, strong image is the one they equate with being a man. In sexual terms, penile-vaginal intercourse is seen as the main and perhaps only means of sexual activity acceptable. When this type of man becomes paralyzed and may no longer able to fulfill these roles, he may experience significant disturbances in his gender role. He may even express that he can no longer be a "real man." Similarly, women have been socialized to be nurturant. They are taught that their role is to care for others. When they are placed in the position of having to be cared for, they too may have difficulties accepting themselves as "real" women. In addition, for women, the physical attractiveness lost through muscle atrophy and being confined to a wheelchair may make them feel particularly sexually unattractive and out of touch.

Finally, many physically disabled people are taught that they will still be able to please their partners sexually, and that they "should" receive their gratification through this other-pleasing. While it is true that spinal cord injured men and women have the ability to please their partners, it is essential to their self-esteem and future adjustment for them to learn that they too can receive sexual pleasure (Weinberg, 1982).

As more rehabilitation professionals have begun to recognize and support the notion of sexual rehabilitation for physically disabled populations (particularly spinal cord–injured people), attention to the format of the rehabilitation has increased. Group therapy and teaching has been most commonly utilized, usually combined with some individual therapy wherever possible.

Dixon (1981) has found that strong group identification occurs with individuals with more visible handicaps, such as amputation, spinal cord injury, and stroke. This identification can be therapeutic in that it allows for information exchange and successfully maximizing the value of modeling. The group identification makes group dealing with stigma and quality of life issues far more salient and effective than individual therapy, particularly with an able-bodied therapist.

In addition, group approaches have been found to be easy and efficient of cost and time (Freeman, 1983; Steger, 1980). The format for sexual education and counseling groups for spinal cord–injured individuals generally includes a balance between didactic coverage of basic sexual information, attitude development, discussion of sexual adaptations, effective communication, maintenance of relationships, and practical issues of individual concern (Melnyk, 1979). Techniques of role play and behavior rehearsal are often utilized in these groups.

Although a group format utilizing cognitive behavioral approaches in counseling spinal cord-injured people has become more or less accepted by those who provide sexual rehabilitation, no comprehensive cognitive behavioral approach has appeared in the literature. This chapter will present a model of such a program. It is hoped that future research can be undertaken using this model.

Although a number of sexual rehabilitation programs for spinal cord-injured populations exist, few have been systematically investigated in terms of efficacy of group versus individual therapy. In two general studies (Rush, 1981; Shaffer, 1981), the findings were contradictory. Given the design flaws of the Rush study, one would tend to place greater credence on the findings of the Shaffer study which supported the greater efficacy of group cognitive behavior therapy for changing depression, anxiety and assertiveness. Although these factors are not the only factors for inclusion in a sexual rehabilitation program for spinal cord-injured people, the findings of the Shaffer study can be utilized to provide a rationale for the use of group therapy in sexual rehabilitation programs, since depression, anxiety, and assertiveness must all be addressed with this population.

Of the progams that do exist, Chipouras (1979) has provided a review of the 10 programs designed as comprehensive sexual rehabilitation programs and has found the following commonalities in approach (note: these programs do not provide firm research statistics on outcomes).

1. Programs are based on the principle that sexuality and sexual functioning are important components of overall rehabilitation.

2. Most programs encourage staff participation through in-service training to ensure sensitive and comfortable treatment of client sexual concerns.

3. Most programs utilize the Sexual Attitude Reassessment (SAR) workshop, adapted for use with spinal cord injured participants, staff and partners. (Note: SAR workshops generally involve the flooding of participants through movies and small group interactions. The purpose has been to desensitize participants in order to enable them to be resensitized with more open and liberal attitudes about sexuality. Most participants of SARs report positive gains, but there has been little work in systematic objective evaluation (Held, 1975).)

4. Programs related to sexuality are offered on a voluntary basis.

5. The spouse/partner is included in the sexuality program whenever possible.

6. A library of reading and audiovisual material is usually available for patient use.

7. Although almost all programs have a formal component, e.g., lectures, film presentations, there is a great deal of emphasis placed on individual needs and preferences.

8. The group approach is used extensively to communicate information, increase awareness and provide a forum for sharing experiences about sexuality.

Formats for courses vary. Most, however, consist of weekly meetings ranging from 1½ to 3 hours over a time span of 6 to 8 weeks (Melnyk, 1979; Steger, 1980). Steger's research project, conducted at the University of Washington Rehabilitation Medical Department Clinic, most nearly approaches the cognitive-behavioral model presented here (Steger, 1980). Several weaknesses in the program have been avoided in the proposed model. First, the heterosexist bias will be eliminated by avoiding use of Steger's evaluation tool, which included a checklist scale of sexual activities ranging from being with a member of the opposite sex to intercourse. This tool also contributes to an unnecessary emphasis on the genital aspects of sex.

Aspects of the research project that have been adopted here include the format of eight 1½-hour sessions with homework assignments and individualized assignments. Unlike the study, however, partners are not required for inclusion in the group proposed.

THE PROGRAM

Format

The program described here is one which will meet for eight 1½-hour sessions. All participants will be spinal cord–injured men and women who have been injured within the past year. They will be inpatients in a rehabilitation hospital. Participants will be medically healthy enough to be able to utilize weekend or day passes.

Homework assignments will include weekly activity scheduling with ratings for mastery and pleasure, and completion of the Beck Depression Inventory (Beck, 1978). All participants will also complete a body image scale on weeks 1, 4, and 8. On weeks, 2, 4, and 6, clients will collect dysfunctional thought records relating to topics covered at those meetings (Secord and Jourard, 1953). Finally, outcome evaluation will be measured using behavioral criterion established by individual group members and by the Sexual Attitude and Information Questionnaire (SAIQ) (Steger, 1980) administered in weeks 1, 3, 5, and 7. Additional individualized homework assignments will be devised with group members.

Rationale

Individuals who experience spinal cord injury are suddenly thrust into a stigmatized group—the group of physically disabled people. The previously able-bodied and now spinal cord–injured person probably participated (albeit passively in most cases) in the stigmatization or at least in ignoring physically disabled people. Now, as members of that group, they experience a great deal of cognitive dissonance. The spinal cord–injured individual has experienced a significant, permanent change in his/her life, requiring great coping without the promise of cure. Since greater coping is the primary goal of cognitive behavioral therapy, this approach seems to be perfectly suited to this population!

On a more pragmatic basis, research has demonstrated the efficacy of group modalities for the physically disabled. Cost effectiveness is another positive point for such a program. Finally, it is realistic to expect that patients will remain in the rehabilitation center for the full eight weeks of the group.

The Group

In proposing that cognitive behavioral approaches are appropriate and useful in the treatment of sexual dysfunction, Steger (1978) has proposed a number of situations in which this approach is particularly useful. Most of the situations are those in which an in vivo strategy of behavior therapy alone is either unsuccessful or for some reason not possible (e.g., lack of partner, lack of carrying out in vivo assignments due to fear). It is felt that indeed CBT approaches can be useful in the treatment of sexual problems in general and need not be restricted to cases in which in vivo work is deemed to be too difficult.

In the intial sessions of this group, the goals are essentially the same as for any individual or group CBT (Young, 1982). They include definition of the specific problems to work on, setting priorities, showing the client that the situation is not hopeless, illustrating the relationship between cognitions and emotions, socializing the client into the therapeutic milieu of cognitive therapy, and stressing the importance of homework. As can be seen in the outline of the group sessions, these goals are addressed fully. Some of the specific cognitive behavioral techniques to be utilized include guided imaging, cognitive rehearsal, thought stopping, assertion training, and social skills training (Steger, 1978; Young, 1982).

Although group members may alter the agenda according to their own needs, this group will generally be a rather structured one in terms of topics covered. Topics do overlap somewhat, but generally each week's group will focus primarily on the topic scheduled.

Outline

Outline of Weekly Group Sessions

Week 1:

1. Introduction: 10 minutes
2. Problem list formulation: 5 minutes

3. Cognitions regarding sex and the physically disabled: 10 minutes
4. Explanation of cognitive behavior therapy and its application to spinal cord injured group: 20 minutes
5. Establishing priorities: 10 minutes
6. Normal sexual response cycle: 20 minutes
7. Homework: 10 minutes
    a. Weekly Activity Schedule (WAS)
    b. Beck Depression Inventory (BDI)
    c. Sexual Attitude and Information Questionnaire (SAIQ)

Week 2:
1. Review of homework: 5 minutes
2. Review of week: 5 minutes
3. Agenda and review of last week: 10 minutes
4. Sexual functioning in spinal cord injured: 20 minutes (alternatives and realistic goals)
5. Role of men and women in sexual activities: 10 minutes
6. The cognitive triad: 10 minutes
7. Problem list in terms of triad: 20 minutes
8. Summary and homework: 10 minutes
    a. Weekly Activity Schedule (WAS)
    b. Beck Depression Inventory (BDI)
    c. Record of Dysfunctional Thoughts

Week 3:
1. Review of homework: 5 minutes
2. Review of week: 5 minutes
3. Agenda and review of last week: 10 minutes
4. Sexual scripts—before and after injury: 20 minutes
5. Movie *(Coming Home)* love scene and discussion: 30 minutes
6. The mechanics: 10 minutes
7. Summary and homework: 10 minutes
    a. Weekly Activity Schedule (WAS)
    b. Beck Depression Inventory (BDI)
    c. Sexual Attitude and Information Questionnaire (SAIQ)

Week 4:
1. Review of homework: 5 minutes
2. Review of week: 5 minutes

3. Agenda and review of last week: 10 minutes
4. Fertility in spinal cord injured: 20 minutes
5. Making social contacts: 20 minutes
6. Dealing with barriers (architectural): 15 minutes
7. Relaxation techniques: 5 minutes
8. Summary and homework: 10 minutes
    a. Weekly Activity Schedule (WAS)
    b. Beck Depression Inventory (BDI)
    c. Body Image Scale
    d. Record of Dysfunctional Thoughts

Week 5:
1. Review of homework: 5 minutes
2. Review of week: 5 minutes
3. Agenda and review of last week: 10 minutes
4. Spinal cord injured speaker: 30 minutes
5. Relationships: 30 minutes
6. Relaxation techniques: 10 minutes
7. Summary and homework: 10 minutes
    a. Weekly Activity Schedule (WAS)
    b. Beck Depression Inventory (BDI)
    c. Sexual Attitude and Information Questionnaire (SAIQ)

Week 6:
1. Review of homework: 5 minutes
2. Review of week: 5 minutes
3. Agenda and review of last week: 10 minutes
4. Sexual assertiveness: 30 minutes
5. Teaching able-bodied partners: 20 minutes
6. Defining sexuality again: 10 minutes
7. Summary and homework: 10 minutes
    a. Weekly Activity Schedule (WAS)
    b. Beck Depression Inventory (BDI)
    c. Sexual Attitude and Information Questionnaire (SAIQ)

Week 7:
1. Review of homework: 5 minutes
2. Review of week: 5 minutes
3. Agenda and review of last week: 10 minutes

4. Sex, relationship, love (including *Active Partners* movie): 50 minutes
5. Teaching able-bodied partners mechanics: 10 minutes
6. Summary and homework: 10 minutes
    a. Weekly Activity Schedule (WAS)
    b. Beck Depression Inventory (BDI)
    c. Sexual Attitude and Information Questionnaire (SAIQ)

Week 8:
1. Review of homework: 5 minutes
2. Review of week: 5 minutes
3. Agenda and review of last week: 10 minutes
4. Community resources: 10 minutes
5. Review: 20 minutes
6. Conclusion: 20 minutes (and last minute concerns)
7. Evaluation of program: 20 minutes
    a. Weekly Activity Schedule (WAS)
    b. Beck Depression Inventory (BDI)
    c. Body Image Scale

Case Studies

The following case studies will illustrate the applications of the cognitive-behavioral strategies with two spinal cord injured patients.

The Case of Jim

Jim was a high school "jock." He was the captain of the football team, the one voted most likely to succeed, and one of the most popular students in the senior class. His motorcycle accident was a tremendous shock to Jim's family and friends. While out one night, Jim's motorcycle was hit by a car driven by a drunk driver. The driver received minor injuries, but Jim was thrown from the motorcycle into a ditch. Jim broke his neck at the C6 level. After several weeks of treatment, the doctors told Jim and his family that Jim would never be able to walk again. In fact, the use of his arms would be limited as well. The full extent of the injury would still take some time to determine.

As with many spinal cord–injured people, Jim went through a period of understandable depression. He felt that his life was over and experienced feelings of hopelessness. The helplessness that accompanies depression was made worse by the fact that indeed Jim was physically helpless. When it was decided that Jim was ready to begin the work of physical rehabilitation, Jim's depression seemed to be lifting. He poured himself into what he called his new "training regime." Jim made tremendous strides exceeding the expectations of even the rehabilitation specialists. Jim began to hope that in fact the prognosis for him was incorrect. After all he reasoned, if he was surprising the professionals so much with his progress, maybe they didn't really know for sure that he couldn't fully recover.

When Jim was transferred to a rehabilitation hospital for further physical and occupational therapy, his denial of the permanence of his disability began to become problematic for him. He did not work toward acquiring general life skills, such as the use of assistive devices for writing, but focused solely on muscle development.

Throughout this time Jim's family had encouraged his belief in his ultimate recovery, since they too were shocked at the severity of his limitations. They just couldn't imagine their able-bodied son as a wheelchair-bound, dependent cripple.

At the rehabilitation hospital, Jim became friendly with one of the hospital volunteers, a high school student from a different school than Jim had attended. Lisa's attention to Jim seemed to help him. She seemed to care for him despite his injuries. When he told her that his situation was temporary, she was surprised enough to relate this to one of the staff.

Jim freely discussed this with several of the staff. When questioned about his future, Jim discussed career goals of law school. He also looked forward to marriage and a family. It was at this point that Jim was approached about joining the sexuality group that was about to begin.

During the first three sessions, Jim's participation and homework assignments were all consistent with his belief in his eventual return to able-bodied status. During the fourth week, however, the other group members confronted Jim with the reality that his disability was as permanent as theirs. The group was very angry with Jim, since his denial constantly reminded them of the reality of their own situations.

When the low level of fertility among spinal cord–injured men was discussed, the reality of the situation seemed really to hit Jim. All of the dreams seemed to crash at once. He could not be a father. He couldn't be a lover. In fact, he couldn't be anything except a "gimp."

At this point, Jim's major dysfunctional thoughts were:

1. "I'll never be able to love and care for anyone else when I can't even care for myself."
2. "No one could ever trust a paralyzed lawyer."
3. "My career goal is impossible to attain."
4. "Lisa has been nice to me because she feels sorry for me."

Jim was withdrawn and quiet during the fifth session until the speaker began to tell his story. George was more disabled than Jim. He was also several years post-injury and older than Jim. George was now married and ran his own business. Jim became verbally aggressive during the presentation, shouting that George was just a fool and didn't realize that he had been married out of pity, not love.

The group members supported both Jim and George. The discussion of relationships took on a different tone during this session. By having another spinal cord–injured person to talk to, other group members finally felt free to ask the questions they felt that the able bodied group leaders could not possibly know about the real "ins and outs" of sexual encounters and of relationships as a physically disabled man.

Jim was particularly helped by this discussion. George candidly told the group his own story. He had also feared that women were staying with him or dating him either because they felt sorry for him or because they thought he had come into money as a result of a legal settlement. This thought had not even occurred to Jim. He began to recognize that in George he had found an individual who had really thought this entire thing out.

After the session with George, Jim's real sexual and social rehabilitation had begun in earnest. The previously unsettling effect he had had on other group members was changed. His strong leadership skills and his verbal eloquence greatly assisted him in re-evaluating his dysfunctional thoughts. He began to recognize that perhaps people could listen to him from a wheelchair and that perhaps he could still be a lawyer.

Lisa became something of a guinea pig for Jim socially. She was willing to go out with him and help him to "check out" places for their accessibility. Lisa drew the line at sexual encounters with Jim. Although initially this confirmed Jim's view of himself as sexually unattractive, Jim had learned to challenge this dysfunctional thought and did eventually accept the possibility that Lisa's refusal to have sex was not a function of his disability but rather a function of her desire to be a virgin at marriage.

Jim was helped to develop more adaptive self-statements regarding his sexual "possibilities." He challenged the negative distortions regarding his performance. With a more adaptive self-view he became less depressed and less hopeless.

By the end of the program, Jim's depression inventory showed remarkable return to acceptable levels. By considering this in conjunction with a body-image rating that reflected a more realistic acceptance of his disability, Jim's progress with sexual and indeed psychological rehabilitation was considered to be highly acceptable. His gains were clearly attributable to the group cognitive behavioral therapy described here.

The Case of Alan

Alan was different from the start. He did not fit into the fifteen- to eighteen-year-old norm for spinal cord–injured men. He was thirty-three years old at the time of his injury. He was also married with two young sons, aged two and six. Alan ran a successful family business prior to his accident.

Alan and his wife Susan seemed to have achieved the American dream. They had a beautiful house, a good marriage, and two healthy children. One summer day, however, this was irrevocably changed. Alan was body-surfing at the beach. It was a common and nondangerous act that he had done many times before. He didn't know what happened this time. He remembered hearing his neck snap. The next thing he knew, he awoke in the intensive care unit.

Apparently, Alan had hit a sand bar and broken his neck. A nearby swimmer pulled him, unconscious and paralyzed, from the water. The swimmer then performed the CPR that probably saved Alan's life. Unfortunately, it may also have contributed to the severity of Alan's spinal cord injury.

When Alan awoke, he was informed that he had broken his neck and that he would never again be able to walk, play the racquetball that he loved, or swim unassisted again. He was a C 5-6 quadriplegic. He was and would remain paralyzed from the chest down. He would have some arm movement and partial use of his hands following extensive rehabilitation.

Alan's adjustment to his new situation seemed too good to be true. He worked endlessly to maximize his remaining function. He wanted to get as well as he could as quickly as possible. He wanted his children to see that he was still their dad and that he was all right.

Like most other spinal cord–injured patients, Alan received no teaching about his sexual options. In fact, the only staff person who mentioned sex at all was the attendant who noticed that he got an erection while he was being bathed. She jokingly said that the erection could come in handy when he was discharged. She failed to attend to the fact that he could not feel the erection or control it.

Alan's other sex education as a quadriplegic came from another patient who told him that as long as he could still use his mouth, he would never be without a companion for sex. He then commented that since Alan already had a woman, he would be just fine.

Almost 6 months to the day from his admission, Alan returned home permanently. Luckily, the ranch-style house that Alan and Susan owned was relatively easy to make accessible for Alan and his wheelchair. Alan also had purchased and learned to drive a specially adapted wheelchair van. Several weeks after his return home, Alan began to go back to work.

In the first months after Alan returned, he and Susan didn't discuss sex. Since they had exchanged their king-size bed for two twin beds so Alan could have a hospital bed at home, they also stopped cuddling during the night. It seemed that both Susan and Alan decided to concentrate on reorganizing their life apart from sex.

One night Alan suddenly told Susan that he would understand if she decided to have affairs with other men. He preferred that she be discreet enough that he wouldn't have it thrown in his face. This offhand statement led to a tremendous fight between Alan and Susan. In fact, it was the first fight they had since the accident.

All of the resentment that had been building up in Susan came out. She said that she was sick of living with his quadraplegia. She hated the fact that they could not longer just jump in the car and go. Now, if they wanted to try out a new restaurant, they had to find out if it was wheelchair accessible. She said that she was tired of being treated as an attendant and not a wife and lover. In short, she just didn't think that she could continue to be the universal nurturer for the entire family.

Susan and Alan decided that Susan would take some time alone. They arranged for after-school care for the children and an attendant to help Alan while she was gone. Susan then went on a 2-week vacation.

While she was gone, Alan finally began to recognize that he had not accepted his disability. He had been using his rehabilitation and his return to work to avoid grieving for his lost status as an able-bodied man. During this time Alan developed an infection that led to his admission to the hospital once again.

While at the admission desk, Alan noticed a flyer on the bulletin board advertising the group CBT sexual rehabilitation workshop. In a flip way he asked to join this group to give him something to do to pass the time in the hospital. Although he would be discharged prior to the end of the 8 weeks, Alan agreed to continue with the program to the end and was therefore allowed to participate.

Alan had a difficult time with the group at first. He was so different. He became the "old man" of the group. He was uncomfortable with the more recently injured members looking up to him. During the third session, Alan informed the group of two facts: that he and Susan had not tried to have any kind of sexual encounter since he had been injured, and that Susan had decided to leave him and the children to live in an apartment until she was sure of what she felt about the constraints his injury placed on their lifestyle.

Alan had begun to keep his record of dysfunctional thoughts the week before this. He had identified himself as weak and dependent. He felt that he would not be able to live without Susan. Although he was able to identify that he was indeed functioning back at work and was caring for his children as well, the feeling of weakness and dependency continued.

As part of his homework, Alan agreed to become the groups' guinea pig. He would try out all of the things they were learning about social contacts, community resources, and the changes in relating experienced by someone who is wheelchair bound. Since he was the only outpatient in the group, and since he was still the "old man" with more confidence than the others, this role seemed fitting.

Alan's depression scores began to reduce as he began to learn firsthand that his preconceived notions of what life would be like were not realized in reality. One of the biggest breakthroughs that Alan experienced occurred when one of the recreational therapists suggested that Alan join her sailing. It was Alan's first return to the beach since his injury. He had been an avid sailor prior to the injury and had thought that this was forever out of his reach. It was a tremendous day for Alan. As the group guinea pig, he shared his day with the group. On that day Alan determined that he could and would have a full and happy life, despite his physical limitations.

At the last group session, Alan reported that Susan had decided that she could not live with the limitations imposed by Alan's injury. Divorce seemed inevitable. Alan had to work very hard to avoid a slide back to his previous dysfunctional beliefs that nobody would love and want to live with a spinal cord–injured man.

Almost 1 year to the day from his announcement that Susan and he were going to separate, Alan spoke to another group of spinal cord–injured men in their sexual rehabilitation group. He recounted his story to them with an update.

Susan and Alan had indeed divorced, as so commonly occurs following severe sudden disability of one partner. Alan was now seeing several women. One of them had become a sexual partner as well as a friend. With her help, Alan had learned that he was indeed capable of receiving as well as giving sexual pleasure. He reported that he was orgasmic with sex. While the orgasm was not a genital one as before, it was still very enjoyable.

Although the reality of sexual life with a quadraplegic is different than sex with an able-bodied man, and although the "quicky" was now a thing of the past, Alan reported that he was very satisfied with his sexual life. In fact, he reported that he was probably a better lover now than he had been before his injury.

Before Alan left after his talk, he agreed to complete a follow-up body image scale and depression inventory. The results were gratifying though not surprising, given Alan's presentation to the group. Alan's depression scores were highly acceptable. His self-esteem, as determined by the body image scale, was higher than it had been a year ago. Alan declared himself sexually rehabilitated on that day. Before he left, he added that he planned to continue to experiment with his sexuality as long as possible.

Conclusion

Cognitive behavior therapy, by its very problem-oriented coping orientation, makes it a valuable approach in the sexual rehabilitation of spinal cord–injured people. Its pragmatic approach to problems helps to make it applicable to all spinal cord–injured people, regardless of their background. The group setting helps these individuals share, learn, and practice effective strategies that will enable them to live more effectively as physically disabled persons in an able-bodied world.

Use of the model described here also can provide hard data by which a group approach to cognitive behavior therapy for spinal cord–injured populations can be assessed. Although the approach is intuitively sound, it awaits rigorous testing.

REFERENCES

American Association of Sex Educators, Counselors, and Therapists. (1979). *Sexual education counseling and therapy for the physically handicapped*, Washington, DC: AASECT.
American Journal of Nursing, August 1977. Rush, J. A. (1981). Group versus individual cognitive therapy: A pilot study. The person with a spinal cord injury. *Cognitive Therapy and Research*, 5.
Beck, A. T. (1978). *Beck Inventory*. Philadelphia: Center for Cognitive Therapy.
Berkman, A. H., Weissman, R. & Frielich, M. (1978). Sexual adjustment of spinal cord injured veterans living in the community. *Archives of Physical Medicine and Rehabilitation*, 59.
Chipouras, S. (1974). Ten sexuality of the spinal cord injured, *Nursing Clinics of North America*, 9.
Dixon, J. K. (1981). Group self identification and physical handicap: Implications for patient support groups. *Research in Nursing and Health*, 4.
Freeman, A. (Ed.). (1983). *Cognitive therapy in couples and groups*. New York: Plenum Publishers.
Held, J. P., Cole, T. M., Held, C., Anderson, C. & Children, R. A. (1975). Sexual attitude reassessment workshops: Effect on spinal cord injured adults, their partners and rehabilitation professionals. *Archives of Physical Medicine and Rehabilitation*, 56.
Melnyk, R., Montogomery, R., & Over, R. (1979). Attitude changes following a sexual counseling program for spinal cord injured persons. *Archives of Physical Medicine and Rehabilitation*, 60.
Miller, S., Szasz, G., & Anderson, L. (1981). Sexual health care clinician in an acute spinal cord injury unit. *Archives of Physical Medicine and Rehabilitation*, 62.
Secord, P. F., & Jourard, S. M. (1953). The appraisal of body-cathexis: Body-cathexis and the self. *Journal of Consulting Psychology*, 17.
Shaffer, C. S., Shapiro, J., Sank, L. I., & Coughlan, D. J. (1981). Positive changes in depression, anxiety and assertion following individual and group cognitive behavior therapy intervention. *Cognitive Therapy and Research*, 5.
Singh, S. P., & Magner, T. (1975). Sex and self: The spinal cord injured. *Rehabilitation Literature*, 36.
Steger, J. C. (1978). Cognitive behavioral strategies in the treatment of sexual problems. In *Cognitive behavior therapy: Research and application*, J. P. Foreyt & D. P. Rathjen, (Eds.). New York: Plenum Press.
Steger, J. C., & Brockway, J. (1980). Sexual enhancement in spinal cord injured patients: Behavioral group treatment. *Sexuality and Disability*, 3.
Weinberg, J. S. (1982). Human sexuality and spinal cord injury, *Nursing Clinics of North America*, 17.
Young, J., & Beck, A. (1982). Cognitive therapy: Clinical applications. In *Short term therapy for depression*, A. J. Rush (Ed.), (pp. 182–214). New York: Guilford Press.

INDEX

ABC model, 110
Absolutistic thinking, 46, 71
Achievement striving, 169–170
Activity scheduling, 31–32, 75, 165–166
Adolescents
  antisocial, 135
  cognitive processes in, 70–71, 134
  hospitalization of, 72, 133
    admission, 72–73
    and behavioral standards, 74–75
    case studies, 76, 77–78
    and families, 73–74
    pharmacotherapy in, 80
    psychoeducational techniques in, 80
    referral information, 73
    staff training programs, 80–81
  retarded, 135
  schizophrenia in, 135
  self-esteem in, 71, 75, 136
  treatment of, 69–72
Agenda setting, 43–44
Aging, 199–210
  changes in, 200
  generalization, 210
  problem behaviors in, 199–200
  problem-solving training in, 200–210
  procedures, 209
  therapy
    alternatives, 207
    decision making, 207–208
    definition of, 206
    educational aspects of, 205
    verification in, 208
Alcohol
  as coping mechanism, 54–55
  effects of, 54

Alcohol *(continued)*
  maladaptive conceptualizations in, 55–57, 58
  therapy for abuse of, 57–65
    day hospital in, 65
    group therapy protocol for, 61–65
    techniques in, 59–61
Alertness, 184
All-or-nothing thinking, 24, 111, 163, 168
Anger, 170, 175–177
Anorexia nervosa, 40, 41
Antabuse, 41
Anthony, W. A., 104
Antidepressants, 37, 38, 39, 41, 80
Antipsychotic drugs, 37, 39, 41
Anxiety disorders, 13
Arbitrary inference, 25, 46, 71, 111
Arnkoff, D., 84, 105
Assertiveness training, 32, 59
Attention-deficit disorder, 134
Attention, selective, 163–164, 169

Bandura, A., 71
Beck, A. T., 20, 22, 59, 71, 105, 162, 164, 174, 191
Beels, C., 108–109
Behavior rehearsal, 32
Belief
  definition of, 27
  distortion of, 28
Belschner, W., 88
Benzodiazepines, 41
Berger, R. M., 204
Berkman, A. H., 214
Berne, E., 95, 133
Beta blockers, 41
Bibliotherapy, 32
Borderline personality disorder, 41
Brain damage
  case study, 192–196
  cognitive changes in, 184–186
  diagnosis of, 188–191

  assessment tools for, 190
  physical changes in, 186–187
  in stroke victims, 183
  therapy for, 191
Breathing, 33, 159
Brunson, B. I., 165
Bukberg, J., 189
Burman, M. A., 165
Burns, D. D., 22, 162, 168, 172
Busemeyer, J. R., 205

Cancer, 14, 155–161
  coping skills in, 155–157, 160
  depression in, 189
  short-term therapy in, 158–160
Carkhuff, R. R., 93
Carnegie, D., 21
Cassem, N. H., 169
Catastrophizing, 25, 111–112
Chipouras, S., 216
Cochran, S.D., 38
Cognitive-behavior modification, 20
Cognitive rehearsal, 31
Cognitive Therapy and the Emotional Disorders (Beck), 32
Cognitive Therapy of Depression (Beck et al.), 104
Collaboration, 20, 75, 104
Communication skills
  affective, 185–186
  in brain damage, 185–186
  in type A's, 166–167
  verbal, 185
Concentration, 185
Cooper, C. L., 174
Coping, 20, 103, 155–157, 160
Coping with Depression (Beck & Greenberg), 32, 44
Coronary heart disease, 162, 172, 173–174, 175, 177

Davison, G. C., 203
Decision making, 207–208

INDEX

Deinstitutionalization, 103
Depression, 21, 22, 38, 39, 40, 70
  in brain damage, 183–196
    evaluation of, 188–191
  chronic, 187–188
  in elderly, 202
  in type A's, 170, 177–179
Diagnostic related groups (DRG), 14
DiGiuseppe, R., 112
Distortions, 22–29
  about drugs, 45–46
  of reality, 149
  treatment for, 28–29
Dixon, J. K., 215
DSM II, 22
DSM III, 52, 188
Dual therapists, 41–43, 44
D'Zurilla, T., 59, 84, 208

Electroconvulsive therapy, 40
Elkind, D., 70
Ellis, A., 20, 22, 107, 133, 141, 176
Emotion
  cognitive model of, 22
  expression of in brain damage, 186
Emotional reasoning, 26

Family therapy, 13
  and adolescents, 73–74
Faulty attribution, 112
Feeling Good (Burns), 32, 168, 169
Fiebel, J. H., 187, 188
Folkman, S., 202
Friedman, M., 166, 174, 175

Gale, M., 175
Gestalt, 133
Gittelson, M., 71
Glass, C. R., 105
Glasser, W., 132
Goals, 19, 20

Goldfried, M., 59, 84, 202, 208
Goulding, M., 133
Grief, 187, 202
Group therapy, 84–101
  for adolescents, 136–147
    constructive behavior tools, 141–143
    rules in, 136–141
    self-analysis, 147–150
    self-observation skills, 144–147
  boredom in, 98–99
  dropouts from, 99
  duration of, 86
  log-keeping in, 85–86, 87, 91
  monopolization in, 96–97
  pretraining screening for, 84–101
  role of the leader in, 92–93, 95
  social reinforcement in, 88
  steps in, 86–92
  wall display in, 91
  "yes-but" activity in, 95–96

Hackett, T. P., 169
Harper, R. A., 133, 176
Headaches, 170
Health care costs and reimbursements, 14
Hibbard, M. R., 190
Holland, J. C., 189
Homework, 33, 80, 135–136, 159, 217
Hostility, 175–177
How to Live with a Neurotic (Ellis), 141
Hussian, R. A., 202, 204
Hypertension, occupational, 173
Hypomania, 40
Hypothyroidism, 39

Idiosyncratic meaning, 29

Jacobs, L. I., 113
Joynt, R. M., 187, 188

Kämmerer, A., 84
Kanfer, F. H., 205
Karasek, R., 174
Kunz, G., 101

Labeling, 27
Lawrence P. S., 202, 204
Lazarus, A., 20, 29, 133, 202
Lithium, 38, 39, 40, 41, 80
Logotherapy, 20
Lopez, M. A., 205

Magnification, 26, 71, 111–112
Mahoney, M. J., 84
Marital counseling, 13
Marshall, J., 174
Matthews, K. A., 164
Maultsby, M., 20
Meditation, 33
Meichenbaum, D., 20, 59, 63, 135, 157
Memory disturbances 84, 185
Mind reading, 26
Minimization, 26, 71, 190–191
Misunderstandings, 21–22
Monoamine oxidase inhibitors, 39, 41
Mood disorders, 13
Moreno, J. L., 132
Multimodal therapy, 20

Negative prediction, 26
Nortriptyline, 39
Novaco, R., 59, 63

Osborn, A. F., 88
Ostfeld, A. M., 175
Overgeneralization, 25, 71
Own Your Own Life (Emery), 32

Pacht, A. R., 167

Pain, 13, 41
Panic disorder, 40, 41
Peall, N. V., 21
Penman, D., 189
Perceptual functioning, 184–185
Perfectionism, 167–168
Perls, F., 133
Perseveration, in elderly, 209
Personalization, 27, 46, 71, 164
Pharmacotherapy, 36–49, 80
 case studies, 46–48
 noncompliance, 80
Phobia, 41
Piaget, J., 70
Placebo response, 37, 44–45
Pleasure predicting sheet, 171
Positive, disqualifying, 25
Price, T. R., 187
Price, V., 162–163, 167, 169, 175, 177
Psychodrama, 132
Psychoeducational techniques, 44, 79–80
Psychosis, 39
 chronic, 14

Rational behavior therapy, 20
Rational-emotive therapy, 20
Reality therapy, 132
Reattribution, 30
Reflections on Perfection (Pacht), 167–168
Relaxation training, 33, 166
Replacement imagery, 31
Reynolds, R.C., 173–174
Robinson, R. G., 187
Rogers, C. R., 107, 132
Role-playing, 91, 216
Rose, S. D., 204
Rosenman, R. H., 174
Rush, A. J., 37, 216

Scaling, 31

INDEX

Schema, 22
  interpretation of, 28
Schizophrenia, 41
  in young adults, 103, 135
Selective abstraction, 25, 46, 111–112
Self-analysis, 147–150
Self-disclosure, therapist's, 108
Self-esteem
  in adolescents, 71, 75, 136
  in cancer patients, 161
  low, in type A's, 170–173, 179
Self-involvement, 172
Sexual disorders, 14
Sexual rehabilitation, 216–221
Shaffer, C. S., 216
Shame, 33
Sheen, Bishor F. J., 21
Shekelle, R. B., 175, 177
"Should/must/ought" statements, 26–27
Shure, M., 83
Siegel, J. M., 84
Silber, S., 205
Slavson, S. R., 132
Social reinforcement, 88, 209
Social skills training, 32, 59
Spinal cord injuries, 14, 213–226
  case studies, 221–226
  and gender role, 215
  group therapy for, 215, 218
  role playing, 216
  and sexual expression, 213
  sexual rehabilitation programs for, 216–221
    agenda, 219–221
    format, 217
    rationale, 217
Spivak, G., 83, 84, 95
Strategies, 29–33
Stroke, 183, 215
  cognitive changes in, 184–186
  physical changes following, 186–187
Substance abuse, 13, 14, 70; *see also*

Alcohol
Suicide, 22, 40, 70
Sweden; *see* Umea, Sweden

Talk Sense to Yourself (McMullin & Casey), 32
Tantrums, 134–135
Terminal illness, 14
Therapies, cognitive behavior, 20
Thinking, 113
Time urgency, 165–167, 174
Toseland, R., 204
Transactional analysis, 133
Transference, 21
Triad, cognitive, 22, 23, 24
Truax, C. B., 93
Turk, D., 59
Type A behavior, 14, 162–180
  cognitive processes in, 163–164
  consequences of, 170
  features of, 165–179
Type A Behavior Pattern (Price), 162–163
Type B behavior, 163–165

Umea, Sweden psychiatric care in, 118–130
  admission beds, 120
  outpatient clinics, 119
  patient screening, 123–124
  staff, 121–128
  wards, 121

Voices, externalization of, 31

Weissman, M. M., 38, 169
Wessler, R. L., 112
Whalen, S.R., 112
Williams, R. B., 175
Wondolowski, M., 101

Work, excessive involvement with, 173–175

Young adults, 103–115

hospitalization of, 104
treatment of, 105–115

Zelazowski, R. R., 101